The International Companion to John Galt

INTERNATIONAL COMPANIONS TO SCOTTISH LITERATURE

Series Editors: Ian Brown and Thomas Owen Clancy

Titles in the series include:

International Companion to Lewis Grassic Gibbon
Edited by Scott Lyall
ISBN 978-1-908980-13-7

International Companion to Edwin Morgan
Edited by Alan Riach
ISBN 978-1-908980-14-4

International Companion to Scottish Poetry
Edited by Carla Sassi
ISBN 978-1-908980-15-1

International Companion to James Macpherson and The Poems of Ossian
Edited by Dafydd Moore
ISBN 978-1-908980-19-9

International Companion to John Galt
Edited by Gerard Carruthers and Colin Kidd
ISBN 978-1-908980-27-4

The International Companion to John Galt

Edited by Gerard Carruthers
and Colin Kidd

Scottish Literature International

Published by
Scottish Literature International
Scottish Literature
7 University Gardens
University of Glasgow
Glasgow G12 8QH

Scottish Literature International is an imprint of
the Association for Scottish Literary Studies

www.asls.org.uk

ASLS is a registered charity no. SC006535

First published 2017

Text © ASLS and the individual contributors

All rights reserved. No part of this book may be
reproduced, stored in a retrieval system, or
transmitted in any form or means, electronic,
mechanical, photocopying, recording or otherwise,
without the prior permission of the
Association for Scottish Literary Studies.

A CIP catalogue for this title
is available from the British Library

ISBN 978-1-908980-27-4

Contents

Acknowledgements vii
Series Editors' Preface ix
A Brief Biography of John Galt xi

Introduction 1
   Gerard Carruthers and Colin Kidd
1. John Galt's Ayrshire 8
   Andrew O'Hagan
2. Satire, Hypocrisy, and the Ayrshire–Renfrewshire
   Enlightenment 15
   Colin Kidd
3. Finding Galt in Glasgow 34
   Craig Lamont
4. Galt the Speculator: *Sir Andrew Wylie*, *The Entail*,
   and *Lawrie Todd* 44
   Angela Esterhammer
5. How John Galt Wrote North America 57
   Ian McGhee
6. Commemorating the Covenanters in *Ringan Gilhaize* 70
   Alison Lumsden
7. The Insider's Eye in the Age of Improvement, Urbanisation,
   and Revolution 82
   Christopher A. Whatley
8. Pioneering the Political Novel in English 98
   Gordon Millar
9. Reading for Something Other than the Plot in Galt's
   'Tales of the West' 110
   Anthony Jarrells
10. Gender and the Short Story in the Twilight Years 125
   Gerard Carruthers

Endnotes 137
Further Reading 165
Notes on Contributors 171
Index 173

Acknowledgements

The editors wish to thank Ian McGhee for compiling the index to this volume. They are also grateful to the General Editors of the series, Professor Ian Brown and Professor Thomas Clancy, for their support of the project.

Series Editors' Preface

Moving the publication of the *Companions to Scottish Literature* series, under the revised title of *International Companions*, to Scottish Literature International, the academic imprint of the Association for Scottish Literary Studies, has had several benefits. One major advantage has been the ability of the new publisher to be open to adding titles to the originally proposed list of Companion volumes in response to new developments in academic research and teaching. While the life of the series is intended to be finite, this openness of mind on the part of our publisher to adding titles has been most welcome to the editors. The present volume, not originally included in the projected series list, is a fine example of the value of this fresher and more open publishing policy.

Under the editorship of Professors Gerard Carruthers and Colin Kidd, this volume recognises and addresses the renewed interest in, and respect for, the novels of John Galt over recent years. While the editors note that Galt also wrote poetry and drama, much of which is not of the quality of his prose – though some may come in future to be reconsidered – they have rightly focused on Galt's novels and short stories. Further, the chapters they have commissioned have been able to set Galt's writing in the broader context of his public life. The result is an engaged and engaging volume whose contributors are in the forefront of scholarship. Its chapters demonstrate in lively and lucid, yet rigorous, language exactly why Galt was and remains such an important figure in Scottish literature. They offer, after a period of some neglect, contemporary understanding of – and incentive to read, appreciate and enjoy – Galt's work and wit.

Ian Brown
Thomas Owen Clancy

A Brief Biography of John Galt

John Galt was born on 2 May 1779 at Irvine in Ayrshire, the son of a ship's captain involved in trade to the West Indies. Sickly as a child, Galt was at first schooled at home, and later attended grammar school at Irvine. In 1789, the family moved to Greenock in Renfrewshire when Galt's father became a shipowner and in 1796 Galt began work as a clerk for a local firm. In 1803 he found some published success as a poet when the *Scots Magazine* published part of his epic poem 'The Battle of Largs'. The poem was published in full in 1804, around the time its author moved to London in an attempt to become a businessman. In 1807 his article 'A Statistical Account of Upper Canada' was published in *The Philosophical Magazine*, and in 1808 his main business partnership was declared bankrupt, though without Galt's suffering liabilities. In 1809 he studied law for a few months, entering Lincoln's Inn, but then decided to travel around the Mediterranean where he met Lord Byron. In 1811, back in London, he published two volumes of his travels and a biography of Cardinal Wolsey, and became editor of the *Political Review*.

In 1813 Galt married Elizabeth Tilloch and published a sequel to his Mediterranean travels, *Letters from the Levant*. In 1814 he became editor of *The New British Theatre* and the following year gave up this position to become Secretary of the Royal Caledonian Asylum, a charity established by the Highland Society in London. In 1816, Galt published *The Life and Studies of Benjamin West*, a biography of the American painter who became President of the Royal Academy. In 1818 his tragedy *The Appeal* was staged in Edinburgh with a verse prologue by John Gibson Lockhart and verse epilogue by Walter Scott. Back in London in 1819, Galt began lobbying Parliament for the Edinburgh and Glasgow Union Canal Company, though this first attempt failed. He also turned his hand to writing school textbooks under various pseudonyms. The following year his parliamentary efforts were successful and he was given a substantial reward by the canal company he had lobbied for. In 1821 *The Ayrshire Legatees* was published in monthly parts in *Blackwood's Magazine*, and in the same year Galt was engaged by a group of businessmen from Upper Canada, attracted by his lobbying reputation, to assist them in obtaining compensation from the government for losses sustained in the War of 1812. *The Steam-Boat* and *Annals of the Parish* were both published in 1821, followed in 1822 by *Sir Andrew Wylie, The Provost, The Gathering of the West,* and *The Entail*. In 1823, *Ringhan Gilhaize* and *The Spaewife* appeared in print.

The following year Galt was a founding party of the Canada Company whose Secretary he became; in 1825, he was one of five government commissioners sent to Canada on a fact-finding mission. Later that same year, Galt was granted the freedom of Irvine. *The Omen* and *The Last of the Lairds* were published in 1826, the same year that Galt was appointed Superintendent of the Canada Company. He travelled via New York to the areas around modern Ontario, including Toronto. In 1827 Galt established the towns of Guelph and Goderich, and in 1829 he was recalled to London, dismissed from the Canada Company in June, committed to King's Bench Prison for debt in July, and discharged in November. In 1830, *Lawrie Todd, Southennan,* and *The Life of Lord Byron* appeared, and Galt briefly became editor of *The Courier*, a London evening newspaper. In 1831, *Bogle Corbet* was published and Galt played an instrumental role in forming the British American Land Company (to do in Lower Canada what the Canada Company was doing in Upper Canada) and was appointed as its Secretary. In 1832, *The Member* and *The Radical* were published and Galt suffered the first of a series of strokes. In 1833 he published his *Autobiography* and the following year his *Literary Life and Miscellanies*. In 1834, he retired to Greenock where he continued to write articles, short stories, novellas, and poems. On 11 April 1839, John Galt died.

Introduction

Gerard Carruthers and Colin Kidd

John Galt's standing as an author has waxed and waned. There is nothing unusual about this. The course of literary reputations is as quirky as a game of Snakes and Ladders, and Galt's trajectory is no exception. More surprising perhaps is the recognition Galt enjoys in the top tier of 'Scottish Romantic literature', for Galt is the least romantic of authors.[1] Unlike Robert Burns (the 'heaven-taught ploughman'), Walter Scott ('The Great Unknown' or 'The Wizard of the North'), or James Hogg ('The Ettrick Shepherd'), Galt lacks the mystery of a romantic alter ego, a striking identity, or a compelling marketing-image. While, like all of these writers, Galt owes a debt to the Scottish Enlightenment, he is seen as being more thirled to that 'pre-Romantic' period than Burns, Scott, or Hogg, because of the 'theoretical histories' – his own words – which sit at the heart of his fiction.[2]

The personality of Galt as a rather dry rationalist was established in the twentieth-century mind by George Douglas Brown in his *The House with the Green Shutters* (1901). The work of an Ayrshire novelist, it took a flamethrower to what Brown regarded as the tired literary parochialism of nineteenth-century Scotland and to a dour Presbyterian-capitalist-imperialist mindset that constrained the imagination; Galt – also an Ayrshire novelist – was an obvious local target of Brown's ire. Brown identifies the Scot as

> the best of colonists. Galt is his type—Galt, dreaming in boyhood of the fine water power a fellow could bring round the hill, from the stream where he went a-fishing (they have done it since), dreaming in manhood of the cities yet to rise amid Ontario's woods (they are there to witness to his foresight).[3]

Galt, a thoughtful Presbyterian who believed in Providence, a man of business, the founder of Guelph, Ontario, Secretary to the Canada Company, and, of course, the author of that parochial novel par excellence, *Annals of the Parish*, possessed a curriculum vitae guaranteed in almost every essential to provoke Brown. Yet matters are not entirely straightforward. Brown had worked as a research assistant to David Storrar Meldrum as he produced new editions of Galt's fiction in the 1890s.[4] Moreover, Brown's novel is a deliberate caricature, and Brown's tongue was firmly in his cheek as his novel raged, darkly comical, against the literature of the Kailyard. 'Kailyard' was a recently coined term of disparagement for a brand of wilfully escapist and trivial Scottish fiction. The ironic dissection in *The House with the Green Shutters* of the parish-pump mentality owed much – both as target and as indirect inspiration – to Galt's *Annals of the Parish*, not least in its signalling of the larger realities in the world beyond the village community. Nevertheless, while Galt's village is ultimately warm and benign, Brown's is stifling. However, Brown's debt to Galt's oeuvre, and in particular to the sombre constraints and grim, dysfunctional family saga of Galt's *The Entail*, are obvious to any reader acquainted with two of Ayrshire's finest novelists.[5] Notwithstanding these unacknowledged affinities, Brown's negative assessment has become the standard modern reading, not only of Galt, but of the near-entirety of nineteenth-century Scottish fiction, which is regarded as deficient for its buttoned-up religiosity, reserved unionist defeatism and obvious failure to confront the matter of Scotland.

In his own day, Galt was largely admired by the literati. Henry Mackenzie in a review in *Blackwood's Magazine* for May 1821 saw Galt as a scintillating realist, and Francis Jeffrey in the *Edinburgh Review* for October 1823 wrote a review of Galt and others under the title of 'Secondary Scotch Novels'.[6] This secondariness, however, did not necessarily imply that Galt was a second-rate Walter Scott; rather Jeffrey was pointing, obviously enough, to Galt's métier as a painter of the more intimate spaces of national life. Galt tended to eschew – at least as his primary concern – the large-scale historical canvas (though, of course, broader brushstrokes are far from absent in Galt). However, Thomas Carlyle, an arch-definer of the nineteenth-century Romantic sensibility, described Galt in his journal of 1832 as altogether lacking in literary glamour, 'deafish [with] the air of a sedate Greenock burgher; mouth indicating sly humour and self-satisfaction'.[7]

Galt's contemporary admirers included the proto-feminist and fellow-novelist, Christian Isobel Johnstone, who lauded what she described as Galt's 'vulgar, *outré* characters'.[8] As incoming editor of *Tait's Edinburgh*

Magazine, Johnstone had, in *Tait's*, sponsored into print his short-story, 'The Howdie', which, in its rumbustious female-character, had been disliked by the group around *Blackwood's Magazine*.⁹ The greatest of William Blackwood's authors, Walter Scott, also had a keen sense of Galt's merit even if he did not always recognise its provenance. Consider the passage from Scott's Journal for 1826 where he misidentifies the authorship of Galt's *The Omen*: 'Read a little volume called the OMEN – very well written – deep and powerful language. *Aut Erasmus aut Diabolis*, it is Lockhart or I am strangely deceived.'¹⁰ The fact that Scott fails to identify Galt and misidentifies Lockhart (his own son-in-law) ought to give pause to the generic label of the 'Blackwood Group', often applied to Scott, Galt, Hogg, Lockhart, and others around Blackwood the publisher and his 'Maga'. In 1961, David Craig damned the Blackwood's phenomenon as a

> well-knit milieu, literary, academic and business. [...] Yet the spirit in which [Blackwood's writers] did their work was hardly a strength to their culture, so given over were they to reactionary and provincial cults.¹¹

Craig, a Marxist critic, disliked the Tory politics of Scott and Galt, but what caused him even more disquiet was the 'provincialism' he detected in the Blackwood's writers. His account of Scottish literature in the eighteenth and nineteenth centuries is a very presentist one, where Scottish literature is judged anachronistically by twentieth-century standards for its failures to do justice to the presumed aspirations of the Scottish people and the Scottish nation. For instance, while Craig saw Scottish religious fiction as commendably immersed in the life of the people, too often this genre, in his assessment, did not represent 'the whole life of the people', by which he means essentially a full *national* life.¹² Craig's is a secular cultural nationalism aligned with an enduring twentieth-century tradition of Scottish criticism, inaugurated by Edwin Muir in the 1930s and which later flourished in the work of David Daiches. This strain of criticism condemns eighteenth- and nineteenth-century Scottish literature as insufficiently Scottish.¹³ Muir in his poem 'Scotland 1941' had condemned Robert Burns and Walter Scott as 'sham bards of a sham nation', and therein lies the crux for critics of the generalist tradition: that Scotland is a broken nation and therefore cannot really help but produce anything other than a broken literature. These cyclopean critics reduce a wide range of literary concerns to questions of national wholeness, integrity, and supposed authenticity. Why, it is asked implicitly (and sometimes explicitly), are Scotland's writers writing about religion rather than about 1707 and Scotland's *real* problem, the loss of political nationhood? And, as corollary to this secular prejudice, the 'provincial' or regional focus of Galt is read as representing an incapacity or perhaps reluctance to portray the Scottish nation as a whole.

The reductive terms of nationalist criticism derive from the inter-war period, the age of Hugh MacDiarmid and Edwin Muir, which sought out a literary language and broader cultural tradition separate from those of England. Critics of this type were insensitive to the complexity and sophistication of Galt, and more broadly to a nineteenth-century value system that did not accord with modern nationalist assumptions about Scottish priorities. Nevertheless, some critics did diverge from the nationalist consensus, including William Roughhead who in the 1920s and 1930s produced some excellent editions of Galt, based to some extent on the earlier work of Meldrum and S. R. Crockett in the late nineteenth century. However, the dominance of the nationalist outlook in mainstream Scottish criticism and university courses long remained unchallenged. In the case of Galt, the challenge emerged unobtrusively in the work of Ian A. Gordon, New Zealand-based critic, author of a very fair-minded study of Galt in 1972 and of a series of carefully annotated editions of the fiction which demonstrated not only that Galt was in the first rank of British political novelists, but also – who would have thought it? – through his fictional microhistories a supremely skilful and adept chronicler of Scottish life. Gordon's editions of *The Provost* (1973), *The Member* (1975), *The Last of the Lairds* (1976), *The Entail* (1984), and *Selected Short Stories* (1978) encapsulate fine textual scholarship and incisive critical acumen.

Galt could no longer be dismissed as a lightweight Tory hack. F. R. Hart in *The Scottish Novel from Smollett to Spark* (1977) rejected Craig's curt dismissal of the Blackwood's grouping: 'Its nationalism was sometimes authentic, its romanticism Germanic or Coleridgian, its radical Toryism the immediate ancestor of the Fraserians and Thomas Carlyle. Blackwoodian reaction is the manifestation of a Scottish counter-Enlightenment.'[14] By 'nationalism' Hart does not mean an explicitly political nationalism, while his invocation of a 'counter-Enlightenment' draws attention to the ways in which Scott, Galt, and their colleagues were simultaneously heirs to the intellectual legacy of the Enlightenment, yet also sceptical of unalloyed narratives of progress (such as the complacencies of the Whig interpretation of British history). The 'Toryism' of Blackwoods emerges as a countercultural critique of established pieties, as 'radical' in its own way as the Leftism of the following century.

Hart, moreover, perceives a profound sociological primitivism in the regional fictions of Scott, Galt, and their contemporaries, which anticipates the anthropology of Sir James Frazer's *Golden Bough* (1890). Here the 'provincial mind' – nothing parochial about it – plays a pivotal role in the development of western literature.[15]

Nor should we forget another major contemporary critic who diverges in interesting ways from the tired canons of secular nationalism. In *The Rise of the Scottish Novel* (1989), John MacQueen devotes a lengthy, intellectually incisive chapter to Galt. Here he examines the intersection of Newtonianism, Scottish Enlightenment sociology and political economy, and Galt's Presbyterian conception of Providence.[16] Paying explicit tribute to the editorial and critical work of Gordon, MacQueen distances himself from the received assumption that the Enlightenment was baneful, alien, un-Scottish, and altogether anglocentric. MacQueen's appreciative appraisal of Galt also owed something to Hart's earlier work of rehabilitation.

This more positive appraisal of Galt was in its turn followed by the recovery of 'Scottish Romanticism', a phenomenon whose existence Scottish critics from Lockhart onwards had denied. Galt features prominently in Katie Trumpener's landmark study *Bardic Nationalism: The Romantic Novel and the British Empire* (1997) where the supposed backward-looking antiquarians of the Blackwoods circle are repositioned as contemporary heirs of confident Enlightenment ideas. However, these inherited ideas needed reformulation, for they had come into collision with the shocks of the agrarian, urban, and political revolutions that were transforming western Europe. Moreover, there was a spatial dimension to these upheavals: 'The romantic period is one not only of literary centralization but also of literary devolution [where] London is no longer the center of novelistic consciousness.'[17] The Scottish fictions of Galt and his contemporaries are reinvested with their original purpose as meditations, from the Scottish periphery, on the state of the nation. Trumpener places Galt in a context that is fully native and culturally nationalist. A decade later the idea of Scottish Romanticism had become uncontentious. Ian Duncan's *Scott's Shadow: The Novel in Romantic Edinburgh* (2007) sees Galt as a brilliant generic experimenter in both 'Theoretical History' and romance. Summing up the trajectory of *The Entail*, Duncan describes 'a narrative of a postnational, commercial, private society regulated by property laws […] a resolutely modernist version of historical fiction, eschewing political history as well as romance tropes and topics — as though these are all residual forms belonging to a receding past'.[18] Like Trumpener, Duncan offers us a Galt who is vitally contemporary deploying a sophisticated mode of fiction in the face of modern, western complexities. In the wake of these critics, older assumptions about Galt as 'reactionary' and 'parochial', or as a 'hack' writer guided in his publications by financial interest, no longer convince.

It is important, meanwhile, that, while we regard Galt's achievements as a novelist to be his primary claim to literary fame in our times, and these form the focus of this *Companion to John Galt*, we bear in mind he also wrote poetry and drama. His poetry is now seen as over florid to modern tastes, while his drama is neglected. The neglect of his drama, if not his poetry, can be seen in the context of difficulties many modern critics and readers, not to mention theatre-goers, have with the conventions of the Georgian stage, both as to dramaturgy and performance modes. Drama was always important to Galt: as Angela Esterhammer has observed,

> Persistent allusions to dramatic performance throughout Galt's fiction testify to his lifelong involvement with the world of theatre. Although he never achieved success as a playwright, he continued writing dramas throughout his career; he also wrote theatrical reviews and dramatic criticism, edited a series of his own and other writers' plays (*The New British Theatre*, 1814–15) and published a volume of brief biographies of actors and actresses (*The Lives of the Players*, 1831).[19]

It would be idle to argue that Galt's current reputation as a dramatist is likely to grow, despite the fact of performance in his lifetime of several plays in leading theatres as well as by less-prestigious touring companies. These included, for example, *The Witness*, performed under the title *The Appeal* at Edinburgh Theatre Royal in 1818 with a prologue one of whose authors was John Gibson Lockhart and an epilogue written by Walter Scott.[20] Nonetheless, whatever qualified success his poetry and drama may have had in his lifetime, his reputation now rests firmly on his prose.

Recent years have seen Galt's reputation grow, including the launch of the John Galt Society in 2014.[21] More importantly, perhaps, Edinburgh University Press has agreed to a new edition of selected works of Galt under the General Editorship of Angela Esterhammer. Professor Esterhammer and her advisory board take the view that not all of Galt is worth publishing. This is a pragmatic decision to make manageable an edition of Galt's best writing. It marks an interesting break, however, with the more comprehensive recent editions of other Scottish Romantic writers: Robert Burns, Walter Scott, and James Hogg. The EUP edition is surely the final part of a decades-long process that will have cemented Galt's importance in Scotland, Britain, and Canada. The present volume, *The International Companion to John Galt*, attempts to build on a steady stream of excellent Galt criticism over the past forty years (see Further Reading), including a recent landmark volume edited by Regina Hewitt, *John Galt: Observations and Conjectures on Literature, History and Society* (2012).[22] The themes pursued in the current volume serve as a reminder that literature does not exist in ivory-towered isolation from life itself. Galt especially was a gifted miniaturist from whom no aspect of life, however apparently trivial, was alien. Understanding Galt properly requires deep immersion in such areas as theological controversies, matters of commerce and policy, and the practicalities of emigration. The chapters which follow investigate the thick context in which Galt's writings are enveloped. Galt – the novelist of the West of Scotland, Scotland, and the United Kingdom, their communities, religion, and politics; the perceptive chronicler of commerce, the transatlantic passage, and emigrant life in Canada; the champion both of the local and the global, as well as the Enlightenment and a Romantic counter-Enlightenment – has, for now at least, achieved the recognition his remarkable and distinctive fictional voice deserves.

CHAPTER ONE

John Galt's Ayrshire

Andrew O'Hagan

Overlooking the graveyard in Greenock where John Galt is buried, there is now a sheltered housing block named after him. Its residents remember the Renfrewshire town as it used to be, but they also feel remembered by the town itself, as if 'Greenock' was fully personified, not just a collection of buildings and bus stops and alleyways and drains, but an organism of history with a powerful memory of its own. Thirty-four miles down the coast, in Ayrshire, the ancient burgh of Irvine has a plaque to Galt at the house where he lived, and, for years, John Galt Primary School stood to remind locals of the town's most famous literary son. Galt was born in Bank Street in 1779 to a sea captain and a seamstress. He moved away with his family at the age of ten, trying his hand at Greenock, then in London, Canada, Edinburgh, and Glasgow, but for reasons known to capable nostalgists the world over, or to literary archaeologists of selfhood, it was his birthplace that took root in his imagination and grew large in his work.

I used to trace the contours of that plaque with a small finger. It seemed incredible to me as a boy that a writer could be remembered in iron, that his name could go forward through the centuries, and that the faces he captured – so alive, fresh, and ruddy – could rhyme with the faces coming down the road in the Irvine of my own day. Galt was Coleridge's favourite novelist, the first of his kind to draw on the industrial revolution, inventing the political novel whilst exhibiting a Flemish touch for portraying small-town interiors and common faces. The painter David Wilkie loved Galt, and he shared a similar talent for capturing small-town Scots at their social and political business, 'characters' in a way people would still recognise, animated by settled notions of their nature and their economic reality, but lightened by laughter, embodying a simple and powerful notion of truth. In his fiction, our little towns cohered into 'Gudetown', 'Irville', 'Garnock', 'Dozent', or 'Dalmailing':

it is in essence a place fully dimensioned nowhere on earth but in the imagination of the author, a place of ghosts, moreover, whose grief and laughter haunted Galt's own sense of life. The rustic, pre-industrial West Coast town was on its way out in Scotland as Galt sat down to write; the world of Robert Burns – of holy fairs, kirk supremacy, and excisemen inspecting old ladies' barrels – was dying as Galt conjured with the spectre of his dirty old town. Yet, in some proto-Modernist manner, he brings the place ceaselessly back as a manifest of his own native psychology: his Dalmailing is the blazing negative of a world he can never have fully known, a place that was lost to him, as innocence is lost and one's parents are lost in the frugality of time, and yet the world of literature, we see, is forever a sphere of newly arriving sunlight. In this way, Galt's vision of the town is an auspicious and poetical new dawn for the Scottish novel, a magnification of the psychic relationship that can exist between place and character in modern works, nearly a hundred years before the arrival on the page of Proust's distant Combray, William Faulkner's Yoknapatawpha County, or Samuel Beckett's luminous Emptiness.

In a manner later taken up by Thomas Hardy – whose Wessex feels like a more serious enbrownment of John Galt's western world – we find that the action is wholly mediated through the kenspeckle witnessing of a chorus. In Galt's tales, indeed, it is as if events emerge from the 'gossipry of the town', a phrase to be found in his short story 'The Mem' (1834), about a fifty-something schoolmistress, Miss Peerie, whose frugal and sedentary ways appear to cheat her both of lover and love. Galt's examination has the quality not of an individual dissection but of a common observance. We know as much, not because Galt tells us so, but from the energy of the telling, where a loquacious social discrimination is raised into common sense:

> At first her forlorn condition made her constant sadness not remarkable: it seemed, in the opinion of every body, natural and becoming; and though many condoled at the way she lived aloof, none thought that she could be drawn from her retirement. Maybe they were right; but they made no effort, and the poor woman was habituated to neglect long before those that were to blame suspected themselves of committing any wrong towards her. Thus she was far above the thirties before it was thought that the carelessness of her neighbours had been in any degree that cause of her loneliness. She was far advanced in life when it was by-hand noticed, and it had grown in to a second nature with her, that would not be altered.[1]

The reader might delight at the delineation of a type, but we might also perceive the tolling of a local bell in the grey edifice of this voice, for it is the voice of the Reverend Micah Balwhidder, the parish's chief spiritual guide as well as its fiercest gossip. Balwhidder, an embryo of the great gentleman that had narrated Galt's *Annals of the Parish* (1821), brings the town to life as if he owned it, but also as if possessed by it.[2] 'In the Sabbath evenings,' our narrator says, 'when all nature was sedate' – presumably thanks to his pluming sermons – when 'the sounds of the blacksmith's hammer and the wheels of the wagon and market-cart were at rest, Miss Peerie might be seen walking by herself by the river side, or meditating among the whins on the green. As long as I recollect, this was the case. Every one that saw her spoke in passing by, and her words in answer were few and well chosen; but they gave no encouragement to communion.'[3] And by similar means we find ourselves in the company of a whole town, a whole town with one woman at the edge, venturing into herself as a person of her sort might. Nothing happens in the story, and yet a whole life happens. Miss Peerie is eventually seen no more by her neighbours. Our douce narrator tells us she remained by her spark of a fire and one day quickly died. Yet, in Galt's hands, it is the town that is characterised in its reaction to the lonely woman's death. The mothers of the town took heed and worried at the possible course of life for their own unmarried daughters.

This is the painterly Galt – all stasis yet all vision, wherein a seemingly gossipy portrait of a Scottish schoolteacher can become a manifestation of the town's anxieties, filtered through the consciousness of its greatest worthy. Galt had that tendency of some novelists to understand the world to some extent backwards, returning to the scene of the original blessing, the birth of his own consciousness and love of language, and seeking to find there the kind of wisdom that nature only makes available, to some, in retrospect. For him, Irvine was a magical location, holding a secret beyond the secrets of Paris or Edinburgh or London, for it came to seem, at least when he wrote, to hold the key to the essentials of human nature as he understood it. And this may be the ruling passion in the house of fiction: how life can appear more vivid when recollected, showing us in the deep realms of metaphor a structure of reality beyond the actual. Each of Galt's fictions of the Ayrshire town are animated by his unbridgeable absence from it, by a certainty that he can only visit it in his mind, making a world whole again. For Galt, as for many a Scottish writer, this uncanny procedure was chiefly a matter of dialect. He only had to apply a word from his youth – the word 'eyedency', for instance, meaning 'industry' – and suddenly he could see an Irvine spinster at her spinning wheel, a glint in her eye, 'a reminiscence of our youth,' he wrote, 'in itself at once simple, interesting, and pathetic'.[4] If we take the poet Wallace Stevens at his word, and believe, as Coleridge also did, that reality is nothing without the imagination, then the novelist's task is one of pure felicity to what is known, inflected by a passion for the invisible. The town becomes a simulacrum for the entire world at the same time as it embodies what is lost to the novelist himself.

By the time Galt came to write 'The Mem' – taking readers through the closes of Irvine, by the Low Green and down to the harbour – he had lived away from the town for over forty years. It is a fixation, not a location, and we see it in the best of the fiction he wrote in the golden years of his creativity, 1821 to 1823. Galt was to enjoy several decades as a star writer on literary journals and as an adventurer, but he returned to his old town as if returning to himself, a man in search of first essences. It was in these few brilliant years that he produced his four best novels, *The Annals of the Parish*, *The Ayrshire Legatees*, *The Provost*, and *The Entail*. 'Galt's best books do not contain even the rudiments of a plot,' wrote the critic S. R. Crockett. 'One day progresses after another, much like a douce householder's life in the quiet town of Irvine, punctuated only by the yet greater peace of the recurrent Sabbath-day. There is no plot in the lives of such men, no intrigue save that comical one of couthy self-interest, which Galt treats with a kindliness and an understanding that are unparalleled.'[5] In the smallest way, the drama is of the political sort, the sort, as Crockett says, 'that you get into the habit of running to the window to see',[6] and the essence of these people's lives can be located in a single person's voice, that of the ironical narrator who subtly conveys the very meaning of the town, caught so perfectly, so freshly, twenty years before the arrival of the railway. There's a Wordsworthian gladness in the telling, a Burnsian relish in the 'birr and smeddum' of the Scottish tongue, whilst the intricate, local heart is warmed there, contained there, and wrung out. 'Irvine is the foster-mother of most of what is excellent in the writing,' Crockett adds.[7] It is a habit of characterisation with some writers that their people seem, in some measure, to be made of the same stuff as they walk upon, as if they are in some fundamental way constituent with the earth and the air around them. We taste Galt's milieu. There is always a better world foretold in his fiction, but the town, for all its corruption, for all its gossip, may seem to the reader to be the only heaven that its inhabitants will ever know.

Micah Balwhidder, the narrating minister in *Annals*, has a certain delicacy and grace, and comedy proceeds from the sureness of his footing. Those are real cobbles under his feet, and yet the mind that lights on them is as manufactured and beautifully maintained as Uriah Heep's or Isabel Archer's, whom Henry James saw as a lucid echo from a store of values, some of them set up for her by society and some by her own imagination. 'The question comes back,' James writes in his preface to *The Portrait of a Lady*, 'to the kind and the degree of the artist's prime sensibility, which is the soil out of which the subject springs'.[8] In this respect, our Reverend Balwhidder is a supreme representative of Galt's home-loving sensibility, the Reverend being local to the point where a person from Glasgow might seem to him a foreigner. His heroism may be comic, and his comedy heroic, but there is something serious in Galt's regard for him; he is a chief among the men and women of a particular parish, in whom he finds an authentic pulse. The author's genius was to make the concerns of the south-west of Scotland commensurate, in imaginative terms, not only with the Edinburgh of Walter Scott or the Hampshire of Jane Austen, but with any literary world where the panopticon of human wishes is laid out in a clearly designated field. *Annals of the Parish* shows us a Hogarthian parade of small-town, couthy neighbours and gossips, errant politicos, smugglers, drunken town drummers, spaewives, nosey lawyers, recruiters, farmers, and their docile sons. They tumble through the pages like the blown furze of time itself, landing year by year in these annals, before blowing out again into a vast and unknowable universe of the dead. Galt for me is a wizard of time, bringing a psychology of loss to our understanding of social pattern. I see a graveyard at the back of his work and a sunlit amphitheatre to the fore, where the reader stands. If it snows in Ayrshire, I think of Galt and the snow faintly falling as it does in 'The Dead' by James Joyce, another writer for whom the past was a vital spur to vision. Like the lonely graveyard where Michael Furey lies buried in that famous story, Ayrshire exists, for me, as both the centre of things and a backwater of the mind, irrigating everything.

In his *Literary Life and Miscellanies*, Galt writes of *The Annals of the Parish* and *The Provost* as attempts 'to exhibit a kind of local theoretical history, by examples, the truth of which would be at once acknowledged'.[9] It would be a hundred years on, with the publication of John Hersey's *Hiroshima*, or later, with Truman Capote's *In Cold Blood*, that the parameters between fiction and non-fiction would be blurred to such effect. He believed the books to be deficient as novels, lacking in plot; The

Ayrshire Legatees, he adds, 'cannot be justly appreciated as a novel'.[10] He felt very keenly the closeness of the real-life model: the idea of contrivance did not come naturally to his way of thinking, and yet the work of the heart, the stock of emotion and blatant connection which give to his 'Tales of the West' such vigour and such colour, was very much in evidence for every character and every scene. Yet he persists in the idea that inventions are not the same as 'things of nature' – indeed, it was by the careful distillation and bottling of the latter that he wished to be remembered, as if art's true vintage was always discernible in the isolation of a local truth. He wrote biographies of the town. 'My wish is to be estimated by the truth of whatever I try to represent,'[11] he wrote simply, or not so simply. Galt later told the story of how he eventually came face to face with his real-life model for the Provost, sitting, years after the book was published, among the magistrates of the town during a ceremony at Irvine tollbooth, aged but unbound, and unchanged by his famous depiction. 'His speech partook of his character,' Galt wrote, 'and evinced a degree of good sense, of tact, and taste, though delivered in the Scottish dialect, quite extraordinary'.[12] (I don't know about that 'though': Galt knew well enough what could be achieved in the way of good sense in the Scots tongue.) He flatters the town's reality over his own artistry in a way that commends him. Yet I continue to wonder if the old town isn't a little deeper and more memorable in his rendering, a little more inflected by the durable vision of the artist. 'Fiction reveals truth that reality obscures,' Emerson wrote, and the idea of the town in Galt's novels is more indelible than its stonework.

'It is important to recognise that Galt was groping towards the modern science of psychology,' wrote his biographer, Jenny Aberdein. 'He writes to Blackwood (12 April 1826), "If there is any merit in any of my sketches it is in the truth of the metaphysical anatomy of the characters".'[13] But we will usually find, in assessing Galt's gift as a stylist, that he embedded that curiosity about the growth of the mind in an unmistakeable landscape, the Irvine of his childhood. He knitted all interior drama to the seasonal qualities of the town and its environs, which is what affords his style its tremendous demotic power and gives his prose its elasticity and its precision. As with speech, style is place with some people; it relates to primary conditions. 'My Autobiography will enable the courteous reader to determine what I owe to Irvine,' Galt wrote, but in fact it is not his memoir but his fiction that most fully displays the debt. His fictional method bears a Wordsworthian grandeur in its attraction to the lyricism of childhood, to the moral openness of country habits, common speech, and local character. These could, of course, be the hallmarks of a sentimental novel of home truths and beaming hearths, what would become, in the Scottish novel, the kailyarders' paradise, but Galt is never sentimental. There is feeling, but it is held to account always and everywhere with original humour, and his style was forensic, drawing blood from the customs of the town as opposed to wrapping them in sweet-smelling roses. Decency and diligence live in Galt's fiction beside delinquency and sloth; his towns are multiplicities, and none of his characters is from a stockpile of familiar types. A novelist does not haunt his old house, he is haunted by it, and Galt's biographer, furthermore, sees a man inching forward, a brilliant literary snail with a town on its back:

> Galt frequently alludes in later years to his possession of what he calls 'local memory' (today we should call it *visual memory*) – a faculty for registering a scene in all its detail, even when its full import is not realised, and for retaining the impression throughout life. Galt's mature reflective powers – powers of analysis, interpretation, philosophy – had thus rich store of remembered experience on which to work. Pictures as well as actual scenes were thus remembered, and a picture of Niagara, seen at a relative's house in Kilmarnock, so filled his mind with notions of grandeur as for a time to spirit him away from the actual world.[14]

And the 'actual world' can bear it, for what is left, after a novelist had done his bit, but a heftier, more subtle town, a more variegated local soul, one in which a recalled story about Robert Burns or a deathless character of John Galt's can make the town into something glorious, a place in the national literature and a domain where people can live imaginatively. Let the tourists arrive, and let the bands play, for Irvine is rich on the page, and its son, John Galt, can remind readers in his own words that the humanity of the place is a moveable feast. It can go all over the world. There was no baseless fabric to Galt's vision, and when I close my eyes in 2016 and think of Irvine and its neighbouring town of Kilwinning, I see not only the places of my own childhood, the place where I went to school and where I paddled in the burn, where I sold 'tablet' round the doors and played rounders with now-vanished friends on summer evenings, I also see Galt's town at the same time, and I recognise no great distance between our human stations. In fact, I see a deep connection between then and now, the same closes and wynds, the same harbour, and the same sky as the nights draw in and people make their way home under the lamps.

CHAPTER TWO

Satire, Hypocrisy, and the Ayrshire–Renfrewshire Enlightenment

Colin Kidd

The fiction of John Galt lives. The observation might seem gratuitous, if not redundant, except this is not the case with Galt's close contemporary Walter Scott. With every passing generation in the anglophone world, Scott's Waverley Novels become – it seems – that much harder to appreciate. For Scott's sedate narrative tempo is not that of the modern world, and much less so as the analogue age gives way to the digital era. Moreover, his historical novels make serious historiographical demands of their readers. Even those of us who love Scott can see that his oeuvre appears forbidding, like the toppled statue of a bygone literary Ozymandias. Galt's novels, on the other hand, are not simply monuments to a lost literary sensibility, to be visited out of respect for Scotland's cultural heritage, but can still be read for sheer enjoyment. Indeed, Galt's fiction lives in a way that makes his obscurity not only undeserved, but also a trifle mystifying. Possibly it has something to do with Galt's unromantic subject matter or the apparent density of local dialect in his fiction. Although Galt's use of vernacular Scots does deter some readers, those who persevere – even just a little – soon find themselves caught up in his novels.

While nothing in literature dates more rapidly than humour, readers continue to laugh in an unforced way at Galt's jokes. In their day, of course, Scott was recognised as a greater comic genius than Galt; certainly, Scott's comedic range was far wider than Galt's. Nevertheless, much of Scott's humour now falls flat; though recognisably droll, it seems today ponderous, overwrought and contrived. Yet, notwithstanding the passage of two centuries, Galt remains very funny, perhaps not quite laugh-out-loud hilarious, but certainly capable of provoking chortles as well as smiles. Indeed, not only do we moderns easily find the wavelength of his humour, but Galt's deadpan comic style also anticipates somewhat eerily the tragi-comic ventriloquism of a dominant figure on today's literary scene, Kazuo Ishiguro. To a reader brought up on the first-person self-deceptions of the Reverend Micah Balwhidder, Archibald Jobbry and Provost Pawkie,[1] Ishiguro's unreliable narrators – an artist-printmaker or a butler caught up in the intrigues of inter-war Fascism – seem uncannily familiar.[2] Ishiguro's world is much darker than Galt's, and his personae lack something of the avuncular warmth with which Galt imbues his characters; yet, these important differences notwithstanding, the self-deceiving narration is articulated in a very similar kind of voice.

There is, of course, more to Galt than his mastery of first-person narrative self-deception. Galt was indebted to the pioneering sociology and political economy of the Scottish Enlightenment,[3] and described his 'Tales of the West' as a kind of 'local theoretical history'.[4] Indeed, it is part of Galt's narrative sophistication, and his comic brilliance, to splice together in his tales sociological, providential, and personal narratives. Events happen, and the reader is presented – directly by the ostensible first-person narrator, indirectly and sotto voce by Galt – with various kinds of explanation operating on different layers: the ingenuity of the narrator himself on which he immodestly congratulates himself, or the invisible hand of the Deity, or changing economic practices and social arrangements, or mere accident and chance happenings – or, perhaps indeed, some combination of these. Galt is also a novelist who knows the way the world works. Commerce, agriculture, manufacture, emigration, burgh governance: all are presented with authority and expertise. Galt's is a very worldly realism, and his novels have provided a rich seam of material for the social historian.[5] However, is it too much to insist that his primary claim on our attention stems from his gifts as an ironist, and most especially for his sublime mastery of destabilised first-person narration?[6]

Where does Galt get this gift of subversive ventriloquising? He was not above borrowing literary techniques from others when it suited him. Galt acknowledged that *Annals of the Parish* was a Scots Presbyterian homage to Oliver Goldsmith's *Vicar of Wakefield* (1766),[7] and the form of epistolary travelogue deployed in *The Ayrshire Legatees* derived in some measure from an earlier Scottish epistolary classic, Tobias Smollett's *The Expedition of Humphry Clinker* (1771).[8] Nor can we discount direct inspiration for Galt's teetering style, though – significantly – only in parts. While, to be sure, Jane Austen in *Emma* (1815) provided a template for a kind of third-person interiority, which depended on the ironic interplay of blinkered perspectives, carefully misled expectations, and conventional assumptions within a small communal setting,[9] this literary model approximated only in certain regards to Galt's unsettling first-person narration. In so far as one can detect prose echoes in Galt of disquieting first-person narrators, these derive from Jonathan Swift's Gulliver and his Modest Proposer,[10] neither of whom is situated in a realistic domestic environment. In the realm of poetic monologue, of course, there was the vivid, nearby example of Robert Burns's Holy Willie,[11] whose voice – suitably modulated – endures in Galt. Of course, the very idea of the Puritan hypocrite has a longer (and wider) literary provenance, and can be traced back to Shakespeare's Malvolio,[12] to Molière's influential character Tartuffe,[13] and to Samuel Butler's Hudibras, which became a defining model among Scots Episcopalians for anti-Presbyterian satire, but was later appropriated by liberal Presbyterians in their own internecine disputes with unbending Presbyterian orthodoxy.[14] However, none of this is to detract from Galt's originality. He did possess special gifts: not only an eye for the blurry conjunctures where providential happenings and deeper sociological trends appeared to coincide, but also a keen awareness that here a novelist might marry self-subverting psychological acuity and a fully realised depiction of local community with the persona and lilt of Burns's superb comic creation. However, the connection with Burns went beyond matters of voice and literary technique.

It is the argument of this chapter that the heated ecclesiastical debate in Galt's counties of Ayrshire, where he spent his first ten years, and nearby Renfrewshire, where he spent his early manhood, dominated public discussion in the second half of the eighteenth century and into the nineteenth, supplying the matter for much of Galt's oeuvre. There is a further crucial strand to this line of local investigation. The literature generated by ecclesiastical controversy – imaginative as well as polemical – revolved around issues of sincerity, humbug, and deceit. Hypocrisy was the common currency of religious disputation and partisanship in these counties, and was the notorious crux of two local heresy trials.[15] At their ordination into the Kirk, ministers were required to testify their adherence to the Church of Scotland's doctrinal standard, the Westminster Confession of Faith. Yet, as it appeared to ultra-orthodox diehards, several prominent ministers, in Ayrshire especially, flaunted beliefs quite happily which stood at some remove from the rigidly Calvinist theology embodied in the Westminster Confession. Did this mean that these two-faced Ayrshire ministers had entered the Kirk in a dishonest way, publicly endorsing a set of beliefs which at the time they privately disbelieved, and then once safely ensconced within the citadel of the Kirk had bruited their doubts and disagreements with escalating confidence? Throughout the second half of the eighteenth century, Auld Lichts in the counties of Ayrshire and Renfrewshire satirised the crafty dissimulation of New Licht Moderate ministers, men who happily took stipends without believing the Calvinist creed to which they subscribed. In particular, John Witherspoon (1723–1794), minister of Beith in north Ayrshire, and later of Paisley in the neighbouring county of Renfrewshire, devoted his brilliantly scathing satire the *Ecclesiastical Characteristics* (1753) to attacking the hypocrisy of New Licht ministers who subscribed to a Calvinist Confession in which they did not believe. But that was not the only front in the Ayrshire wars of hypocrisy. Decades later, Burns, as the leading literary voice among the enlightened New Lichts of Ayrshire, turned the tables in his own ecclesiastical satires. For Burns inverted the well-established orthodox critique of Moderate hypocrisy, satirising rather the hypocrisies of ostentatiously orthodox Holy Willies, men whose morals fell short of their dogmatic self-righteousness – a sanctimony which barely masked earthier propensities. Yet in the next generation still – as older controversies subsided – this obsession with hypocrisy was indirectly to inspire in Galt a new strain of literary ventriloquism. Here the charge of hypocrisy dissolved into a more rounded portrayal of self-deception, not only among ministers and elders of the Kirk but more broadly among other walks of life. While Galt displayed a traditional local mastery of the pietistic boast, he operated nonetheless in a lighter register than his predecessors. Developments in novelistic technique owed something to this change in tone. Certainly, Galt was objective and unsparing in his dissection of cant and self-interest, but these, in lieu of harsh satirical censure, were also granted a humane comic novelist's warm indulgence.

Galt's primary debt, it is argued here, is to his local context, which underpins not only the stuff of his ecclesiastical fictions, but also, more generally, his acquisition of a distinctive narrative voice. In Galt, the novelist par excellence of parish-pump locality and county community, the vernacular Tartuffe-figure of eighteenth-century Ayrshire–Renfrewshire satire became a more rounded and fully developed comic character. The battles between Enlightenment and counter-Enlightenment were sharper and fiercer in Ayrshire and Renfrewshire, it seems, than elsewhere in Scotland. By the time of Galt's adulthood the heat of polemic had cooled considerably, but the din of auld battles still lingered in the communal memory; moreover, hypocrisy, the stock motif of ecclesiastical satire – on both sides of the Ayrshire–Renfrewshire culture wars – long continued to enjoy a central place in the region's literary concerns. Hypocrisy in its various manifestations was to the life of late eighteenth-century Ayrshire and Renfrewshire central, compelling and ubiquitous – and Galt was a connoisseur.

Hypocrisy seemed implicit in the mechanics of the eighteenth-century Kirk. The Church of Scotland, re-established on Presbyterian foundations at the Revolution of 1689–90, had as its subordinate standard the Westminster Confession of Faith (1647).[16] This hardline Calvinist document became the primary determinant of doctrinal orthodoxy. Indeed, it was enshrined in the Union of 1707, whose accompanying Act for securing the Church of Scotland obliged Scotland's ministers, university professors and schoolmasters to subscribe the Confession.[17] In 1711, by an Act of the General Assembly, the Church's chief legislature, probationer ministers were required to own 'the whole doctrine' contained within the Confession prior to licensing, and ministers at their ordination were quizzed on their sincere commitment to 'the whole doctrine contained in the Confession of Faith'.[18] By the mid eighteenth century there had been no relaxation of these terms of admission to the ministry, yet the Church of Scotland, or at least the influential Moderate party within it, had become the Scottish Enlightenment at prayer. In particular, Francis Hutcheson's philosophy of moral benevolence[19] had somehow insinuated itself into a Kirk still nominally and legally founded on the grim predestinarian Calvinism of the Westminster Confession. Cynical hardliners within the Kirk began to question aloud the seemingly flagrant incompatibility of the Church's Calvinist base and the seemingly heterodox culture which had arisen on these unlikely foundations. Such a situation could only have come about, conservatives reckoned, through deceit: the hypocrisy of non-Calvinist ministers who perjured themselves by seeming to endorse a Calvinist formula of belief.

The arch-critic of the hypocritical Moderates was an underappreciated comic genius, the Reverend John Witherspoon of Beith; underappreciated perhaps because of Witherspoon's girning illiberal reaction, at least at that stage of his career (he appears to have mellowed when he later became the President of Princeton College in New Jersey, and adopted major elements of the Scottish Enlightenment into its curriculum).[20] Witherspoon's *Ecclesiastical Characteristics* was a masterpiece of subversive ventriloquism by way of an adopted Moderate persona, which wickedly parodied the form and content of New Licht confessional subscription: 'The Confession of Faith, which we are now all laid under a disagreeable necessity to subscribe was framed in times of hot religious zeal; and therefore it can hardly be supposed to contain anything to our sentiments in these cool and refreshing days of moderation.'[21] According to Witherspoon, it was 'a necessary part of the character of a moderate man never to speak of the Confession of Faith but with a sneer; to give sly hints, that he does not thoroughly believe it'.[22] Indeed, he went on to suggest an alternative semi-pagan formula of subscription that aligned more closely with the inner beliefs he attributed to his Moderate New Licht opponents within the Kirk. He concocted a profane 'Athenian Creed' that captured, so Witherspoon surmised, the true beliefs of the Moderates: 'I believe in the beauty and comely proportions of Dame Nature, and in almighty Fate [...] I believe that the universe is a huge machine wound up from everlasting by necessity [...] I believe that there is no ill in the universe.'[23] In a later published sermon of 1759, Witherspoon castigated both the Kirk's 'open enemies and treacherous friends', drawing particular attention again to false subscription, which constituted 'so direct a violation of sincerity', notwithstanding the bleating 'excuses and evasions' accompanying such acts of 'gross dishonesty'. 'What success,' Witherspoon wondered, 'can be expected from that man's ministry, who begins it with an act of such complicated guilt'.[24] Witherspoon's disgust at Moderate pretensions was a major theme in *History of a Corporation of Servants* (1765), a Gulliverian satire of shipwrecked sailors who come upon a strange society in the wilderness of Amazonia, whose 'northern province' is an irreverent caricature of Enlightenment Scotland. In particular, Witherspoon followed the successful comic precedent of the Academy of Lagado – Swift's spoof Royal Society in *Gulliver's Travels* – distinct echoes of which can be detected in the precise ways he mocks Moderate claims to philosophical sophistication, scientific achievement, and agrarian improvement. The Moderate Enlightenment is encapsulated, for instance, in the absurd hobbyhorses of ministers who collect 'salted butterflies' or 'make a gold chain for binding a flea to a post',[25] and the reader is immediately reminded of Swift's Academician who attempted to extract sunbeams from cucumbers.[26] By contrast, the lines of influence between the thorny counter-Enlightenment satires of Witherspoon and Galt's more latitudinarian *comédie humaine* were, at best, circuitously indirect. Nevertheless, there was a degree of cross-appropriation, as we shall see, between Enlightenment and counter-Enlightenment camps of the Ayrshire–Renfrewshire region. Indeed, the keen emphasis on hypocrisy which Witherspoon imported into the rough-and-tumble Kirk politics of the south-west was long lasting and in time was picked up by enlightened critics of the Auld Lichts, enduring as a stock theme of debate well into Galt's youth and beyond.

Witherspoon's attack on the Moderates significantly raised the temperature of ecclesiastical faction-fighting in north Ayrshire and nearby Renfrewshire. The Reverend John Adam (1720–1792) of West Kilbride, an outspoken Auld Licht, delivered a provocative sermon in 1765 at the opening of the Synod of Glasgow and Ayr, which identified the presence of false shepherds within the Kirk. There were 'too many such shepherds', contended Adam, 'as God denounces a woe against'.[27] Adam's insinuations against liberal New Lichts got under the skin of another nearby minister, the elderly New Licht, the Reverend Alexander Fergusson (1689–1770) of Kilwinning. Fergusson sent an injudicious but anonymous letter to the *Scots Magazine* (significantly perhaps the favourite reading matter in *Annals of the Parish* of another Ayrshire minister, the fictional Reverend Balwhidder)[28] in which he complained that 'you would pronounce them villains who had signed the Confession of Faith, and did not believe every proposition'. This was, the anonymous Fergusson argued, a 'censure unworthy of a Christian', which his colleague had acquired 'from your leader': a pointed allusion to Witherspoon.[29] A series of letters to the *Scots Magazine* castigated the anonymous New Licht minister for his blatant defence of insincere subscription. A pseudonymous author, 'F', accused the anonymous Fergusson of being a kind of Protestant Jesuit: he was advocating, it seemed, a kind of 'mental reservation' at the point of confessional subscription: 'So the Jesuits' morals allow. But it is a new thing for a Protestant minister to avow.'[30] Another angry correspondent castigated the New Licht champion as 'a friend to double meaning', who was complicit in 'deceit and perfidy'.[31]

The controversy in the press prompted the Synod of Glasgow and Ayr, which met in October 1767 in Irvine, to condemn in general terms the notorious letter in the *Scots Magazine* 'justifying the grossest dishonesty in the subscription of ministers to the Confession of Faith'. The Synod expressed its 'disapprobation and detestation of all disingenuity or equivocation in subscribing the Confession of Faith'.[32] Fergusson had hidden his authorship of the letter to the *Scots Magazine* under the initials A.B., but it seems, everybody knew A.B.'s identity. His clerical colleagues were sufficiently constrained by professional courtesy, or indeed embarrassment, to avoid mentioning Fergusson by name, but unfettered by caste or its etiquette, James Macconnel, the town-drummer of Beith (very possibly a proxy for Witherspoon and his allies), issued a specific complaint against Fergusson, which the Synod directed to the Presbytery of Irvine as the appropriate jurisdiction. Fergusson's heresy trial – in which ecclesiastical faction was compromised by jurisdictional questions and collegial inhibition – became bogged down and eventually becalmed in the operations of the lower court. The Presbytery moved so slowly that eventually the Synod tried to wrest the case back into its own jurisdiction, and in April 1769 denounced any 'opinion that tends to promote or encourage dissimulation or disingenuity' in signing the Confession. However, the Synod recognised Fergusson's 'great age and infirmities', and referred the case back to the Presbytery of Irvine 'to take such prudent measures as may appear to them to be most for edification'.[33]

Meanwhile, the press war raged on. According to Witherspoon's uncle, the Reverend Thomas Walker (1704–1780) of Dundonald, who wrote under the pseudonym Philalethes, Fergusson's mode of confessional subscription was 'so grossly and obviously deceitful, that even a Jesuit would be ashamed openly to espouse it'.[34] Another pseudonymous author, Philorthodoxus, condemned 'evasion', 'sophism', and 'subterfuge' in the admission of cryptic heretics into the Kirk,[35] a position reinforced by the editor of an anthology of letters to the *Scots Magazine* on the topic, who denounced ministers who successfully managed to 'creep in unawares' to the Kirk by way of 'cowardly and hypocritical dissimulation', and their 'clandestine way' of 'smuggling' into the Kirk 'heretical sentiments' utterly at odds with the Church's supposed doctrinal standards.[36] On the other hand, Fergusson's defenders, who continued to uphold his cause after his death in 1770, argued that the quintessence of true Protestantism was the natural right of ministers to private judgment. Of course, the divine word of scripture set limits to Christian orthodoxy, but mere human formulae such as confessional documents should not constrain interpretation. Therefore, liberals argued, what conservatives smeared as hypocritical dissimulation was nothing of the sort, but rather an exercise of Protestant independence.[37]

The furore surrounding Fergusson brought a doctrinal starkness to ecclesiastical division in Ayrshire and Renfrewshire which was missing in other parts of Scotland. In Glasgow's south-western hinterland, liberal Enlightenment clashed with conservative counter-Enlightenment. Elsewhere in Scotland and at the national level, differences within the Kirk were largely muted, or displaced onto procedural questions regarding the role of lay patronage in the appointment of ministers.[38] The milieu in which Galt was born and grew up was, it seems, different from the rest of Scotland. Moreover, these local battles focussed precisely on issues of hypocrisy and insincerity. The matter of Galt's art was the currency of ecclesiastical debate in late eighteenth-century Ayrshire.

The battles over Fergusson, which continued to rage after his death and well into the 1770s, were followed by a further phase of conflict which came to focus first on another set of heresy proceedings directed against the New Licht liberal minister, the Reverend William McGill (1732–1807) of Ayr, and then on the outspoken ecclesiastical satire of McGill's poetic champion Burns. McGill, who had been Fergusson's assistant at Kilwinning, was himself alert to the problem of Christian hypocrisy. In an early latitudinarian work, *Christian Unity Illustrated* (1766), he identified a species of hypocrisy very different from insincere subscription, namely the problem of a fanatical, legalistic religion devoid of love: 'People may pretend zeal for the interest of our dear Saviour; but by whatever marks they endeavour to manifest it, if their zeal be without love, everything else is gross delusion or hypocrisy; and hypocrisy extremely prejudicial to our common Christianity.'[39] McGill's *Practical Essay on the Death of Christ* (1786) offended as a heretical Arminian-cum-Socinian betrayal of Calvinist doctrine, which brought McGill notoriety and the enmity of Ayrshire's Auld Licht diehards.[40] However, it was the anti-subscriptionist appendix which McGill added to his published sermon on the centenary of the Glorious Revolution in 1788,[41] which, together with his *Practical Essay*, brought McGill before the Presbytery of Ayr in 1789. This heresy-hunt brought forth some of Burns's most powerful ecclesiastical satires, including 'The Kirk of Scotland's Garland', an ironic jab at McGill's persecutors.[42] The Synod of Glasgow and Ayr eventually found a tepid compromise solution to the McGill affair, which ignited still louder expostulations from orthodox blowhards and made Ayrshire a byword across Scotland as a seat of heresy.[43] Indeed, as late as the 1840s there are references in the ecclesiastical literature to the 'Ayrshire heresies'.[44]

However, better known still was Burns's major recasting of the debate on hypocrisy, a liberal strategy aligned with the perception of his theological hero McGill that a loveless Christianity was a counterfeit of true religion. In 'Address to the Unco' Guid, or the Rigidly Righteous', Burns outlined the dangers of a hollow, uncompassionate Puritanism:

> O ye wha are sae guid yourself,
> Sae pious and sae holy,
> Ye've naught to do but mark and tell
> Your neebours fauts and folly![45]

The brutal coarseness of Burns's 'Holy Willie's Prayer' made all too vivid the ways in which a canting, self-regarding pharisaism – self-righteous yet fervent in pursuit of theological deviation – might provide a deceptive outer mask for lechery and vindictiveness (and, of course, for an assured indulgence of the venial lapses of the elect):

> O Thou that in the heavens does dwell!
> Wha, as it pleases best Thysel,
> Sends ane to Heaven and ten to H_ll,
>   A' for Thy glory!
> And no for ony gude or ill
>   They've done before Thee.—
> [...]
> Yet I am here, a chosen sample,
> To shew Thy grace is great and ample:
> I'm here, a pillar o' Thy temple
>   Strong as a rock,
> A guide, a ruler and example
>   To a' Thy flock.—
> [...]
> O L__d—yestreen—thou kens—wi' Meg—
> Thy pardon I sincerely beg!
> O may't ne'er be a living plague,
>   To my dishonour!
> And I'll ne'er lift a lawless leg
>   Again upon her.—
> [...]
> L__d hear my earnest cry and prayer
> Against that Presbytery of Ayr!
> Thy strong right hand, L__d, mak it bare
>   Upon their heads!
> L__d visit them, and dinna spare,
>   For their misdeeds![46]

Burns was cautious during his lifetime about an open avowal of Holy Willie's Prayer. Nevertheless, it seems that Holy Willie did appear in chapbook form in 1789, and it also appeared in various outlets after Burns's death, from 1799 onwards.[47] However, the former Auld Licht accusation against hypocritically insincere subscription to the Westminster Confession continued as a theme of Ayrshire–Renfrewshire polemic, not least in the Paisley poetaster James Maxwell (1720–1800), who puffed himself up as the orthodox answer to Burns:

Our Church likewise, bless'd be the Lord,
Hath such a bond of sweet accord,
And ev'ry preacher that would join
With her, must her Confession sign.
But hypocrites who this have sign'd,
And with the Church by falsehood join'd;
Yet afterward would this despise,
And disregard their solemn ties;
Let them henceforth excluded be,
That all their base deceit may see.[48]

Hypocrisy would long remain a prime ingredient of Scottish literature, not least in the literature of anti-Calvinism. Famously, Burns's Holy Willie's self-righteous assurance finds echoes elsewhere in Scotland, most obviously in James Hogg's much darker exploration of the antinomian psyche in *The Private Memoirs and Confessions of a Justified Sinner* (1824).[49] However, much less well signposted is the local debt in Galt's rich cast of hypocritical and self-deluding characters to the staple obsession of late eighteenth-century Ayrshire and Renfrewshire. However, hypocrisy for Galt was not, as it was in different ways for Witherspoon and Burns, an accusation, but rather a point of departure for a deeper psychological exploration of the processes of self-deception. On the other hand, Galt, as a precise observer of social and political practices, did attend to the various nuances of Presbyterian culture in his home counties.

In retrospect Galt's North Ayrshire, including the fictional parishes of Dalmailing, Garnock and Gudetown, constitute a Scots Presbyterian anticipation of Barsetshire: the habitat of some finely limned ministers – most notably the Reverends Balwhidder and Pringle, and a tableau of variations in ecclesiastical outlook, rhetoric, and temperament among distinctive brands of kirkmanship, as well as the scene of ecclesiastical plotting and lay-clerical intrigue. In Gudetown, the wily Provost Pawkie takes the death of the Reverend Swapkirk as the occasion to inveigle into the vacancy the limp Reverend Pittle, an undiscerning match for Mrs Pawkie's unsuitable tippling cousin, who was fast running through her inheritance and likely to become a financial burden on the Pawkies; however, so cold and dreary are Pittle's sermons that – as it were, through the cunning of providence – the devious scheme is seen to rebound on its originator.[50] In *Annals of the Parish*, we glimpse a variety of preaching styles: the Reverend Keekie of Loupinton, 'a great expounder of the kittle parts of the Old Testament, being a man well versed in the

Hebrew and etymologies'; the Reverend Sprose of Annock, 'a vehement and powerful thresher of the word, making the chaff and vain babbling of corrupt commentators to fly from his hand'; the Reverend Waikle of Gowanry, 'a quiet hewer out of the image of holiness in the heart'; and the young William Malcolm, who reads an 'Englified' sermon typical of enlightened Moderatism, but which is not entirely to Balwhidder's taste.[51]

Balwhidder, it transpires, is something of an Auld Licht, but entirely lacks the ideological rigidity of the fanatic; rather, Balwhidder's laziness and infirmity of purpose cut him adrift from new theological developments. He is auld-fashioned as much as Auld Licht, knowing nothing of theology other than what was inculcated during his ministerial training, 'the old and orthodox proven opinions of the Divinity Hall'.[52] When, in 1779, Balwhidder is invited to preach before the King's Commissioner at the General Assembly, he innocently revives a comically archaic brand of apocalyptic sermonising that is decades past its expiry date, at least in polite, metropolitan circles. Unwittingly, the nervous bumpkin preacher from an Ayrshire backwater deploys imagery and robustly intemperate politico-theological argument reminiscent of the late seventeenth-century Covenanters. Where once his audience of the great and good might have been scandalised by his references to 'the gorgeous Babylonian harlot riding forth in her chariots of gold and silver' and the 'everlasting destruction of Antichrist, and the worshippers of the beast', Balwhidder's oratorical excesses are now so redundant as to garner only suppressed snickering in the form of ironic faint praise. Eventually Balwhidder himself cottons on to the unwelcome fact that this set-piece sermon – in other respects the highpoint of his modestly obscure ecclesiastical career – 'had rather gone beyond the bounds of modern moderation'.[53] The fervent, primary-coloured factionalism of late eighteenth-century Ayrshire – a polemical battleground of Moderate Enlightenment and Auld Licht counter-Enlightenment – emerges in strangely subdued tones: a quite different scenario, featuring backward yokels and their difficulties keeping abreast of changing fashions in churchmanship.

Ecclesiastical differences also spill over into the neighbouring county of Renfrewshire, where in *The Ayrshire Legatees* Galt describes two contrasting preaching styles that the travelling Pringle family encounter near the start of their journey in the pulpits of Greenock. These are representative of the orthodox Auld Licht and Moderate New Licht factions within the Kirk. Dr Drystour, the Auld Licht minister of Greenock, is 'rather costive in his delivery' and preaches on the Old Testament, the tenth chapter of Nehemiah; Dr Eastlight, his New Licht rival in the town, supplies 'a correct moral lecture on good works' to his 'genteel congregation'.[54] Indeed, *The Ayrshire Legatees* features a comic gallery of ecclesiastical types, briefly sketched in its minor characters and more fully developed in the central protagonists. Back in the Ayrshire parish of Garnock, Zachariah Pringle's young assistant, Reverend Charles Snodgrass, is another New Licht, a fan of novels and other forms of profane literature, who preaches in Garnock during the Pringle family's absence, while Mr Micklewham is the pragmatic session-clerk of the parish, who unobtrusively runs things after the fashion of its incumbent. More fully portrayed are the Reverend Zachariah Pringle himself, an amiable and indulgent old hand, sagaciously gentle on the tiller when it comes to the administration of his parish and, in particular, the normal run of human frailties with which he has to deal; Mrs Glibbans, the 'polemical Deborah of the Relief Kirk',[55] a body of schismatic Presbyterians disappointed in the backsliding of the established Kirk itself; and Mr Craig, an elder of the Kirk in Garnock, 'rigidly righteous',[56] but something of a Holy Willie in his inclinations. In the course of the novel, Galt is seen to align himself, of course, with the New Lichts, yet he extends a humane compassion and the very spirit of toleration championed by the New Lichts to their Auld Licht opponents. The self-righteous Auld Lichts of the novel – Mr Craig and Mrs Glibbans, 'whose knowledge of the points of orthodoxy had not their equal in the three adjacent parishes'[57] – are figures of fun, but without any sinister aspect.

Strictly speaking the *Ayrshire Legatees* is only quasi-epistolary, for letters are interspersed with passages of third-person narration, though this allows a skilful Galt to navigate between the voices of his letter-writers and third-person impersonality, and to generate different kinds of comedy within the short compass of the tale. Much of this light, high-spirited novel concerns the doings of the Pringle family on its extended trip to London to claim a legacy. This allows Galt to introduce a pointedly baroque exaggeration of Auld Licht responses back in Garnock to the Anglican ways in the south of England that the visiting Presbyterians report on in their letters.[58] However, towards the close of the *Ayrshire Legatees*, attention shifts back to happenings in Garnock. This brings into focus questions of hypocrisy, and in particular the consistency of Mr Craig, the pious, unforgiving scourge of illicit coupling within the parish, but equally a man whose sexual continence is open to question. Nevertheless, Galt treats Mr Craig more indulgently than Burns did Craig's prototype Holy Willie.

The Reverend Pringle himself is not beyond tweaking the tail of his Auld Licht – and *ipso facto* old-fashioned – elder. Writing to Micklewham from London, Pringle recounts a visit he paid to a sparsely attended St Paul's Cathedral, a semi-popish Anglican citadel: 'You may, therefore, tell Mr Craig, and it will gladden his heart to hear the tidings, that the great Babylonian madam is now, indeed, but a very little cutty.'[59] Snodgrass too has his sport with Craig, on the occasion when the substitute minister and his elders are discussing arrangements for the christening of a child born from an irregular relationship within the parish. At the suggestion that the well-to-do in the parish have a whip-round to pay for the poor baby's 'baptismal frock', Mr Craig, characteristically, is appalled, 'stigmatising it with good emphasis "as a sinful nourishing of carnality in his day and generation"'. The Reverend Snodgrass remarks that it is a Christian obligation to support the poor and the helpless. But, the uncharitable Craig replies, the 'wean' is far from helpless – quite the opposite, 'a sturdy brat' – which prompts Snodgrass's jest at the elder's expense:

'I fear, Mr Craig, ye're a Malthusian at heart.' The sanctimonious elder was thunderstruck at the word. Of many a various shade and modification of sectarianism he had heard, but the Malthusian heresy was new to his ears, and awful to his conscience, and he begged Mr Snodgrass to tell him in what it chiefly consisted, protesting his innocence of that, and of every erroneous doctrine.[60]

However, it is not Craig's hair-splittingly scholastic attention to the finer points of doctrine nor his uncharitable inflexibility that brings him decisively into the sights of the connoisseur of hypocrisy.

Rather it is the strange 'miracle' of his 'servant-damsel' Betty, under the name of Mrs Craig, sending for Nanse Swaddle, the midwife, to come to her assistance.[61] The Reverend Pringle, who was 'of that easy sort of feather-bed corpulency of form that betokens good nature',[62] writes to his session-clerk with a reticent and carefully triangulated forbearance that does not entirely obscure the otherwise charitable minister's inner waspishness:

Dear Sir, I have read your letter of the 24th, which has given me a great surprise to hear, that Mr Craig was married as far back as Christmas, to his own servant lass Betty, and me to know nothing of it, nor you neither, until it was time to be speaking to the midwife. To be sure, Mr Craig, who is an elder, and a very rigid man in his animadversions on the immoralities that come before the session, must have his own good reasons for keeping the marriage so long a secret. Tell him, however, from me that I wish both him and Mrs Craig much joy and felicity; but he should be milder for the future on the thoughtfulness of youth and headstrong passions. Not that I insinuate that there has been any occasion in the conduct of such a godly man to cause a suspicion.[63]

However, had some other person been caught in such a predicament, Pringle adds, 'Mr Craig would have sifted with a sharp eye how he came to be married in December, and without bridal and banquet'. But, Pringle noted, 'it's done now, and the less we say about it the better'. After all, as Pringle reminds his session-clerk, 'Where does hypocrisy not abound?'[64] Hypocrisy was accepted as a part of normal life. Another kind of careful triangulation occurs in the response of the ultra-orthodox Mrs Glibbans. While taken aback by the news from the Craig household, the theologically nimble widow is able to conjure up a casuistical defence of her Auld Licht ally, which explained to her satisfaction the unusual but blemish-free chronology of Betty's quiet marriage to Craig, and his own embarrassed silence for a while about the nuptials. All was for the best; though '"it would have been an awfu' judgment had Mr Craig turn't out no better than a Tam Pain or a Major Weir"'.[65]

In fact, Betty turns out to be something of a shrew, and Mr Craig soon feels 'the ourie symptoms of a henpecked destiny'.[66] But Galt is far from harsh in his treatment of his own Holy Willie, and allows him to escape his apparent fate. The new Mrs Craig dies, and the novel concludes, as do so many early nineteenth-century plots, with another marriage in prospect, in this case 'the general opinion in Irvine, that the union of Mr Craig with Mrs Glibbans is a happy event drawing near to consummation'.[67] The lecherous hypocrite remains within the compass of the community. Normal human failings do not constitute grounds for ostracism or division. With a kindly twinkle, Galt – through the medium of his benevolent clergyman Pringle – winks at inconsistency and appears to recommend the turning of a blind eye in the interests of communal accommodation. A kindly cohesion – however messy or fudged – is preferable to a strict code of moral or doctrinal accounting, which only leads to the making of invidious distinctions between sheep and goats. In pastoral leadership the overall good of the community, in all its rich diversity of human types, blatantly hypocritical behaviour notwithstanding, trumps all.

The Ayrshire Legatees is a spry reworking of the genteel, post-picaresque travelogue, after the fashion of the Bramble family's tour in *Humphry Clinker*. However, *Annals of the Parish*, while seemingly another ecclesiastical tale similar in its register and good humour, depends in its telling upon an underlying machinery of a very different sort. *Annals of the Parish* belongs to a new genre that Galt pioneered and made his own: a singular, first-person narration, where the reader both warms to the perceptively unperceptive narrator, and is able to pass affectionate judgment on the narrator's vanity and other venial flaws. The Reverend Micah Balwhidder is as rounded and plausible a narrator as can be found in fiction: his perceptiveness fluctuates within a narrow band, from a simple-mindedness grounded in an old man's wisdom and village-wise sagacity to a sharp, penetrating simplicity. He means well, but is not immune to long-windedness, self-congratulation and a capacity to reach for the wrong end of a stick. His prudence and parochial cunning do not inhibit an engaging, but inappropriately earthy, command of language and allusion. As a pastor otherwise keen to elevate the sights of his parishioners to the grand truths of the gospel, and notwithstanding a series of prudently genteel but half-hearted retreats into delicate euphemism, Balwhidder seems never more than a moment or two away from expressions of tavern vulgarity and farmyard bathos.[68] Galt represents Balwhidder's interior world as a midden, where scraps of Old Testament erudition and fragments of high-flown Puritan moralising are to be found scattered indiscriminately alongside coy allusions to dung itself, 'the very scent-bottle of the whole commodity'.[69]

Balwhidder's Ayrshire parish, like Pringle's, also contains the inevitable – perhaps obligatory – case of hypocrisy, in this case a licensed preacher working as a tutor in a gentry household, who carries a suggestively Auld Licht name, Mr Heckletext. The 'hidden hypocrisy of the ungodly preacher' comes to light when Heckletext fathers a child with a servant girl. However, both mother and child die in childbirth, itself brought on by the shock of the servant girl when she sees Heckletext preaching in Balwhidder's pulpit, and without the mother having named the child's father, though Heckletext is suspected. Heckletext is summoned before the kirk-session, brusquely denies everything, sues the local elders for defamation, marries the housekeeper of his employer, moves with her to Edinburgh, and, then, as Balwhidder notes, 'within three months of the day that I myself married them, Mrs Heckletext was delivered of a thriving lad bairn'. The moral of the tale is obvious to Balwhidder: the mysterious workings of 'a chastising Providence', which afflicts Balwhidder with a toothache, and thus brings Heckletext unexpectedly into the pulpit and his offences to light.[70]

However, Galt's real achievement in the *Annals*, and elsewhere in a series of deliciously ironic first-person narratives, was to sublimate the Ayrshire–Renfrewshire obsession with hypocrisy into something much less barbed. He eschews local polemic and the satirical mode for a more rounded portrayal of human life in the complex and treacherously ambiguous web of networks and connections which exists even in a village parish or small burgh. Straightforwardness, it transpires, is an Arcadian ideal, and the demands of society compel something other than robust directness, indeed on occasions a measure of guile – sometimes, it is true, of a Machiavellian sort, but often, as it were, an innocent guile, perhaps no more than harmless indirection or a benign economising on the truth. However, Galt's subject is not only the way in which social pressures trim our responses to the world; his first-person narratives also relate to the basic workings of the human mind itself. Arguably, these themes represent Galt's engagement with the Scottish Enlightenment science of man, and its preoccupations with both the philosophy of mind and the ethics appropriate to a modern commercial society. However, Galt's novels are saturated in local flavours, and it seems far from implausible that the tang of long-running debates in Ayrshire and Renfrewshire about the different forms of religious hypocrisy endows Galt's self-subverting first-person narratives with their distinctive spice. Galt derives immediate inspiration from the regional culture in which he grew up, but also transcends it. Instead of focussing directly on the stock Ayrshire trope of hypocrisy, Galt explores how the human mind filters out unwanted information, including its possessor's awareness of his (in the case of Galt's male narrators) own inconsistencies, flaws, half-truths, petty deceits, and – of course – hypocrisies. In Galt's oeuvre hypocrisy becomes merely one aspect of the way individuals construct self-serving, self-protective, compensatory, and partially self-deceiving narratives about their own lives.

Ecclesiastical partisanship and ideology yield to psychological insights of a more general and less polemical character. Indeed, Galt uses his insight into personality and its fickleness to construct a modest bridge across the old ecclesiastical divisions between Auld and New Lichts. Balwhidder is something of a hybrid: very obviously an Auld Licht by inclination, he is depicted unobtrusively as a 'man of feeling',[71] who, as often as not, follows his benevolent instincts rather than the harsh dictates of orthodox righteousness. Notwithstanding his Auld Licht attachments,

Galt's creation functions as an emblem of the Scottish Enlightenment's highest ideals, the moral sense identified by Francis Hutcheson and the associated philosophy of sentiments and sympathy elaborated by Hume and Adam Smith.[72] The reader warms to Balwhidder's generous humanity in spite of his uncouth anti-Catholic rhetoric and Auld Licht homilies.

In fact, Balwhidder comes to discern sociology – of an intuitive sort – lurking beneath Auld Licht idioms. He concludes late in life that there was 'no merit' in his 'foresight' and acknowledged capacity to read historical portents: 'I had only lived longer than the most of those around me, and had been all my days a close observer of the signs of the times; so that what was lightly called prophecy and prediction, were but a probability that experience had taught me to discern.'[73] Moreover, he humbly acknowledges that 'experience teaches fools', and that he has found his 'experience mellowing' and 'discernment improving'.[74] Yet as late as 1804 Balwhidder starts to stew, Auld Licht style, about a Catholic priest, Father O'Grady, who is ministering to poor Irish labourers at a nearby cotton mill. Notwithstanding his own personal, instinctual enlightenment, he lapses, just as instinctively, into the well-worn grooves of anti-Popish claptrap. Not only does he resort to the millennialist identification of the Papacy as the 'old dragon [...] with its seven heads and ten horns', but he sees the mass as a scene of 'mummeries and abominations', the crucifix – absurdly – as 'that memento of Satan'.[75] Balwhidder urgently convenes the kirk session to see what can be done; nevertheless, his elders – recognising that 'the days of religious persecution were past' and that the 'vehement infidelity' of the Jacobins posed a greater threat than the Counter-Reformation – recommend that 'no step be taken, but only a zealous endeavour to greater Christian excellence on our part, by which we should put the beast and his worshippers to shame and flight'. Balwhidder accedes reluctantly to this prudent course of inaction, and only comes years later to endorse this advice 'now that I have had years to sift its wisdom'.[76] Later, in a touching tribute to their elderly minister, the members of Balwhidder's kirk-session offer to pay for a helper, who would carry the burden of his ministry, but Balwhidder is reluctant, for he still feels at the height of his powers as a preacher: 'I felt no falling off in my powers of preaching; on the contrary, I found myself growing better at it, as I was enabled to hold forth, in an easy manner, often a whole half hour longer than I could do a dozen years before.'[77]

We should not forget, however, that Galt has a darker side, which is visible only occasionally in his comedies of Ayrshire church life. However, it comes to the fore in *Ringan Gilhaize*, a pious family saga of the

Reformation and Covenanting eras, which ends with its main protagonist – its heroic but increasingly unstable narrator – no longer able to distinguish truth from delusion.[78] Gilhaize's sense of righteousness has been corrupted, and distorted into a species of extreme puritanical enthusiasm. At the novel's brilliantly precipitous conclusion, we can no longer tell whether Galt's voice is heroic or ironic, for his hitherto heroic narrator has become a self-appointed instrument of providence, a godly killer.[79] When required, Galt could vary the register of narrative delusion in his novels, in *Ringan Gilhaize* taking self-deception to a level well beyond holy hypocrisy, to the psychologically disturbed depths of religious fanaticism.

However, this reminder serves only as a complicating postscript to Galt's primary alchemical achievement: the transmutation of hypocrisy into something lighter and less harshly pejorative, where the reader is able to extend a measure of sympathy towards the all-too-human flaws of an unreliable and untrustworthy narrator. Galt took hypocrisy – the leitmotif of Ayrshire–Renfrewshire pamphleteering for the previous half century or so – and gave it a subtle modulation. His early ecclesiastical fiction smooths the hard-edged satire of hypocrisy into the milder comedy of self-deception, a process later extended to the political realm, and the pointedly destabilised memoirs of a provost, an MP, and a radical.[80] However, the ultimate provenance of this cod-Machiavellian persona is in the wars of hypocrisy that dominated the Kirk politics of late eighteenth-century Ayrshire. The presiding genius of the Ayrshire–Renfrewshire Enlightenment's late autumnal phase, Galt should be recognised too as the indirect successor of an inventive and ingenious provincial counter-Enlightenment. The New Lichts had no monopoly on wit, and the illiberal Witherspoon deserves a place alongside Burns in the local lineage of satirical brilliance that produced Scotland's most assured comic novelist.

CHAPTER THREE

Finding Galt in Glasgow

Craig Lamont

In 1834, John Galt said: 'Although Irvine was my birthplace, and Greenock the town of my adoption, yet I have ever regarded my obligations to Glasgow as paramount to those due to every other place.'[1] Those familiar with Galt's oeuvre will know that Glasgow was one of his regular settings. His shrewd eye and sharp memory for the characters and topography of a place mark one of the most celebrated features of his oeuvre. But Galt's personal regard for Glasgow flags up the need for a closer inspection of the city's role in his life and writings. Arguably, Galt was the leader of the 'Glasgow school of fiction'.[2] The authors Thomas Hamilton (1789–1842) and Michael Scott (1789–1835) also fall into this category, and with Galt they share the uncertain ground that falls between Enlightenment and Romanticism. Galt's presiding role in this 'school' helps us appreciate these two periods in literary history as intertwined rather than antithetical and entirely distinct. In this chapter there will be an emphasis on Galt's references to Glasgow in the process of becoming an imperial city. The impact of its growth on the rest of Scotland and North America will be considered, as will the work of authors in the Glasgow school. But before this process can be fully explored it is essential to contextualise Galt's Glasgow: both the post-Enlightenment city he himself experienced and the legacy of the Glasgow Enlightenment.

The Glasgow Enlightenment and its Influence

Most scholarly works on the Scottish Enlightenment inevitably focus on Edinburgh, its institutions and personalities.[3] Indeed, Nicholas Phillipson went as far as to suggest that 'there is an important sense in which the history of the Scottish Enlightenment *is* the history of Edinburgh'.[4] In recent decades, however, there has been a growing recognition that Aberdeen and Glasgow had influential Enlightenments of their own, with distinctive hallmarks and regional characteristics. Roy Campbell in a robustly argued essay entitled 'Scotland's Neglected Enlightened', laid down the gauntlet: 'The hotbed of genius which was appropriated by Edinburgh had its intellectual foundations in the work in Glasgow. Glasgow led; Edinburgh followed.'[5] The first serious comprehensive survey of Glasgow's place in the Scottish Enlightenment was *The Glasgow Enlightenment* (1995), a collection of essays edited by Andrew Hook and Richard Sher.[6] Not only does it draw attention to a succession of distinguished philosophers and social theorists at the University of Glasgow – Francis Hutcheson (1694–1746), Adam Smith (1723–1790), Thomas Reid (1710–1796), John Millar (1735–1801) – but it also points to institutional developments in the city. It emphasises, for example, the role of the Glasgow Literary Society, founded in 1752, in helping to shape and refine the thinking of its members in a gamut of disciplines that ranged well beyond literature. In 1753, Robert and Andrew Foulis established their Academy of Fine Art in Glasgow. The brothers had earlier set up their own press, which was renowned throughout Europe for its fine productions, simple aesthetics, and near-immaculate renderings of ancient classical texts. The Foulis Academy furnished students, who included the renowned Scottish painter David Allan (1744–1796) and the innovative modeller and engraver James Tassie (1735–1799), with a diverse portfolio of artistic skills.[7] By the time the Hunterian Museum opened in Glasgow in 1807, the classic period of the Scottish Enlightenment was past, and the very presence of the Hunterian served as a memorial to Glasgow's Enlightenment.

Nevertheless, Glasgow was much less central to Scottish literary history. The vernacular renaissance of the eighteenth century in the work of Allan Ramsay and Robert Fergusson was largely an Edinburgh-based phenomenon; even the Ayrshire poet Robert Burns, riding the wave of success of his *Poems, Chiefly in the Scottish Dialect* (1786), chose the capital as the host city of a much-anticipated second edition (1787). Glasgow could claim no such renaissance in poetry.[8] It was not until the end of the next century when a Glaswegian literary tradition was retrospectively summoned into being in *Literary Landmarks of Glasgow* (1898), where several distinguished figures including Defoe, Smollett, Burns, Scott, and Dickens were brought into association with the Second City of the Empire. Oddly, Galt features as a poet and a dramatist and as a friend of Thomas Campbell, but nowhere as a novelist.[9] It is this initial exclusion of Galt from Glasgow's literary history that has, until recently, prevailed.

This serves to obscure the strong connection between Galt and an earlier writer from Glasgow's hinterland, Tobias Smollett (1721–1771), from Renton in Dunbartonshire. Smollett studied at Glasgow University and became a medical apprentice to William Stirling and John Gordon.[10] There is a parallel between Galt's nostalgic reminiscences of his favourite towns and cities in *The Literary Life* and Smollett's praise for Edinburgh and Glasgow in *The Expedition of Humphry Clinker* (1771). Smollett's Welsh squire Matthew Bramble, after famously describing Edinburgh as a 'hot-bed of genius', is said to be 'in raptures with Glasgow'. His nephew, Jery Melford, calls it 'the pride of Scotland'.[11] Bramble then becomes the mouthpiece for Smollett's memories of his time at the university: 'a respectable pile of building, with all the manner of accommodation for the professors and students, including an elegant library, and an observatory well provided with astronomical instruments.'[12] Galt's first novel *The Ayrshire Legatees* (1820–21) takes on the same epistolary style as Smollett's *Humphry Clinker*. Moreover, there are striking similarities between Galt's Pringle family in London and Smollett's characters, in particular Mrs Pringle, who – like Smollett's Tabitha Bramble, Lydia Melford, and Winifred Jenkins – is 'independent in her spelling'.[13]

Ideas specific to the Glasgow Enlightenment survive in Galt's work. Anand Chitnis has reminded us that Galt would have had access to the great works of the Scottish Enlightenment in the collection of the Greenock Library.[14] In particular, Keith Costain has argued that Adam Smith's famous 'invisible hand' motif, described as a 'secularized Providence directing man', occupies a central place in Galt's work.[15] Indeed, all of Galt's major novels make sport with the operations of providence, and as often as not with misinterpretations of providence by Galt's self-deluded characters. In *The Literary Life*, Galt muses on the nature of Providence. Galt stumbles towards the paradoxical character of free will, which he defines in terms of both 'motive' and 'impulse'. 'Motives clearly imply choice', he explains, 'and a man may be held responsible for the effects of motives which he chooses to allow to actuate his conduct; but the case is different with impulses. He has no choice—he must go on as the impulse directs him.'[16] Galt reveals the crux of a problem that many of his characters are made to handle directly. It is worth mentioning that Galt's legacy from the Scottish Enlightenment was very different from that inherited by his contemporary Sir Walter Scott. Ian Duncan notes that Galt eschews the balance found in Scott's Waverley Novels between 'empirical social history', which Galt employs, and 'antiquarian romance', which he disdains.[17] Nor was the commercial progress of

Glasgow a straightforward matter of celebration; indeed, the Enlightenment in Scotland was concerned as much with the supposed fragility of commercial society as with the motors of improvement. In *The Entail* (1823), much of which is set in eighteenth-century Glasgow, the city becomes the scene of Claud Walkinshaw's corruption.[18]

The Post-Enlightenment Entrepôt and the Glasgow School

Galt is the novelist of Glasgow's hinterland. Indeed, Liam McIlvanney has said that *Annals of the Parish* (1821) can be read as a Glasgow novel. The *Annals* comprise a set of memoirs narrated by the Reverend Micah Balwhidder, the minister of the fictional north Ayrshire parish of Dalmailing between 1760 and 1810, but it is the all-too-real expansive city of Glasgow that determines changes in the ways and rhythms of life in the small towns and villages of Ayrshire. Glasgow is not just a centre of commerce and industry, but an explosive force whose energies radiate outwards into nearby counties. As McIlvanney puts it:

> It is the Clyde's Virginia trade that brings the first luxuries [...]. It is the burgeoning city that creates a market for the second Mrs Balwhidder's lucrative commerce in butter and cheese, and Glasgow is where Balwhidder's son becomes a flourishing merchant [...]. The new toll road to Glasgow [...] opens up the parish to new fashions, new ideas and the newspapers brought by the Glasgow carrier. It is Glasgow money (presumably the profits of the sugar and tobacco trade) that establishes a cotton-mill, with its politicised weavers, a bookshop and a sprawling new settlement.[19]

The sense of awe is genuine: material novelties in Dalmailing are repeatedly described 'such as no one in our parish had ever seen'. Galt shows how landscape and society are changed by the broadening horizons of empire, in many cases literally, when improvements make frequent travel easier and mobility becomes commonplace. A new chaise proves 'a great convenience' for Balwhidder, who discovers a new partiality for travel: 'one of the best means of opening the faculty of the mind, and giving clear and correct notions of men and things.'[20] Yet Galt makes it clear that the spoils of empire – though welcomed initially – become less welcome the more they abound. In 1765, the establishment of a whisky distillery and three new 'coal-heughs' in the parish is said to be a 'Godsend'.[21] By 1788, 'in the midst of all this commercing and manufacturing',

Balwhidder notices 'signs of decay in the wonted simplicity of our country ways'.[22] In 1808 a cotton-mill is built alongside the new town of Cayenneville, and Balwhidder admits: 'we had intromitted so much with concerns of trade, that we were become a part of the great web of commercial reciprocities, and felt in our corner and extremity, every touch or stir that was made on any part of the texture.'[23] A similar image was used to describe Glasgow's westward spread in *The Ayrshire Legatees*, when Zachariah Pringle says: 'at Greenock I saw nothing but shipping and building; at Glasgow, streets spreading as if they were one of the branches of cotton spinning.'[24]

In fact, it is this particular infatuation with weaving that Galt uses to express improvements in Glasgow during the tumultuous time of the French Revolution, when certainty in Providence is tested by the 'impulse' of men: that 'itch of Jacobinism' he uses to describe the artisans of Cayenneville. In *The Gathering of the West* (1822), Galt satirises the different groups attending the Royal Visit of George IV to Edinburgh in that year. Here Glasgow is described as 'that classical and manufacturing city'.[25] In this we might read that Galt is remembering the days of the Enlightenment in his emphasis on 'classical'. However, in the course of the movement from Glasgow, Galt's signature weaving metaphor is spun again: 'all the roads from Glasgow to Edinburgh were like so many webs of printed calico, stamped with the figures of coaches and carriages, horses and noddies, men, women, and children.'[26] The Glasgow poet Dugald Moore (1805-1841) provides an echo in *The Bard of the North* (1833):

> See what a change trade's golden wand can do!
> As if by magic make a village spring
> To all the glories of a capital.
> Her towers rise high in heaven, while far around
> The hum of nations, gather'd like stray'd bees
> By blooming commerce, to one busy spot,
> Rolls like low thunder o'er the settled scene [...].

As with Galt's portrayal of civic development in *Annals of the Parish* and colonisation in *Bogle Corbet* (1831), Moore seems to have encapsulated a Smithian notion of imperial connectedness. Thomas Hamilton's novel *The Youth and Manhood of Cyril Thornton* (1827) suggests further comparisons with Galt can be drawn. There is a nod to Galt's *The Spaewife* (1823) when Cyril refers to the 'Provost Aulay MacAulay of Dumbarton (probably a descendant of the very amusing personage commemorated by my friend Galt)'.[27] When he first enters Glasgow, Cyril describes the bookshelves in the home of his intended host, a Mr Spreull, among which he notes 'Swift's Works and De Foe's, the Tatler, Spectator, and Rambler, Smollett's Novels, a translation of Rabelais, the Institutes of Scottish Law, Burke's Letters on a Regicide Peace, an odd volume of Hume's History, and a considerable body of Calvinistic divinity'.[28] In this passage Hamilton condenses the literary culture of his time: the waning of the Scottish Enlightenment (Hume its only survivor, and as a historian rather than philosopher) and the rising popularity of periodicals alongside the inevitable religious texts. The inclusion of Smollett's novels is suggestive of his broader influence on the Glasgow School. In providing before-and-after views of Glasgow's topography, Hamilton stands with Galt in acknowledging the encroachments of commercial and imperial activity into the countryside. When leaving Glasgow, Cyril says:

> With reverted eyes I gazed upon the lofty towers of the Cathedral, till, by the increasing distance, they could no longer be distinctly traced in the dense canopy of smoke which overhung the city.[29]

Upon his return ten years later, he recalls the familiar sights of the 'high black towers and spires of the Cathedral, overtopping the dense volumes of vapour that lay spread like a canopy above the city':

> The dirty and miserable suburbs by which it is surrounded, now extended a mile or two further into the country, and the smoke of innumerable coal-works and factories, which had sprung up on all hands, infused a new and uncalled for pollution in the atmosphere.[30]

Robert Crawford takes this same line in noting that Glasgow was 'one of the first cities in the world to beget a poetry of industrial pollution', citing an 1842 poem by John Mitchell, 'written in Standard Habbie and spoken in the voice of the city's newest northern chimney, or lum'.[31] But more revealing, perhaps, than these expressions of ecocriticism is Hamilton's portrayal of Glasgow's intellectual torpor, which sits awkwardly with its industrial dynamism. The Hunterian Museum was built in 1807 on the site of the Old College in Glasgow's High Street. Until then, Hunter's collections had been held in London and were still in use for teaching purposes.[32] Once built, the Hunterian formed a new quadrangle with the library that once housed the Foulis Academy and the professors' houses. The area became known as Museum Square. In *Cyril Thornton*, Hamilton states that the building, 'barbarously discordant with the prevailing character of the place', was a shock to his eye: 'It almost seemed to have dropped from the clouds, and stood staring on the dark and time-honoured masses, by which it was surrounded, as if wondering by what extraordinary chance, it had been thrown into such company.'[33]

Indeed, the move towards memorialisation in the nineteenth century, wherein ideas are commemorated rather than questioned, appears to mark the end of the Scottish Enlightenment itself. Within the new Hunterian Museum, the university was not averse to remembering its own role in the Scottish Enlightenment. The posthumous portrait of Hunter (1787) by Sir Joshua Reynolds commissioned by the university tells us that a conscious effort was being made to remember the forgotten connections between the city and its intellectual heyday. Beside Hunter's portrait sat several other paintings and artworks from Hunter's house in London. There were, however, three exceptions. As Thomas H. Bryce tells us, these are the portraits of the chemist William Cullen (1710–1790), Smollett, and Hutcheson.[34] These surely represent a Glaswegian triumvirate suitable for the commemoration of the University of Glasgow's contribution to the Scottish Enlightenment.

Given the centrality of Glasgow to the plot of *Rob Roy* (1817), we should not overlook the claims of Sir Walter Scott to be an honorary member of the Glasgow School. Kilpatrick's *Literary Landmarks* takes the reader on a literary tour of the different scenes found in the novel: taverns, inns, the old Glasgow Bridge, the College gardens, and the ancient Cathedral. Moreover, *Rob Roy* presents a wonderfully rounded portrait of an eighteenth-century Glasgow merchant, Bailie Nicol Jarvie, after whom a tavern and, more recently, a whisky have been named. Jarvie's famous comment on the Union's profound impact on Glasgow's development ('Now, since St Mungo catched herrings in the Clyde, what was ever like to gar us flourish like the sugar and tobacco-trade?') is a popular Unionist line in the debate on whether an independent Scotland would have recovered from the colonial disaster at Darien in the late 1690s without a Union with England.

Galt's own colonial experiences lend his later novels a rare insight into the practical world of empire, but it is sometimes forgotten that these works also carry a strong Glaswegian inflection. However, before delving into Galt's colonial novels, we should address the troubling issue of Glaswegian attitudes to transatlantic slavery. In *Annals of the Parish*, Galt edges towards criticising slavery in his characterisation of Mr Cayenne, whose 'blackamoor servant', Sambo, is in one scene portrayed as a victim of his master's violent temper. In the comic scene, the docile Sambo has forgotten to serve mustard and incites the rage of Cayenne who, in his attempt to throw the jar at his servant's head, misses and spills the mustard on his own face. Balwhidder considers the result 'a providential reproof', suggesting Galt's own dismay with the treatment of people as 'property'.[35] This is not to say that Balwhidder is used in this case as Galt's mouthpiece. If anything, Balwhidder's passing reference to Sambo's loyalty ('it was an affectionate creature, and as fond of his master as if he had been his own father') reveals his unenlightened views when the reality of slavery is made local and commonplace.[36]

In his *Autobiography* (1833) Galt takes on the subject more directly, declaring: 'the abolition of slavery I never thought could be a question, the justice of the measure was indisputable.'[37] He goes on to form a theoretical plan 'to divide the field negroes from those of the boiling-house, and to consider the former as a peasantry, and the latter as manufacturers'.[38] This scheme has obvious Smithian undertones, which themselves have been overplayed in the inter-relationship between the Scottish Enlightenment and slavery. Galt seems to echo the common concern of the time that immediate emancipation would encourage strife in the plantations. These concepts are at play in *Bogle Corbet*, which begins with the titular character's recollections of his childhood in a Jamaican plantation, followed by his life in Glasgow during the late eighteenth century. In a letter to D. M. Moir, Galt described the novel as 'a Glasgow story' and, in comparison to his earlier work, said: 'The object of the work is a view of society generally, as *The Provost* was of burgh incidents simply.'[39] Yet *Bogle Corbet* seems to embody Galt's own concerns with the emancipators in his thinly veiled attack on English anti-slavery societies: 'I moralised on Negro slavery, wondering how, among the bumpkins and philanthropists of England, it should have been so much forgotten that charity begins at home.'[40]

In *Tom Cringle's Log* (1829–1834) by Michael Scott, a fellow member of the Glasgow School of novelists, the narrator details his time as a planter in Jamaica, offering more insight into Glasgow's imperial connections. In Scott's work he renders the Jamaicans' speech phonetically, and there are more than a few instances invoking the 'happy Negro' myth; for instance when Aaron Bang says to Tom Cringle: 'Strange [...] I had expected to see little else amongst the slave-population here than misery and starvation; whereas, so far as I can observe, they are all deucedly well cared for, and fat and contented'.⁴¹ Perhaps this is done to offset the growing support for this myth with cutting scenes of suffering:

> A little farther on, the bodies of an old man and two small children were putrefying in the sun, while beside them lay a miserable, wasted, dying negro, vainly endeavouring to keep at a distance with a palm branch a number of the same obscene birds that were already devouring the carcass of one of the infants.⁴²

In chapter five, Cringle is at a loss to believe that the black shipmate has a Scottish accent, saying: 'Yes, we are [going to Jamaica ...] but we will not sail with the devil; and who ever saw a negro Scotchman before, the spirit of Nicol Jarvie conjured into a blackamoor's skin!' The mate claims to have been born in 'the good town of Port-Glasgow'.⁴³

We can find a more direct imperial connection between Glasgow and the New World in *Bogle Corbet*. Significantly, when the text was reprinted in 1977 much of the original content was cut. But what does the 1977 edition erase from our understanding of Galt's treatment of Glasgow? What might be regained from a new reading? First, several accounts of Glasgow's city centre as it was in 1789 were removed. These scenes are important, complementing the depictions of the Trongate found in *Annals of the Parish* and *The Steam-Boat*. Having been raised overseas, Galt's narrator encounters Glasgow with the eyes of a tourist, echoing that sense of awe inspired by Smollett in *Humphry Clinker* and by Hamilton in *Cyril Thornton*.⁴⁴ In addition, attention is drawn to the confluence of accents, revealing the audible impact of Empire on everyday life: the 'almost English tongue of Mr Macindoe' from his years in the West Indies; the English-American 'decisive and energetic vernacular' of Dr Leach; and the 'genuine Trongate' of Mr Aird.⁴⁵ As Bogle comes to work in Mr Aird's weaving workshop, there are signs of radicalisation among the weavers who transform the shop into a Jacobin club: that same revolutionary 'itch' referred to in *Annals of the Parish*. Furthermore, the Revolution's interference with Glasgow's trade is said to 'thin' the 'canopy of smoke that overhung its spires and chimney-tops'.⁴⁶ In this chapter Corbet describes the cathedral and the Molendinar burn, contrasts the young men of the College against those who visit the Exchange, and finds himself in the Tontine coffee-room where 'the gorgeous and grand of the town' talk of their trade.⁴⁷ The abundance of detail here tells us that Bogle Corbet had Glasgow's diverse metropolitan social structure in mind when he moved to Canada. Gilbert Stelter has outlined Galt's fascination with

Glasgow, Edinburgh, and London and how they 'formed' his 'conception of cities' and, eventually, led to his interest in the foundation of towns like Ardrossan in 1805.[48] Therefore, we can say that Galt's time in Glasgow had a large influence in founding Guelph in 1827, fictionalised in *Bogle Corbet* when the narrator describes the felling of the first tree, and the subsequent naming of the town:

> I left the name to be given by the settlers themselves, and in the course of the day heard that they had fixed on one; both appropriate, as it referred to themselves, and agreeable to me, as applied to a new place. In Glasgow there is an old well-known street called "The Stockwell" [...]. Several of the Glasgow men being artisans and crafts' men, Stockwell was intended chiefly for them, and those who might come after of the same kind.[49]

This crucial event, being fundamental to Waterston's shortened text, is unfortunately disconnected from the sections of Glasgow that had been edited out. This dislocation thwarts Galt's intention, which was precisely to portray *Glasgow's* emigrant communities in the New World. After all, the 'New World' implies a history, an 'Old World' from which it was forged. As Galt says in *The Literary Life*, the 'discovery of America' is 'equivalent to the creation of another continent, purposely to relieve the oppressed of the old'.[50] Galt's conclusion to *Bogle Corbet*, an optimistic argument that emigration should be undertaken when people are young and their prejudices are not hardened, may seem unrealistic and condescending, but we should not ignore the particular route that drew Galt to this conclusion. Nor should we forget the stamp of the Glasgow Enlightenment upon Galt's wider oeuvre.

CHAPTER FOUR

Galt the Speculator: *Sir Andrew Wylie, The Entail,* and *Lawrie Todd*

Angela Esterhammer

John Galt lived, worked, and wrote as a speculator in an age of speculation. His major fiction dates from the 1820s, a decade in which historians often locate a paradigm shift in economic behaviour.[1] During this decade, stock markets in Britain experienced a severe boom-and-bust cycle brought about by a system of easy credit and rampant enthusiasm for speculative investments, including foreign government bonds as well as canal, railway, and mining projects at home and abroad. In intellectual and imaginative contexts, too, speculative behaviour pervades the 1820s, an era of experimentation with new technologies, media, and genres when the word 'speculation' itself was ever more frequently used. It was during this time that Galt founded and directed the Canada Company, an ambitious land-speculation project. Due in part to the setbacks he suffered in this commercial venture, he looked to literature as an alternative way of raising capital, investing his writing time in genres and media that were trending amongst readers and, in some cases, directly supported his business interests by promoting emigration to North America. Galt's on-the-ground experience with the business of speculation is reflected in his fictional works, where risk-taking entrepreneurial action drives plot, reveals character, and leads to social progress as well as social upheaval. As literary scholars become increasingly attentive to relationships between nineteenth-century fiction and economic concepts of value and credit, Galt's extensive exploration of the speculative mode promises further insights into a key phenomenon of his age.[2]

The *Oxford English Dictionary* defines speculation in the economic sphere as 'a commercial venture or undertaking of an enterprising nature, especially one involving considerable financial risk on the chance of unusual profit'. The speculator bases present actions on trends, probabilities, and projected values, taking risks on unknown futures and the uncertainties of other people's behaviour. Whether on the stock market or the book market, speculative ventures are vulnerable to accident, contingency, and unforeseeable shifts in public opinion that may cause windfalls or panics. Conversely, the interventions of speculators have varying effects on the social order and the welfare of others, for instance by driving up the price of commodities or by influencing perceptions that in turn affect socio-economic realities.

Galt's fiction is attuned to these reciprocal relationships of power and vulnerability between individual entrepreneurs and the contexts in which they act. Speculation in the form of initiative and enterprise is an essential element of socio-economic progress in his novels, whether for individual protagonists or within local and global economies. On the other hand, speculation can be irresponsible and manipulative, threatening the welfare of families and distorting natural patterns of development. These different valorisations take shape in Galt's fiction within different settings (Scotland, London, America) and with the help of different narrative perspectives (conservative, risk-taking, sceptical, committed). As Galt depicts economic speculation on the level of plot, he also engages in imaginative speculation about possible worldviews and outcomes. The present discussion will focus on three novels to illustrate Galt's contrasting analyses of speculation, reading *Sir Andrew Wylie* (1822) as an allegory of speculative investment, *The Entail* (1823) as a critique of the disruptive effects of speculation on a long-established patrimonial system, and *Lawrie Todd* (1830) as an illustration of the dynamic growth of a new economy based on entrepreneurship. New perspectives on all these fictional texts open up when they are read alongside Galt's little-known non-fictional essays on the history of commerce and financial speculation. Lastly, a late short story entitled 'The Speculawtor' (1838) provides an odd coda to Galt's depictions of speculative behaviour.

All of the above-mentioned tales have a fundamentally entrepreneurial theme, being stories of self-made men who rise from poverty to prosperity. To begin with, *Sir Andrew Wylie, of that Ilk* depicts the progress of Andrew, the orphaned son of a Scottish peasant, as he amasses financial and political capital in London and returns to his Scottish village of Stoneyholm as a propertied baronet and Member of Parliament to marry his childhood sweetheart, the daughter of the local laird. By the time he wrote *Sir Andrew Wylie*, Galt had been working for many years as a mercantile agent and would-be entrepreneur, and he had researched and written texts on economic policy and history. These include an 'Essay on Commercial

Policy' published in the *Philosophical Magazine* in 1805 and a long treatise on the history of English commerce that he wrote while he (like his hero Andrew Wylie) was working as a partner in a factors' company in London.[3] Incorporating Galt's interest in economics into a *Bildungsroman* of sorts, *Sir Andrew Wylie* can be read as a history of the economic moment in which it was written – that is, the boom market of the early 1820s – and as an analysis of speculative investment. Seen from this perspective, Andrew himself functions as an investment opportunity: an unknown commodity due to his obscure origin, and yet a stock character whose behaviour confirms people's expectations, Andrew Wylie is a vehicle in which other characters invest their confidence and their patronage. Like any stock, Andrew's perceived value rises and his ability to attract further investment increases the more that people invest in him. *Sir Andrew Wylie* is thus 'a veritable econometrics of character-*Bildung*', to use a phrase coined by Emily Apter to describe nineteenth-century French novels.[4]

As Andrew lives through the actual economic events of the years around 1800, the key to his steady career progress is the interplay between the assumptions that others impose on him and his own performance of character. Andrew Wylie's most memorable trait proves to be an odd combination of naiveté and the 'wiliness' suggested by his name, all of which is manifested in his ability to act the frank, natural, unaffected Scotsman in a manner that plays extraordinarily well among London's *beau monde*. After moving from rural Scotland to London, Andrew's introduction to the highly theatrical society of the metropolis quickly teaches him that he can ingratiate himself with the upper classes by continuing to perform his identity as a simple Scotsman. The transformation by which Andrew realises the value of his native identity in the urban marketplace occurs when he is unexpectedly invited to a high-class dinner-party hosted by the Earl of Sandyford:

> Andrew was agitated and confused; but, in ascending the stairs [...] the idea suddenly flashed upon him, that he owed the honour of the invitation to the simplicity of his Scottish manners and appearance. [...] [A] moment's reflection set all things right with our hero, and he seemed [...] to undergo a marvellous transmutation, from an awkward vulgar boy, into an easy and confident gentleman. [...] [H]e went forward in that agreeable state of self-possession, which a man feels when he knows it is in his power to dispense pleasure. Lord Sandyford, who possessed an acute perception of the latent powers of character, perceived, by the change, on the instant he threw his eyes on him as the door opened, that he was not the entire

simple oddity which he had first imagined, and immediately went towards him, and shook him by the hand, in a manner that raised him at once, as it were, into the equality and footing of a friend.[5]

In the course of this passage Andrew recognises the part he is to act, which is precisely to impersonate himself – or, one might say, to capitalise on his commodity value as the typical Scotsman. Throughout the novel, it remains ambiguous whether Andrew's patrons give him so much credit for his unique personal qualities, as the Earl of Sandyford implies by calling him 'a singular being'[6] – or for precisely the opposite reason, because he reassuringly fulfils a Scottish stereotype. Andrew is universally regarded as an 'original'[7] but also, paradoxically, as a commodity in the sense that he fills roles predefined by the socio-economic order, being in turn an apprentice, an entrepreneur, and a capable advisor and agent. Similarly, Andrew's identity conforms to the roles offered by various novelistic genres: picaro, orphan hero, stereotypical Scotsman, even at times an unlikely romantic hero. Andrew Wylie – and, on another level, Galt as the creator of the character Andrew – thus show themselves to be what Jerome Christensen has called 'masterful speculator[s]' who derive profit 'from the manipulation of the readymade as a commodity in the market'.[8]

Typically for Galt's fiction, the reader, too, is expected to make judgements about Andrew's credit-worthiness. Throughout the novel it remains undecidable whether Andrew is authentic – whether this investment is 'the real thing' – or whether he is exploiting his own marketability, possibly even to the point of fraud. The novel's final sentence sums up the source of Andrew's success as a harmonious combination of character and contingency ('prudence and good fortune united'),[9] but other descriptions imply a greater discrepancy between hidden cleverness and the mere appearance of naiveté: he is a 'sly simpleton'[10] who presents a face of 'supposed rustic simplicity',[11] yet maintains 'a degree of system in the simplicity of his manners'.[12] More than any other of Galt's characters, Andrew Wylie paradoxically performs candour and profits from an economy that values both type (in the sense of a familiar commodity) and hype (in the sense of reputation). With insightful humour, Galt's depiction of Andrew Wylie highlights the way people buy into the vision of Andrew that they want to see, so that he functions as a kind of joint-stock venture whose value rises spectacularly on the strength of the increasingly large investments that speculators from all ranks of society make in him. This story of speculation ends happily for almost everyone

– yet it raises enough doubt about the reliability of appearances and performances to leave the reader with an awareness of the risks of investing too much in them.

Appearing within months of *Sir Andrew Wylie*, *The Entail* tells a more cautionary story about a self-made Scotsman. A family saga set in the west of Scotland from the early 1700s until 1815, *The Entail* follows Claud Walkinshaw and three generations of his family through economic machinations, marriage alliances, and legal manoeuvring by which they seek to improve and secure their status based on ownership of property. The contrast in perspective compared with Sir Andrew Wylie is evident from the opening sentence of *The Entail* onward. In this case, the cause of the protagonist's initial poverty is a disastrous speculation: the Darien expedition of 1698–1700, in which Claud Walkinshaw's father lost his life and his grandfather lost the family estate. Brainchild of the adventurer William Paterson, the Darien venture was a grandiose plan to establish a Scottish colony and trade route on the isthmus of Panama. Within two years of its inception, it left three-quarters of the colonists dead and depleted Scotland of substantial capital sums that had been invested in the expedition.

In *The Entail*, the Darien fiasco functions as the first cause of the protagonist's destructive career of speculating on family alliances and the probability of future events. 'Claud Walkinshaw,' the novel begins,

> was the sole surviving male heir of the Walkinshaws of Kittlestonheugh. His grandfather, the last Laird of the line, deluded by the golden visions that allured so many of the Scottish gentry to embark their fortunes in the Darien Expedition, sent his only son, the father of Claud, in one of the ships fitted out at Cartsdyke, and with him an adventure in which he had staked more than the whole value of his estate.[13]

Claud's grandfather lost the family lands by entrusting his property to a fluctuating and unpredictable element, the sea. The word 'embark' does double duty in the above passage, referring literally to the sailing of the Darien expedition to America while reminding readers that 'embarking' one's fortune on any speculation involves the risk of sudden ruin. For the Walkinshaws, investment in Darien brings not only the loss of the estate but the loss of Claud's parents during his infancy: 'He was scarcely a year old when his father sailed, and his mother died of a broken heart, on hearing that her husband, with many of his companions, had perished of disease and famine among the swamps of the Mosquito shore.'[14] The narrator says little more about the Darien expedition after these lines, leaving the profound irony of the opening sentence to sink in: thanks to this disastrous speculation, Claud Walkinshaw is the 'sole surviving male heir' of nothing at all. Worse than nothing, Claud inherits a loss that becomes his obsession and the driving force of the novel when he schemes to reassemble his ancestors' landholdings, sacrificing the inheritance and the life of his own legitimate heir in the process.

Before taking *The Entail*'s condemnation of speculative ventures at face value, however, it is worth noting that Galt held a very different view of the Darien expedition in his non-fictional writing. He expressed great admiration for the expedition's promoter, William Paterson, and strove to redeem his reputation in a biography of Paterson that he was writing almost simultaneously with *The Entail*.[15] An excerpt of this biography later published in the *New Monthly Magazine* summarises Paterson's grand commercial schemes in the subtitle, calling him 'The Projector of the Darien Colony, the Banks of England and of Scotland, and other Public Undertakings'. In Galt's biographical narrative, the historical William Paterson becomes another self-made protagonist who begins as 'a poor stripling, proceeding from a lone cottage in a remote part of the kingdom, friendless and pennyless'.[16] His 'curiosity' leads him to become an adventurer and buccaneer; then, thanks to his genius for speculation, he mounts the 'grand colonial project' of the Darien Company.[17] Galt's enthusiasm for Paterson's achievements is especially intriguing in light of an uncannily similar venture that was in the news at the time Galt was writing his biography of Paterson and *The Entail*: an investment scheme invented by the Scotsman Gregor MacGregor to promote emigration to the Central American country of Poyais. The Poyais venture echoes the Darien expedition of the previous century in raising a huge investment for a plan to transplant Scottish emigrants to America – with the crucial difference that MacGregor's scheme, one of the most extreme expressions of the speculative climate of the early 1820s, was a perilous scam, for Poyais did not actually exist.[18] Most of the emigrants that MacGregor lured to Poyais, which he claimed was an established nation with towns and amenities, ended up dying, like Claud Walkinshaw's father in *The Entail*, 'of disease and famine among the swamps of the Mosquito shore'.[19] Against this complex background, Galt was laying his own plans for an investment scheme involving the sale and settlement of land in British North America. These plans would coalesce in 1824 with the founding of the Canada Company, by (in the words of the commemorative plaque to Galt in Guelph, Ontario) 'a group of British speculators' with John Galt at their head.

The contrast between Galt's enthusiastic engagement with transatlantic settlement projects and the much more negative attitude toward speculation in *The Entail* points to the novel's narrative perspective, which is that of a risk-averse anti-speculator. Galt's publisher William Blackwood repeatedly urged him to write *The Entail* in the first person; 'I hope you will be able to manage it so as that the hero tells the story himself,' Blackwood wrote to Galt on 11 June 1822, 'for you may depend upon it, that it is always the most effective way, and it is particularly your forte'.[20] But Galt instead chose to tell this story through a third-person narrator who, though unobtrusive, is neither omniscient nor neutral. He appears to be a young 'writer' – that is, a lawyer or Writer to the Signet (but with the double-entendre of writer as novelist) – who is tangentially involved with the affairs of the Walkinshaw family. This writer's own worldview occasionally becomes more prominent; it is the viewpoint of one who respects the law and the inherited social order it is meant to uphold, and who thus disapproves of Claud's moral and legal circumvention of the law of primogeniture. In one of the narrator's few self-referential comments, he characterises himself as settled and risk-averse: 'For all our days we have been naturally of a most sedate turn of mind.'[21] His disapproval of speculation is already evident in the diction of the novel's opening sentences, in the way he describes Claud's grandfather as 'allured' and 'deluded by [...] golden visions', makes clear that landed patrimony is not to be 'staked' or gambled on an 'adventure', and declines to consider any contextualising motive for the elder Walkinshaw and 'so many of the Scottish gentry' to have undertaken the Darien expedition.[22]

Similarly disapproving language surrounds other instances of speculation in *The Entail*. Another infamous new-world venture, the Mississippi Company promoted by exiled Scottish speculator John Law in 1719–20, blights the hopes of Claud's eldest son, Charles, because the family of his beloved Isabella Fatherlans is ruined by it:

> The father of Isabella was one of those unfortunate lairds who embarked in the Mississippian project of the Ayr Bank, the inevitable fate of which, at the very moment when the hopes of the lovers were as gay as the apple boughs with blossoms in the first fine mornings of spring, came like a nipping frost, and blighted their happiness for ever.[23]

Just as the 'Mississippi bubble', as it was commonly called, recalls the Darien scheme in being cast as a reckless speculation, the rhetoric of this passage echoes the oppositions set out in the first sentences of *The Entail*. Isabella's father is 'unfortunate' because he 'embarked' his fortune as liquid assets on a transatlantic speculation rather than remaining invested in land. The unhappy Isabella and her lover Charles Walkinshaw, by contrast, are associated with the rhythms of nature: apple boughs in spring, the produce of the land, the cycle of the seasons. As the Darien scheme leaves the heir without an inheritance, the Mississippi project leaves Isabella Fatherlans without her father's lands.

As Mark Schoenfield has noted, even if Claud Walkinshaw regards his own actions as a contrast to and reparation for his ancestors' reckless speculation on Darien, 'the plot' nevertheless 'asserts the continuity between the two projects'.[24] More than the plot, though, it is the conservative narrator who puts Claud in the same boat with his reckless forefathers by condemning his land dealings as 'cold-hearted speculations'.[25] His persistent suspicion of risky ventures that threaten the land-based feudal order brings about an alignment between various kinds of speculation throughout the novel: gambling; legal manoeuvring based on probabilities of birth, marriage, and death; and transatlantic emigration. Just before he dies, Claud looks back ruefully on his own actions in terms that suggest a game of chance: 'there's nae bail – no, not in the Heavens – for the man that has wilfully raffled away his own soul in the guilty game o' pride'.[26] Among Claud's descendants, American adventures continue to threaten disruption of the Scottish economy, echoing the Darien and Mississippi schemes of the previous century. The anti-speculative worldview of *The Entail* is especially evident when Claud's grandson James, who has a better claim that anyone else to be the sentimental hero of the novel, briefly considers emigrating to America:

> While tossing on these troubled and conflicting tides of the mind, he happened to recollect, that a merchant, a school-fellow of his father, and who, when he occasionally met him, always inquired, with more than common interest, for his mother and sister, had at that time a vessel bound for New York, where he intended to establish a store, and was in want of a clerk; and it occurred to him, that, perhaps, through that means, he might accomplish his wishes.[27]

Seen in the wider context of Galt's career and his oeuvre, this passage shows how *The Entail* reflects and inverts Galt's otherwise pro-emigration fiction. In several of Galt's other tales, a mercantile career, often in North America, is the way to status and success for just such a young Scotsman as James Walkinshaw; in Galt's own life and that of most of the men in his family, America and trade were the chosen paths. But in the conservatively inflected *Entail*, James's conjecture about emigration is immediately aligned with the metaphor of 'troubled and conflicting tides,' and the prospect of embarking on a vessel bound for New York, as his ill-fated great-grandfather did on the Darien expedition, is dismissed by the narrator as the 'sort of self-delusions [that] are very common to youths under age'.[28] In fact, James considers emigration chiefly as a way out of an unwelcome marriage into which he is being forced by the unfortunate entail of the family estate. When this negative incentive is removed by other means, James's desire to embark for America evaporates and is replaced by the (in this novel) more attractive alternative of a commission in the army to fight Napoleon.

Throughout *The Entail*, then, speculation – coloured by the perspective of a risk-averse narrator seeking the security of law and custom – is negatively inflected as a threat to the established order. The Darien scheme and the Mississippi bubble that set the background conditions for the novel's characters form an ominous counterpart to speculative ventures contemporary with the novel's composition, including Galt's soon-to-be-born Canada Company. Over the next few years, Galt would experience the anxieties of a transatlantic speculator first-hand, worrying that the capital he had attracted from investors in the Canada Company was not generating a return, and that he himself might inadvertently have promoted a speculative bubble.[29] In 1829, the Canada Company almost failed and Galt, having fallen out with the other Directors, found himself back in London in debtor's prison. His remedy was to make money by writing another long novel about a transatlantic entrepreneur: *Lawrie Todd; or, the Settlers in the Woods*.

Based on the memoirs of Grant Thorburn, an actual Scottish emigrant to upper New York State, and drawing on aspects of Galt's own practice as a land agent in Upper Canada, *Lawrie Todd* is the tale of a successful land speculator. Lawrie, like Thorburn and Galt, buys wilderness land and resells it at a profit once the advance of settlement and improved services have increased its value. His most important and profitable speculation is founding the town of Judiville (a stand-in for Rochester, New York) by buying a huge parcel of well-located, undeveloped riverfront wilderness around a tract that is being developed by his relative and partner, Mr Hoskins. By sub-dividing the parcel and carefully timing the sale of the lots at increasingly higher prices as he and Mr Hoskins establish a school, a church, and other institutions and trades, Lawrie amasses a fortune that enables him to support his children's careers in America while he retires comfortably to Scotland with his third wife.

Of all Galt's fictional biographies of Scottish lads who rise from humble origins, *Lawrie Todd* is the one most obsessed with speculative ventures. The first-person narrator holds up the founding of Judiville – 'my grand spec of the twenty thousand acres'[30] – as the climax of his career, and proposes to 'conclude the history of my speculations in this part of these memoirs, because I embarked in no other'.[31] Yet Judiville only marks the midpoint of a lengthy tale consisting from beginning to end of speculations or 'specs', as Lawrie habitually calls them. Setting up as a grocer in New York, he buys commodities from coffee beans to cod to flowers and seeds on credit and quickly resells them at a profit. Beyond retail commodities, Lawrie also speculates on people, including marriage partners. 'You should be a-making your calculations for another spec,' he is told after he has mourned the death of his first wife and it is time to look for a second.[32] He makes 'speculations'[33] on well-qualified emigrants by hiring them as schoolteachers, ministers, or bankers when he believes they will increase the attractiveness of new settlements and hence the dollar value of his land.

While *Lawrie Todd* affirms the importance of land speculation in advancing the rapid and efficient settlement of upper New York State, Lawrie occasionally reflects on its more ethically dubious aspects. When he employs subterfuge to make a good bargain for three hundred acres with a salt spring that, by rights, is the discovery of his rival Baillie Waft, Lawrie expresses concern that the reader might cast judgment on his 'hasty predilection for specs'[34] as he justifies himself with the claim that he has done it out of the obligation to provide for his eldest son. Another reflective moment occurs after he has established himself as a New York merchant adept at buying and selling commodities at a profit, when a chance encounter causes him to re-think his entire career path. Lawrie meets a virtuous widow, Mrs Micklethrift, on her way to visit her son the settler, whom she praises for making an honest living in the backwoods: 'as men increase and multiply,' she muses in biblical language, 'the value of his land will rise in the natural way, and without the artifice of speculation'.[35] Lawrie describes this encounter in terms that recall a Pauline conversion experience ('it opened my eyes to a new light'); it prompts him to change his way of life by giving up trade, which 'is likely ever to be fluctuating,'[36] and becoming a backwoods settler himself. For a moment the novel seems to set up an opposition – familiar to readers of *The Entail* – between 'natural' prosperity based on ownership and working of the land, and the artificial practices of commercial speculation. But in this pro-speculation novel, the tension can be resolved. Lawrie successfully brings a speculative economy into the backwoods by launching a scheme to provide supplies to poverty-stricken settlers on credit in the winter until they can pay them off by employment during the summer. This venture, well timed to relieve the wants of the settlers but also to turn a profit for Lawrie, proves to be the 'mustard seed' from which, he claims, 'sprung the great tree of my subsequent prosperity'.[37] Echoing the words of Jesus when he likens faith to 'a grain of mustard seed' (Luke 17.6), this choice of words puts Lawrie's speculative activities under the auspices of Christian faith and natural growth. In contrast to *The Entail*, the narrative perspective of *Lawrie Todd* allows for a reconciliation of speculative intervention with the rhythms of natural development in the context of North American colonisation.

Complicating and counterpointing Galt's novel-length explorations of speculative behaviour in *Sir Andrew Wylie*, *The Entail*, and *Lawrie Todd*, however, is a bizarre short story entitled 'The Speculawtor', published in *Tait's Edinburgh Magazine* a few months before Galt's death. It is in his signature style of fictional autobiography: the first-person narrator Peter Patterns narrates in his distinctive voice and dialect how he rose from being an orphan and 'poor scholar'[38] at the village school to learning the weaver's trade, becoming a partner in a small manufacturing concern, turning merchant and then investor, with the prospect of being elected provost still in the offing. Peter the 'speculawtor' (as he calls himself) thus shares a similar career path with Andrew Wylie, Lawrie Todd, Bogle Corbet, and to some extent with Galt himself. While Galt was not in the weaving business, this frequently occurring motif in his fictional biographies references one of the key industries of the Glasgow area and may figuratively evoke (via the derivation of 'text' from Latin *texere* 'to weave') his role as a 'weaver' of texts.

As the story's title suggests, Peter Patterns speaks from the viewpoint of a commercial speculator, although he claims to have become one accidentally as a result of historical circumstances. After the post-Revolutionary war with France brings about a general depression in the west of Scotland and drives Peter's mercantile business into bankruptcy, another unforeseen event brings about a reversal in his fortunes: the price of cotton skyrockets just after he has bought some, and Peter unexpectedly finds himself a speculator on the commodities market who makes money 'with the scrape of a pen in a *notandum* book, without the fasherie of a warehouse'.[39] But with this economic upheaval comes a spiritual crisis that distorts his internal sense of value: 'I felt in a way that was not creditable to my discretion, putting a value on things by the difficulty of getting them; reckoning those of the best that were farthest aboon my reach – a left-handed wisdom, in which the blighted are apt to indulge.'[40] In contrast to his steady socio-economic progress up to this point, Peter suddenly comes to desire those things that he cannot have, those that are most difficult or risky to attain, simply because they *are* risky.

Even as he proves adept at commodities trading, Peter worries that it is too much like gambling – and worse than gambling in the effect it has on other people's lives by withholding from them the goods that they most need:

> I had often an inward grue, even when I had made a sappy profit; for I thought the trade of a speculawtor no unlike that of a gamester. Many, many a time has a seroon of indigo reminded me, blue as it was, of a pair of dice, and a weel-spread out sample table, of a dambrod – saying to myself, verily the one is just as beneficial to the world as the other; but cards and dice are the least harmful; for surely to buy commodities, and hold them, that they may become scarce, to fetch a better price when sold, is not a right merchandising.[41]

Peter's narrative quickly turns from autobiography to a diatribe against speculators of a certain kind. Careful to excuse colonial speculators who do the public a service by importing scarce commodities from abroad, Peter – who now claims to have given up the speculating business – rails against domestic speculators who inflate prices merely for their own profit, and even calls on the public to rise up against them:

> Therefore, what I have now to counsel is, that, although some, like me, may make a bawbee by buying and selling commodities, it's a line that's no orthodox; only I dinna think it may well be put down by the law; but it's a duty we all owe to our species, to laugh and gaffaw at it when we can, till we make all sort of speculawtors gang by with their tails atween their legs, and as their noses were bleeding. It's for that I indite this.[42]

From public shaming of speculators, Peter goes even further to recommend violence: 'For God's sake, folk, crunch the speculawtors under your heels, like yird toads.'[43]

Peter Patterns, the rueful speculator, gives Galt one more perspective from which to ponder early-nineteenth-century socio-economic behaviour. The evils of speculation, according to this narrator, are legion: it is parasitic on real labour; it wilfully causes scarcity among those who are in need of commodities; it relies on a suspect system of values involving potential rather than actual capital; it leaves too much to fortune or accident. 'It's no a good line,' Peter concludes, 'and chiefly for this reason, it depends more on good luck than good guiding, which no right trade does'.[44] While analysing the distorting effects of speculation on the local economy, 'The Speculawtor' simultaneously exposes the speculative pattern that underlies Galt's characteristic tales of self-made men. Like the financial markets of the 1820s, Peter Patterns' status and net worth rise beyond expectation until a crisis in confidence brings about a reversal of values and a quick descent into self-doubt and recrimination. This bitter indictment suggests that the entrepreneurial progress of Galt's protagonists, which takes comic form in the case of Andrew Wylie or Lawrie Todd, is always vulnerable to accidents and reversals, and that the activities even of successful speculators cause distortions in the local economy that may or may not be admitted within the narrator's point of view.

Does Peter Patterns express Galt's last word, or is he only one among many projected voices? Galt's ability to imagine and express a variety of worldviews allows for a multifaceted exploration of speculative behaviour, a phenomenon that shaped material conditions and literary production during the 1820s and beyond. His narrators and protagonists include prosperous speculators and failed ones; observers, promoters, and victims of the market; schemers within a landed economy and projectors of settlements in the wilderness. Galt's real-life familiarity with many of these roles informs his approach to weaving texts and tales. The simultaneous performance and analysis of speculation that takes place in his fiction thus makes a signal contribution to the imaginative literature and social commentary of an economically eventful age.

CHAPTER FIVE

How John Galt Wrote North America

Ian McGhee

John Galt set sail from Falmouth in October 1826. He was bound for New York and then overland to Upper Canada where he was to take up his post as the Canada Company's first commissioner. For Galt, this was not merely a job. He believed that this was his opportunity to make a lasting mark and to win renown as a community builder in a still unpolished jewel of the British Empire. Things did not quite go according to plan and, though he did achieve fame in the colonies, it came posthumously, after much personal difficulty and disappointment. The experience produced two novels, *Lawrie Todd* and *Bogle Corbet*, as well as a number of magazine articles, and in their different ways they tell us much about Galt's precepts and ideas in relation to settling the wilderness.

Galt became involved with Canada in 1820. He was enjoying success as a parliamentary agent – what we would now call a lobbyist or fixer – having secured the passage of an Act to allow the building of the Union Canal to join Edinburgh to the existing Forth and Clyde Canal at Falkirk. In that capacity, he was approached by a group of Canadians who were seeking compensation from the British government for losses incurred when they repelled a US invasion of British Canadian territory during the War of 1812. These Canadians engaged Galt in December 1820[1] to progress their claims and offered him commission of three per cent on any monies recovered but explained that it would not be possible to advance any money for expenses.[2] Galt was therefore committing himself to a great deal of work on a purely speculative basis.

Galt soon discovered that the government, while generous with sympathy, would not be forthcoming with any money. He realised, however, that the Crown held a vast acreage that had not yet been surveyed or assigned to townships and hit upon the idea that a company could be formed to buy undeveloped land in Canada from the government. In effect the company would buy land wholesale, divide it into smaller parcels, carry out some development in the way of roads and other infrastructure, and then retail individual lots to settlers and immigrants. The price paid by the company would be used by the government to meet the claims of the 1812 war victims and to contribute to the expenses of the colonial administration.[3]

The Canada Company was duly formed in 1824, was granted a charter in 1826, and bought almost 2.5 million acres from the government, which took the money but did not compensate the settlers. Nevertheless, Galt was now enthusiastically committed to the project and drove it forward. He was already a successful author but Galt's true ambitions lay in business. This was the arena in which he wished to prove himself for, as he said, 'I have ever held literature to be a secondary pursuit'[4] and 'a mere literary man – an author by profession – stands but low in my opinion'.[5]

Circumstances, and his own personality, conspired against Galt's work in Canada. The provincial establishment, including the Lieutenant-Governor Sir Peregrine Maitland, were staunchly Anglican and regarded Galt, a Presbyterian, as a threat to their established order. Presbyterianism especially carried the taint of a democratic form of church governance and Galt could well be bringing in dangerously radical ideas. In fact, Galt was a lifelong Tory, as he makes clear in his *Literary Life*.[6] He defended the existing class system, as can be seen in one of his magazine articles about North America.[7] And he was never a sectarian in religion. When he founded Guelph he reserved three prime sites for the Anglican, Roman Catholic and Presbyterian churches and persuaded the Canada Company to gift the land rather than sell it.[8]

Galt did remarkably well in Canada. He founded the cities of Guelph and Goderich and established a business model that kept the Canada Company profitable for over a hundred years. Unfortunately, recognition for his efforts had to wait until long after he had left the country. He was undone by a combination of his own failings, the impatience of his directors and shareholders, and the difficulties of communication over time and distance. He had warned the company that this was a medium- to long-term investment but did not do enough to secure the company's commitment to that goal. He failed to realise that its directors were intent, primarily, on short-term profits. More seriously, Galt did not pay sufficient attention to the details of his accounts. In mitigation, it should be noted that he had to operate without adequate staff and he frequently had to be a one-man band. There is no suggestion that he misappropriated money, but there is considerable evidence that he did not keep proper financial records. For a company worried about the drain on its finances before profits were made, this was a serious matter. Finally, Galt's own personality was a major contributor to his downfall. He tended to behave as though whatever he believed to be right should be equally evident to everyone else. Consequently, he seldom tried to prepare the ground adequately for his policy proposals and, when faced with opposition, resorted to affronted self-justification, as in the attack on Maitland's policies accompanying Galt's application to him for a grant of land at Burlington.[9] As J. K. Herreshoff puts it, 'frequently the letters written by Galt during his Canadian years reveal a considerable degree of self-delusion and a continuing pattern of self-destructive behaviour'.[10] Greater awareness of the consequences of his actions on other people and a much more diplomatic approach to the provincial government would have buttressed Galt's position both locally and with the company in London.

As it was, the company recalled him to London; he left Canada in April 1829, receiving on the morning of his departure an address of gratitude from the settlers.[11] Matters then became worse for he was sued for a debt that he could not pay, and he entered the King's Bench prison in the British capital for three months. The one thing Galt could do was write and, rather like Sir Walter Scott in a similar predicament, he became astonishingly productive. Novels and articles poured from his pen. *Southennan* was published in 1830, his *Life of Lord Byron* in the same year, and a book of biographical sketches, *The Lives of the Players*, in 1831.

This period also saw the publication, in 1830 and 1831 respectively, of Galt's two novels with largely North American settings, *Lawrie Todd, or, The Settlers in the Woods* and *Bogle Corbet, or, The Emigrants*.[12] Both books attempt to impart the lessons Galt learned from his North American experiences. They were intended to be primers for prospective emigrants, but they also set out the policies that Galt believed governments should adopt to promote effective colonial settlement. *Lawrie Todd* is, apart from a visit to Scotland by the eponymous protagonist, set wholly in the United States, but *Bogle Corbet* switches locations from the West Indies to Scotland, to London, and finally to Canada. The differences in the related experiences reflect Galt's perceptions of US and British attitudes and foreshadow significant literary tropes associated with the south and the north that pertain to the Forty-Ninth Parallel.

Both novels are arguably too long. Galt tended to be happier, and better, with shorter forms, but his publisher demanded triple-deckers and, possibly because *Lawrie Todd* was padded out with appendices and other extraneous material, the contract for *Bogle Corbet* stipulated not only that the novel was 'to consist of at least three volumes' but also that each volume was to extend to 'at least three hundred and twenty pages'.[13] Nevertheless, both novels contain much that is good in literary terms and even more that is worth consideration from cultural and historical viewpoints. Both are written as faux autobiographies, a form that is Galt's favourite narrative mode of presenting truth and reality, often of course implicitly. It is a method that served him well in his successful early texts set in Ayrshire. Kenneth Simpson describes the technique as giving scope for ironic 'self-revelation' with *Annals of the Parish* and *The Provost* 'masterpieces' of the technique.[14] The North American novels are not quite on a par with these predecessors but the elements of self-revelation are equally devastating in their psychological propensities. Although 'faux', the first of the novels, *Lawrie Todd*, takes an actual autobiography as its starting point. Grant Thorburn, a penniless nailmaker, skipped bail on a charge of sedition and hurriedly left Scotland in 1792, at the height of the democratic ferment occasioned by the early stages of the French Revolution. He emigrated to the United States, where, having done well for himself, he wrote his life story. Galt met Thorburn in New York and tells us that he bought the manuscript from Thorburn for 'an author's, not a publisher's price'.[15] Thorburn subsequently sought to capitalise on his association with Lawrie Todd and when he published his book under his own name Galt willingly gave up his rights to the manuscript and contributed a preface to the work.[16]

Given that Thorburn states in his preface that 'I have thought for many years that it was a debt I owed to society to publish my life', it is easy to see why his manuscript attracted a novelist of ironic bent. Galt underscores the trait by having Lawrie say that 'I was never slack of giving good advice when a fitting opportunity came in the way, always considering it a duty incumbent to benefit the rest of the world with the fruits of my experience' (I, p. 135). Thorburn's story is, however, only the starting point. In a novel of nine parts, only the first two are closely modelled on it. From the beginning of Part III, Galt takes the narrative into, literally, new territory and away from Thorburn's life although he retains Thorburn's character in the overtly religious but sharp businessman who ascribes his success, in a self-satisfied way, to the workings of Providence and the favour of God. New York, the setting for Parts I and II, reveals Galt's primary purpose to let Britons know the nature of the wilderness and how best to settle it. He thus moves the action to the Genessee country of northern New York State. On his overland journey to Canada, Galt, as instructed by the directors, studied the operations of two of the most respected land companies in that area and wrote back that his 'visits to the Pulteney and Holland land companies was most satisfactory'.[17] The primary didactic purpose of the novel is to let those on the other side of the Atlantic understand something of the nature of the wilderness; thus, there are descriptions of snakes (I, p. 189), forest fires (I, p. 216), encounters with wolves (I, p. 226), and with bears (I, p. 248). Galt seeks to avoid the obvious in his didacticism; cleverly, each of these episodes has the dual purpose of providing a dramatic moment in the plot as well as an opportunity to instruct readers about what may be encountered in this new wild land. He also shows what must be done to make the wilderness habitable. He demonstrates the method of building shanties, or temporary dwellings, (I, p. 188) and then houses (I, p. 212), taking care to note that unseasoned timber will shrink in warm weather (I, p. 213), and the best way to clear the ground of trees (I, p. 212). He warns prospective settlers about the weather conditions that will be encountered by describing a flood (I, p. 196) and by unobtrusively pointing out that work is impossible 'during the wet weather, in which no man could work' (I, p. 229). Such conditions also make travelling very difficult so that after a short journey by wagon 'my hips and knees were both black and blue, and I could scarcely lift a limb' (I, p. 253). It was possibly surprising for British readers but he makes it clear that during the winter the best means of travel is by sleigh (I, p. 259). All in all, Todd says that 'the discomforts of the first few years of a new settlement are unspeakable' (II, p. 103). Apart from being true, these descriptions serve to warn the would-be settler that he should read the agents' advertisements with a healthy degree of scepticism.

Case studies of good and bad practice are offered in *Lawrie Todd*. On the one hand, there is a Paisley weaver and his family who bring far too much baggage and meet great difficulty and loss as a result. Settlers should acquaint themselves with what is actually required in the wilderness and limit themselves to the necessities. On the other hand, there is the Cockspur family who emigrate from England and are 'a genteeler class than migrants commonly consist of […] and were, for settlers the best prepared of all I have ever met with' (II, p. 116). They pay for their land cash down and are examples of the type of middle-class emigrant that Galt continually implored the Colonial Office to encourage. This idea was a recurrent theme in the articles he wrote about government emigration policy. At a time when emigration was seen as the answer to surplus numbers of the working class in Britain, Galt was preaching a version of trickle-down economics: the middle class with capital to make the land work would in time provide opportunities for tradesmen, labourers, and servants.

But even the Cockspurs need advice about their attitudes to their new country. Todd tells one of the young men of the family:

> You will be much mistaken if you expect to find America like England, and still more so if you think it may be made so. I have seen many self-conceited emigrants, who imagined it might: not being able at home to make England like America, they come here, and their first work is to make America like England. It is wonderful how much this is the case with the reforming gentry (I, p. 239).

It is perhaps noteworthy that Galt uses England rather than Britain for this warning. His Scottish characters seem to be more inclined to take things as they find them and, while reminiscing fondly about the old country, adapt more readily to their new circumstances. Todd is himself the prime example of this trait, and, while he makes a great deal of his national identity, he chooses English people to exemplify refinement of education and character.

Of the principal characters in the novel, the Cockspurs and Mr Herbert are English and Mr Zerobabel L. Hoskins is American; all the others are Scots. The Cockspurs and Mr Herbert are conspicuously the most 'genteel' middle-class characters in the book. Todd reinforces the point by saying that 'no gentlewoman can ever be properly genteel that speaks with the Scottish accent' (III, p. 175). Galt had shown no cultural cringe in his previous, and best-selling, novels and personally made few concessions in terms of Scottish speech. Here, however, he is not only reflecting via Todd a common attitude among Scots in relation to language; he is writing for prospective emigrants and is keen to make sure that they get the best possible start in their new land. It is also, of course, a way to flatter his target market, the majority of whom would be English. Mr Hoskins is Galt's typical American. Virtually the same character occurs as Mr Peabody in his short story 'Scotch and Yankees, a Caricature'.[18] Mr Hoskins meets all the specifications of what was to become emblematic of the American character. 'He is plain speaking and entrepreneurial and was one of those who thought Laws and Governments often inconvenient and always troublesome' (III, p. 197).

Nationality is a recurrent theme in the novel and is especially pertinent to the conflicting patriotic emotions of the emigrant, torn between the emotional bond to his roots and the practical realisation that America is his home and the future for himself and his family. The successful Todd does make a return visit to Scotland, which 'of all the passages of my life [...] was the most unsatisfactory' (III, p. 117). He recognises that he has been away too long and that the country and people he remembers are changed, just as he is changed by his years in America. He has, like many travellers, retained in his imagination a picture of the place he left, and, while his conscious mind accepts the inevitability of change, his subconscious is disappointed that things are not as he left them. Galt was by no means a political nationalist. The Hanoverian succession and the British state were perfectly acceptable to him, but he could be described as a cultural nationalist for the way he deployed Scottish speech in this book and, even more so in his West of Scotland novels, for the way he defended Presbyterianism as Scotland's established religion and a beneficent inheritance for its people. Like Walter Scott, Galt was a unionist who was fascinated by Scotland's independent past, but the two men viewed that history through very different lenses. Scott romanticised Highlanders and Jacobites, as in *Waverley* and *Rob Roy*; Galt had little time for Highlanders, as we will see in *Bogle Corbet*.

In *Lawrie Todd*, Galt attaches a glossary at the end of the book to explain Scots and American words and expressions. This is a departure from his previous practice. In his early novels, with more frequent and broader Scots therein, readers are trusted to deduce the meanings of unfamiliar words from the context. This proved no great barrier to sales, even in England. There are two possible and plausible explanations for the inclusion of the glossary. The first is the simple practical point that Galt needed the extra pages to fulfil his agreement to provide Colburn and Bentley with a full three volumes. The second and more fundamental reason, perhaps, is that this is a novel of instruction and Galt would have been keen to ensure that his readers were as fully prepared as possible for emigration. He would not have wanted any misunderstanding about what the Scots settlers or American natives were saying and he would have wanted the would-be emigrants to be aware that they would encounter unfamiliar words and forms of speech. Unlike his novels set in Scotland, these North American texts had a specific didactic purpose, and Galt was seeking a wider and possibly less well-educated readership. The Americanisms he glosses include 'boozer' and 'boss', which are defined as 'a drunkard' and 'an overseer of mechanics' respectively (III, p. 317). A 'cocktail' is 'a dram of bitters' (III, p. 318) and a 'snack' is 'a hasty refreshment' (III, p. 322). The *Oxford English Dictionary* confirms that 'boss' in this sense is American and cites Galt as one of the first users.[19]

For 'cocktail', however, the first use is shown as 1856 and refers to a person who is 'cocktailed' or the worse for drink. It is not used to mean a mixed drink until 1936, while 'snack' is quoted as originating in England. The words were obviously sufficiently unfamiliar to Galt to warrant explanation to his readers. The Scots words also represent a departure from his previous practice. There are no glossaries in the West of Scotland novels with which he made his name, but here he is concerned to be fully understood by all his readers. That does not prevent him from sometimes adopting a Johnsonian approach to his lexicography. 'Gausy' is defined as 'comfortably fat. See many landladies, aldermen and church dignitaries' (III, p. 319) and 'spider', the implement that causes Todd so much trouble with Bailie Waft, as 'an iron utensil for some kitchen purpose, the exact use not known to me' (III, p. 322). Language always matters to Galt, and he takes great care with it.

The novel tells us much about Galt's views on class, gender, religion, and the professions, about which he always maintained a healthy scepticism. He would certainly have agreed with Shaw that 'all professions are conspiracies against the laity'[20] and seldom missed an opportunity to deliver an ironic slap to bankers and, especially, lawyers. These are, however, side issues to the main theme, which is the instruction of prospective emigrants and the desirability of promoting the kind of emigration policies that Galt espoused. An unexpected consequence of such an approach is that Galt has here produced the prototype novel of the American dream. A penniless immigrant arrives in New York, works hard, lives soberly, fears God, overcomes setbacks, and eventually becomes a wealthy and respected member of the community. Lawrie Todd appears to be an example of the Protestant–Capitalist nexus, but Galt puts this in perspective. He shows that Todd puts the Capitalist part before the religious one in any conflict, that his loudly declared morality is no barrier to sharp practice in business and that immigrants are conflicted, at both conscious and deeply subconscious levels, in attitudes to their old and new countries.

Bogle Corbet is also a novel of instruction, but Bogle Corbet is a very different kind of character, in both class and temperament, from Lawrie Todd. Corbet is, on the face of it, the type of middle-class emigrant with modest capital that Galt is trying to encourage. Yet he is a strange choice to carry this message, lacking the simple goodness of Micah Balwhidder or the roguish charm of James Pawkie. He is indecisive, fearful of losing his position in society, and driven to emigration by business failure, but he is recognisably human. The text is much more wide-ranging geographically than *Lawrie Todd*. Corbet is born in the West Indies, quickly orphaned, brought to Scotland to be brought up by a relative, moves to London as a young man, and emigrates to Canada in middle age. He also finds time for lengthy excursions to Jamaica and the Highlands. Kenneth McNeil describes the book as a Circum-Atlantic novel[21] which reflects the nature of trade mainly in grain from North America to the West Indian plantations, sugar from there to Britain, and textiles and manufactured goods from Britain to both destinations. Commercial flows required complementary labour and capital flows including, of course, the slave trade. This Circum-Atlantic commerce was a subject that interested Galt. He wrote an article in 1830 for *Blackwood's* promoting tariff preference for Canadian corn and predicting how the United States would not only in time produce for itself the agricultural products of the West Indies but also acquire the manufacturing capacity to dispense with imports from Britain.[22] As a political economist Galt's forecasts ran counter to contemporary received opinion but generally turned out to be more accurate. McNeil says that Galt's output, including the earlier west of Scotland novels, represents an 'effort to provide a broad overview of the economic forces that shape a society of a given space and over a given time'. He also says that 'Galt rejected the category of romance altogether, which he felt was too devoted to the contrivances and artifices of plot. Instead, historical "truth" is grounded in the logic of probability and exemplarity'.[23] This is what Galt called 'theoretical histories', borrowing the term from the Scottish Enlightenment philosopher Dugald Stewart and in the case of *Bogle Corbet* refining it, as described in the preface, to 'theoretical biography' (I, p iv). We might today classify such work as dramatised documentary.

Like *Lawrie Todd*, the primary purpose of *Bogle Corbet* is didactic. Galt is 'desirous to exhibit the causes which now in this country induce a genteeler class of persons to emigrate than those who did so formerly'.[24] These are his views on emigration policy cast in the form of a novel, but he is also led to extensive animadversions on class, social mobility, and race. Threats to class status permeate the text. Corbet is obsessed and frightened by Eric Pullicate, who enters the story as a radical weaver but ends up as a rich burgess and landowner; 'from a democrat of the very jacobine order he had evolved into a temperate Whig. Had he acquired an estate, he would undoubtedly have been a Tory' (I, p. 190). Yet he 'inspired [Corbet] with something like the antipathy entertained for Doctor Fell' (I, p. 45), despite the fact that 'I could not trace to him one single event by which my happiness had in any degree sustained detriment, I yet felt an involuntary aversion at the sight of him – an antipathy which reason condemned' (II, p. 154). In part, this fear is occasioned by the admission that Pullicate has divined Corbet's own weaknesses, but it is more about the way in which a member of the working classes, by superior intelligence and application, can overtake those who were formerly his superiors. Corbet believes that society should be organised along class lines, and he takes this belief to Canada. Shortly after the party of Scottish emigrants arrives in Ontario, he suggests that 'they only wanted a gentleman with capital to come among them, who would take a magisterial interest in their general affairs' (III, p. 2). Corbet, who by temperament seems unfitted to be a leader yet has greater education and refinement, and who has slightly more money, feels obliged to assume the role, and the working-class emigrants accept this situation as representing the natural order.

Corbet here is reflecting something of Galt's outlook. The writer personally tended to favour tolerance and assimilation rather than repression of radicals. Corbet believes in hierarchy, but he feels forced to admit the attraction of democracy and upward mobility to young radicals. When he is studying the weaving business he sympathises with them for being 'undeserving of the contumely with which they were regarded by the higher ranks' (I, p. 42) because they were simply trying to better themselves. The novel notes that it is the more intelligent workers who are democrats and that if they had a legitimate outlet for their ambitions they would soon dispense with extreme politics. On the other hand, some of the emigrant party express a desire to cross the border into the United States because, their spokesman declares, 'every residenter in the States has the privilege of a hand in the Government, which, considering what we have suffered from the want of that at home, ye will alloo is a fine thing' (III, p. 19). Corbet makes a temporising reply but thinks that the speaker 'was leavened with the radical leaven. And like all those who are so, though not unplausible, self-willed and witless at bottom' (III, p. 20). Corbet is not therefore a model of consistency, attesting again to Galt's acuity as an observer of human behaviour.

Galt found slavery particularly difficult. One of the surprising things about *Bogle Corbet* is the large part of the novel set in Jamaica and the details given of plantation life. Galt never set foot near the Caribbean though his brother died in Montego Bay[25] and his father was a skipper in the West India trade before he became a shipowner and moved the family from Irvine to Greenock.[26] Galt is therefore relying on secondary testimony and source, but this does not prevent him from reaching large-scale conclusions. Galt foresees that emancipation is inevitable but worries about 'the state that awaits the negroes when the control of their proprietors shall have been withdrawn' (I, p. 298). In his autobiography, he is more explicit about his concerns. There must be the 'the necessity of making some provision for the negroes before emancipation, and claiming for the planters compensation for depriving them of their property'.[27] Galt's description of the plantations is Panglossian in its depiction of contented, well-treated 'negroes' and it ignores the harsher realities. There may be no 'inferiority imputed' and abolition may be inevitable, but Galt suggests that slavery is not all bad and that slaves not only have a better life than British paupers but also may not be ready for freedom. Despite such a paternalistic attitude, there is acknowledgement that the owners are demeaned by keeping slaves and there is some criticism of their domestic arrangements in terms of taking black mistresses. Nonetheless, Galt is content to record what he has observed (or, more accurately, been told) and in a manner worrying to modern minds notes concern for the owners in relation to the potential loss of property.

If Galt had mixed messages to deliver about black people, he was unequivocal about Highlanders, at least those below the rank of gentleman. They are mocked mercilessly for a number of supposed faults. They are, perhaps unsurprisingly, clannish and 'have but little kindness to spare for the common offspring of Adam' compared to their own 'kith and kin' (III, p. 83). Galt ignores the fact that lowland Scots were equally guilty of congregating together when they emigrated to Canada, as is the case in this novel. The language of the Highlanders is mocked as 'the dislocated Celtic gibberish in use among the lower classes who frequent the Lowlands' (II, p. 213), and when they speak English it is an excuse for more mockery as in: 'Thank Got we are true clansmen, though we pe in Canada, och hon, umph!' (III, p. 13). The Lowland emigrants consider the Highlanders to be dirty and lazy, declaring that 'they'll no' be overly industrious anent improvement' and that they have 'splendid propensities for dirt and indolence' (III, p. 11). These attitudes towards Highlanders were not uncommon among Lowland Scots at that time, but it is still surprising to see Galt adopt them with fewer qualifications or caveats than he would apply to black people or Indians. His empiricism and judgements based on observation rather than prejudice seem to have deserted him when considering what were, after all, his fellow-countrymen.

Galt succeeded in his declared aims of 'exhibiting the causes which now in this country induce a genteeler class of persons to emigrate' and, having shown why such people emigrate, equipping them with the knowledge to make the best way they can in a sometimes frightening wilderness. Galt's problem is that not only does he have to wrap this didactic purpose in a cloak of entertainment but also stretch that cloak to cover at least three volumes each of three hundred and twenty pages. The lengthening process leaves the material very thin in places, and it has to be patched with extraneous back-stories about some of the characters such as that of Mrs Paddock or Colonel Jocelyn. Tacked on at the end is a gazetteer of places in Upper Canada. Ian A. Gordon, in his biography of the literary Galt, states that 'the extent of my commentary on each [work] being largely a measure of my estimate of its importance' gives a paragraph and a sentence to *Bogle Corbet*.[28] This, though, is too harsh a judgement. The novel is not without merit. It contains too many longueurs to be wholly satisfying, but it is worth reading for descriptions of the wilderness and the lifelike characterisations, and for the depiction of Corbet as he develops from a complaisant younger man with very little motivation to one who can be decisive and commanding when required to direct the efforts of a group of settlers in establishing a functioning community in the wilderness. It is also, as usual with Galt, full of a pawky humour, and it perhaps bears out Paul Scott's criticism of the 'flat and fushionless English'[29] in which it is sometimes written that the best of the humour and the easiest flowing passages are those concerned with the Glasgow merchant Mr Macindoe and with the west of Scotland settlers in Canada. Shining through the entire text is the consistency of Galt's views on what is required by the governments in London and Ontario, for colonisers like the Canada Company, and for settlers themselves, to create successful new communities. The same policies that Galt had been promoting in his journalism and in his dealings with the Colonial Office are repeated here within the different medium of the novel, which he possibly believed would have greater effect.

Bogle Corbet and *Lawrie Todd* have obvious similarities. They are faux-autobiographical in form, didactic in purpose, and based on real, observed experience. Both demonstrate in practical terms the benefits of Galt's favoured emigration and community-building policies. But they are different in tone and outcome. Lawrie Todd is a successful man who has remade himself in the United States, where entrepreneurial spirit is encouraged to flourish and the state, in Galt's view wisely, allows private enterprise the lead in the creation of new settlements. Indeed, so much is this a keystone of Galt's approach that he puts it in block capitals in one of his articles. 'THE BUSINESS OF SETTLING A NEW COUNTRY

IS MUCH BETTER MANAGED BY PRIVATE ADVENTURERS THAN BY GOVERNMENTS' is the ringing conclusion to a *Blackwood's* piece of 1826.[30] *Bogle Corbet* is much more downbeat. The eponymous hero is in many ways a failure, and although he finds some personal redemption in Canada the book ends with him accommodating himself to a modest future rather than triumphing against the odds. In this respect it is probably a more representative example of the lives of the vast majority of emigrants. It can also be seen as reflective of the different countries, independent state, and colony, or at least Galt's experience of them. He was impressed, without ignoring the concomitant faults, by the business-friendly capitalist ethos of the United States, whereas he felt badly bruised by the provincial government in Ontario and the short-sighted attitudes of his board of directors. Nevertheless, he persisted in believing that he had been taking the right path in his own colonial adventures and, arguably, he was vindicated by subsequent events. As he predicted, 'although it cannot be said that I have myself in my own person accomplished much, I have yet sown the seeds of things that in the course of nature may attain magnitude and afford shelter'.[31]

CHAPTER SIX

Commemorating the Covenanters in *Ringan Gilhaize*

Alison Lumsden

It is a critical commonplace to recognise that John Galt's *Ringan Gilhaize* was written in response to Walter Scott's tale of the Covenanting Wars, *Old Mortality*. The controversy that Scott's novel caused is well known. While popular with the public it met with an angry response from the Seceder minister Thomas McCrie, who berated it for its 'partiality to the persecutors' and its 'injustice to the persecuted Presbyterians'.[1] Scott responded to these criticisms in his own review of the work and an ideological battleground was staked out as different factions fought for the right to give voice to what was still a highly resonant, and potentially still relevant, moment in Scottish history.[2] It was this political controversy that dominated criticisms of the novel by both John Galt and James Hogg.

While Hogg claimed that he had written his own Covenanting novel, *The Brownie of Bodsbeck*, long before Scott published *Old Mortality*, he was certainly revising it after Scott's novel appeared. But, whatever the chronology, Hogg makes it clear that the novels were set in opposition to each other. Hogg reports that when Scott read *The Brownie* he noted: 'I like it very ill – very ill indeed [...] Because it is a false and unfair picture of the times and the existing characters altogether' but that he (Hogg) retorted 'It is the picture I hae been bred up in the belief o' sin' ever I was born and I had it frae them whom I was most bound to honour and believe [...] An' that's a good deal mair than you can say for your tale o' Auld Mortality.'[3] John Galt's objection to Scott's representation of the Covenanters was on equally ideological grounds. As Crawford Gribben notes, Galt claimed that Scott 'laid an irreverent hand' on the great national cause[4] and in his *Literary Life* he reports that he

> was hugely provoked that he, the descendant of Scott of Harden, who was fined in those days forty thousand pounds Scots for being a

Presbyterian, or rather for countenancing his lady for being so, should have been so forgetful of what was due to the spirit of the epoch, as to throw it into what I felt was ridicule.⁵

Set in opposition in this way by their own authors, these fictions by Scott, Hogg, and Galt apparently offer radically alternative readings of the Covenanters and the legacies they had left for nineteenth-century Scotland. While Scott is figured as offering a straightforward critique of the Covenanters and an endorsement of the Royalist cause, Hogg and Galt are positioned as recuperating a more sympathetic view of the Covenanters in their texts. In spite of much recent reassessment of Scott and Hogg, and to a lesser extent Galt, this view persists; in the recent *Edinburgh Companion to James Hogg*, for example, the notion that Hogg is simply writing an alternative historical novel that casts a kinder eye over the Covenanting cause is reiterated by both Douglas Mack⁶ and Graham Tulloch,⁷ while in *The Edinburgh Companion to Scottish Romanticism* Crawford Gribben claims that Hogg elevates 'the voice of the folk above the voice of the elite'; Galt, similarly, is figured as preparing an 'alternative' account to Scott in *Ringan Gilhaize*.⁸

However, while it cannot be denied that both Hogg and Galt prompt this response by drawing attention to the ways in which they are in opposition to Scott's novel, there are clearly problems in approaching these texts only in this way, something that becomes apparent as critics try to grapple with their complexities and how they may be read. Mack, for example, acknowledges that *The Brownie* 'is not really a [historical novel] about the Covenanters' at all, but rather a novel about community and the underdog,⁹ while others who have attempted to read it within the paradigm of historical fiction have had to account for what emerge as 'failures' within it. Ina Ferris, for example, suggests that in *The Brownie* the 'narrative stances remain unintegrated, and Hogg moves awkwardly among them, producing a general narrative uneasiness'. She concludes that this may be because Hogg is aware that he is writing in the wrong genre.¹⁰ Galt draws attention to the space between Scott's stylistic methods and his own, defining his works as 'theoretical histories' rather than historical fictions, thus suggesting a difference in methodology as well as in political opinion.¹¹

Nevertheless, comparisons between the Covenanting novels of these three authors all rest on the covert assumption that they are 'historical novels' in the classic sense as formulated by György Lukács.¹² This posits that the essential element of historical fiction is that it employs historical detail not only as backdrop but also to interrogate the process of history itself and how it operates. For Lukács, Scott offers the epitome of this model. What is read as his Enlightenment faith in a progressive model of history becomes the exemplar of what historical process means.[13] Ferris's recognition that Hogg is writing in 'the wrong genre' is, however, interesting, and prompts the suspicion that it may in fact be we who are reading in the wrong genre. Moreover, Ian Duncan has suggested that the narrative strategies adopted by Galt and Hogg may have developed as an opposition to Scott's employment of the romance topos as a way of dealing with history, recognising that they are operating within different narrative paradigms.[14] This chapter will suggest that both Scott's and Galt's Covenanting texts may, in fact, be best read not as historical novels in the conventional sense at all but, rather, as acts of commemoration. By reading them in this way we begin to see new dynamics emerge, which may reveal that Scott and Galt have more in common than initially appears.

There are certainly clues within *Old Mortality* that invite us to read it in this way. Recent reassessments of Scott have drawn attention to the fact that his approaches to history and historiography are far more complex than traditional readings would imply, and crucial to any alternative reading of *Old Mortality* is the opening chapter in which the narrator Peter Pattieson describes an encounter with the figure of Old Mortality as he travels the country restoring the graves of the Covenanters in order to 'repair these emblems of death'.[15] The recuperation of Scott's title *The Tale of Old Mortality* by the Edinburgh Edition of the Waverley Novels draws attention to the role of this figure and establishes a somewhat different relationship between the narrative and the figure of Old Mortality. The new title foregrounds his presence in the novel in significant and ambiguous ways: this is either a tale *about* Old Mortality – which it clearly is not – or *by* him, an equally difficult proposition but one at least supported by Pattieson's claim that the novel is based on the anecdotes Old Mortality has communicated to him, even if supplemented by other sources. Read in this way, the status of the novel itself becomes somewhat more problematic, and we are prompted to consider whether its designation as 'tale' further invites a way of reading it beyond the classic framework of the historical novel.

Several critics have been alert to this possibility. Catherine Jones, for example, suggests that forms of memory are central to all of Scott's fiction, and she argues that the dispute that the novel generated was caused by Scott's harnessing of the communal memory of the Covenanters.

Ina Ferris recognises that Old Mortality's acts, and the dying Peter Pattieson's commentary on them, prompt a kind of 'reflection' that may be in opposition to conventional historical process. However, while such criticism acknowledges the significance of memory and commemoration in the novel's opening chapter, it frequently sets this in opposition to the narration which follows. Jones, for example, argues that the novel demonstrates a general tendency by the Author of Waverley to 'renew the traces of the past through reinscription', Old Mortality (the character) voices only 'the spirit of the past rather than the continuing force of radicalism in the present'.[16] Ferris similarly argues that such reflection inevitably also involves a kind of 'forgetting', a 'moving out of violence' that is also embodied in Henry Morton's eventual escape from the legacy of his father.[17] As such she recognises the role that memory plays in the opening chapter but repositions it in ways that are seen as typical of Scott's presumed aesthetic. Ferris accounts for this closing down, this enactment of forgetting, by positing that, for Scott, positioning the Covenanters in the past was a vital political act, due to the connections that could be drawn between the Covenanters and the radicalism of Scott's own time.[18] Ian Duncan reads the opening chapter in similar ways, arguing again that it offers a way of consigning Old Mortality and everything he represents to the past, since the novel ultimately shows that 'the lapse of secular time dissolves political differences'.[19] Such readings, then, recognise that Scott engages with questions of memory and commemoration and how they interact with history in his opening chapter but ultimately see such issues as subsequently contained, driving a wedge between that chapter and what follows.

In a more recent article, however, Ferris approaches memory in slightly different ways and draws attention to the importance of 'remnant figures' in Scott's fiction, suggesting that they may potentially disrupt the present.[20] Tara Gosta elaborates when she suggests: 'I want us to think about Scott as a remembrancer, as a debt-collector of pasts people would have liked to forget', also recognising that the palimpsestic nature of Scott's fictions operates to disrupt the straightforward consignment of memory to the past within the novel.[21] Such critics pay particular attention to the end of the text. Even Duncan sees it as a complicated type of reconciliation,[22] while Ferris acknowledges (along with several other recent critics) that Morton's return is so problematic that it 'saps' the possibility of a vital future, to turn the hero himself into a 'ghostly remnant' haunting the end of the tale.[23] Such readings recognise that Scott is offering a more complex approach to history here, and arguably there is much in the body of *The*

Tale of Old Mortality as well as in the opening chapter to prompt a reading of it that disrupts any straightforward model of historical fiction (its treatment of time, for example, the amalgam of voices by which its story is told, or, indeed, the depiction of the Covenanting characters themselves), but this is not the topic of this chapter. Nevertheless, it is clear that the opening of *The Tale of Old Mortality* does at least invite us to read what follows not as a historical novel in the conventional sense but, rather, as an act of commemoration akin to Old Mortality's act of cleaning the Covenanting graves. I am proposing here that we might consider reading *Ringan Gilhaize* (and indeed Hogg's *Brownie*) in similar ways.

A number of theories circling around the topics of memory, commemoration, and the response of narrative to trauma have emerged within literary criticism and historical discourse in recent years. Such thinking has its origins in a response to the traumatic events that haunted the twentieth century and from a need to theorise via collective memory how such events can be suitably marked or memorialised; it arose, as Kerwin Klein puts it, along with a 'so-called crisis in historicism'.[24] Most famously, Pierre Nora's direction of the *Les Lieux de Mémoire* project interrogated how the concept of the French state is represented not by traditional historiography but by the monuments, civic institutions, and the intellectual markers by which the state is defined.[25] Sites of memory, or *lieux de mémoire*, are thus in some ways opposed to traditional historiography and arise out of a recognition that 'memory has been torn'.[26] While history is posited as a 'reconstruction', a 'representation' of the past, memory is described as 'a perpetually actual phenomenon',[27] and the purpose of '*lieux de memoire* is to stop time, to block the work of forgetting, to establish a state of things'.[28] As such, commemoration may be seen as in direct opposition to a model of historical fiction that is predicated on *process*, and certainly one that equates process, as Lukács does, with a form of *progress*.

Much of the work surrounding memory theory has focused on literal sites of memory: memorials, statues, physical sites of commemoration. To take a Scottish example, the refurbished Culloden Visitor Centre acknowledges the complexities surrounding the commemoration of a battle site by inviting those who go there to reflect by undertaking the Culloden Walk or contemplating the Culloden Stones.[29] Visitors are thus prompted to participate in commemorating the events of the battle in imaginatively constructive, empathetic ways; to borrow Nora's language, a state of things has been established by which the past is brought into an emotional perpetual state of being. Commemoration, therefore, often takes the form of physical object or installation and invites the visitor to contemplate rather than simply learn the details of the historical event. The Covenanters are not, of course, lacking in such physical forms of commemoration, and the number of sites of memory devoted to them across Scotland is perhaps testament to how resonant their cause remained well into the twentieth century.

But what of novels? Can they too be seen as acts of memory or of commemoration? Pierre Nora is sceptical about literature acting in this way and perceives the emergence of the concept of memory as resulting from a failure in literature. ('Memory has been promoted to the center of history: such is the spectacular bereavement of literature', Nora writes.)[30] Confronting head on the question of whether 'every great historical work and the historical genre itself' is not 'by definition *lieux de mémoire*', Nora concludes that only those 'founded on a revision of memory' may be classed in this category.[31] However, recent criticism has begun to realise that fictionalised history (if that term may be employed to distinguish it from the historical novel) may offer precisely this kind of revision and that literary texts may act as ideal sites of commemoration for this reason. Jerome de Groot, for example, notes that 'What is interesting for students of fiction is the ways in which this new theorising of "History" has drawn attention to historical writing's innate literariness' since 'through an engagement with historical texts the reader is invited to "*imagine*" a set of multiple pasts [which] suggests a way of approaching history and particularly the reading of "evidence" as something clearly fictional, in so far as we understand fiction as something which is held in opposition to concrete "fact".'[32] Similarly Astrid Erll argues that 'Literature and film can vividly portray individual and collective memory [...] by coding it into aesthetic forms, such as narrative structure, symbols and metaphors.'[33]

Alyson Bardsley recognises Galt's rejection of the conventional historical novel in *Ringan Gilhaize* and argues that the novel's dramatisation of 'the poverty of repetition and re-enactment [...] mark[s] failed attempts at sense-making in the face of trauma'.[34] As she illustrates, Galt's novel draws attention to the problems inherent in recounting trauma within the strategies of conventional historical discourse. This is evident in Ringan's responses to the events he encounters, and is inscribed within his account as his experiences of the Covenanting wars become increasingly violent and traumatic. As the congregation are evicted from their church, for example, Ringan describes the sound that he hears as 'not a crie of woe, neither was it the howl of despair, nor the sob of sorrow, nor the gurl of wrath, nor the moan of anguish' for none of these metaphors are sufficient to capture the agony of the people; rather it was 'a deep and dreadful rustling of hearts and spirits, as if the angel of desolation in passing by had shaken all his wings'.[35]

Later, the desolation of trauma is articulated (or rather approached because it cannot be articulated) in different ways. The sorrow of Ringan's neighbours at the insults imposed on the church can only be voiced by 'murmuring'[36] but there is no response but silence when Ringan encounters a family hiding in a barn and stumbles over a dead child. The story of what has happened to the family is punctuated by the 'moans' of the daughter and while listening to this 'dismal recital' Ringan 'could not speak';[37] in the face of such atrocity, the novel suggests, the narrative that holds our personal and collective lives together begins to disintegrate and Ringan recounts that he 'fled like a demoniac, not knowing which way I went'.[38] The culmination of Ringan's own narrative disintegration comes at the moment when he returns home to find his wife and children dead:

> My son bounded forward to tell his mother and sisters of my coming. On gaining the brow of the hill he leapt from the ground with a frantic cry and clasped his hands. I ran towards him—but I remember no more,—though at times something crosses my mind, and I have wild visions of roofless walls, and a crowd of weeping women and silent men digging among ashes, and a beautiful body, all dropping wet, brought on a deal from the mill-dam, and of men, as it was carried by, seizing me by the arms and tying my hands,—and then I fancy myself in a house fastened to a chair;—and sometimes I think I was lifted out and placed to beek in the sun and to taste the fresh air. But what these things import I dare only guess, for no one has ever told me what became of my benign Sarah Lochrig and our two blooming daughters;—all is phantasma that I recollect of the day of my return home.[39]

Bardsley described this moment as an example of 'unbearable witness' when Ringan becomes 'lost in trauma' and suggests that through it Galt dramatises the limitations of 'witness' as a mode of coming to terms with history.[40] Faced with such atrocity, Ringan can no longer construct the narrative of his own life (or recount it coherently for the reader) and by the end of the text, when he has been driven mad by grief, he states that his 'pen sickens with the recital of horrors' so that he has no option but to 'pass by the dreadful things that ensued';[41] there are some things that cannot be told, which cannot be brought into the coherence of conventional historical discourse.[42]

But if, as both Bardsley and Duncan acknowledge, Galt rejects the historical novel in any conventional sense does he, like Scott, gesture towards the alternative form of commemoration and, if so, how is this evident in the structures and forms employed in the novel? Galt, as has already been mentioned, mapped out his own distance from the historical novel by describing his work as 'theoretical histories'. Duncan describes the concept of 'theoretical history' as offering a bridge between historical data (of the kind offered by the *Statistical Account* and parodied in *Annals of the Parish*) and the romance offered by Scott, thus positing a kind of dialectical impulse at work within it.[43] However, while this is one way to consider the concept, the most immediate reference is to Dugald Stewart's notion of 'conjectural history'. 'In examining the history of mankind, as well as in examining the phenomena of the material world', Stewart writes, 'when we cannot trace the process by which an event has been produced, it is often of importance to be able to show how it may have been produced, by natural causes. [...] To this species of philosophical investigation, which has no appropriate name in our language, I shall take the liberty of giving the title of Theoretical or Conjectural History'.[44] By invoking conjecture Stewart thus calls into play the role of imagination in filling in the gaps in the historical record. This interaction of historical fact with imagination facilitates the emergence of the historical novel in general, but Galt's specific allusion to it arguably operates to move the terrain of his work away from that of dialectical historical process towards a re-remembering of the past, which is, in turn, perpetually reconstructed through the reader's imaginative engagement. Clearly, such an approach reinforces the idea that *Ringan Gilhaize* should be read not as a historical novel in any straightforward sense but, rather, as an act of commemoration which continually invites the reader to re-engage imaginatively with the events described within it, thus 'blocking the act of forgetting' for those who read.

Galt's desire to open up a space between conventional historiography and his work is also reinforced more specifically in *Ringan Gilhaize*. Its narrator, Ringan himself, repeatedly tells his reader that he is not writing history but some other form of discourse. This is highlighted as early as the first page of the novel where Ringan claims that he is not writing an historical account but intends, rather, to 'bear witness to those passages of the late bloody persecution in which I was myself both a soldier and a sufferer'.[45] Later he reiterates that 'It's far from my hand and intent, to write a history of the tribulations which ensued from the day of the uproar and first outbreaking of the wrath of the people against the images of the Roman idolatry'.[46] Repeatedly Ringan reiterates that the reader must find conventional history elsewhere, stating, for example, 'as I mean not to enter upon the particulars of that awakening epoch, but only to show forth the pure and holy earnestness with which the minds of men were then actuated, I shall here refer the courteous reader to the annals and chronicles of the time'.[47] He thus throws his reader outwith the bounds of his own text to conventional historiography, emphasising the difference between it and what is being inscribed here.[48]

Ringan's statement that he is 'bearing witness' rather than writing conventional history is compounded by the fact that the novel is written as a first-person account. Several critics have drawn attention to this as one of the central problems of the text, and indeed Galt himself comments on it as a choice of style, describing it as 'a transfusion of character' whereby he made Ringan 'give his autobiography, in which was kept out of view every thing that might recall the separate existence of John Galt'.[49] Charles Swann suggests consequently 'that the price of authenticity' in this novel is 'that a broad objective view of change is replaced by a purely subjective response to events', but he argues that 'Galt's handling of the fictional autobiography is marked by his ability to make the narrator tell us more about himself or the world that he is describing than he himself can recognise'.[50] Indeed Galt's first-person account of Covenanting times offers a narratorial tightrope whereby the reader is left trying to find the space between Ringan's position and Galt's own. However, it may be that 'authenticity' is less the issue here than the fact that the adoption of a first-person, overtly subjective form of narration draws attention to the process of memory and its role in recording the past.

Astrid Erll suggests that:

> From a narratological viewpoint, it is interesting to note that the distinction between an 'experiencing I' and a 'narrating I' already rests on a (largely implicit) concept of memory, namely on the idea that there is a difference between pre-narrative experience on the one hand, and, on the other, narrative memory which creates meaning retrospectively. The occupation with first-person narrators is thus always an occupation with the literary representation of individual remembering.[51]

Galt's narrative in fact dramatises the tensions inherent within the literary representation of remembering, the slippage that exists between 'experiencing' and 'narrating'. In spite of Ringan's insistence that he will 'bear testimony', the first volume and a half of the novel recounts not his own but his grandfather's story, which has gone on to define Ringan's life even though he was only eight at the time of his grandfather's death. This prompts two responses: narration, this suggests, is a resonant force, and one which operates along with memory and imagination to form a potent mix. Narration performed in this way thus operates with memory to create an emotional resonance that resists forgetting. As Nora suggests, it provides a 'perpetually actual phenomenon' that resists closure within the conventional voice of objective historical discourse, and this may be said not only of Ringan's grandfather's account but of the account (Galt's novel) which Ringan himself gives and which we as readers encounter. However, Ringan's act of remembering also stretches the 'authenticity' or credulity of narration to its limits, and questions surrounding the ways in which historical accounts are formulated are thus foregrounded. The tensions between a 'narrating I' and an 'experiencing I' and the roles of memory and remembering in formulating them are thus brought to the fore in ways that would be far less visible in a third-person or omniscient account. Nora suggests that it is 'memory that dictates while history writes', and here Galt offers an act of ventriloquising that emerges as a strategy to undercut the 'official' homogenising voice of history.[52]

Ferris notes that, as a consequence of strategies such as these, memory comes to structure the narrative in *Ringan Gilhaize* so that time collapses upon itself to become 'always present'.[53] Indeed, the treatment of time within the novel marks one more way in which Galt may be seen to be replacing conventional historical discourse with commemoration. The account of his grandfather's and to a lesser extent his father's experiences stretch out the time span of the novel beyond that which can be held within any individual memory. Ringan's account thus covers over one hundred and thirty years, bridging the period from the Reformation to the Glorious Revolution. As a consequence, Ringan's narrative moves beyond what can be recalled by any one memory to encompass the collective memory of several generations. Alyson Bardsley describes this strategy as one by which Galt refuses to distance the past by employing a framing device (in the style of Scott) and that as a consequence the text elides slippages between different time schemes.[54] However, John MacQueen suggests that it in fact draws attention to the presence of multiple (if at times hidden) perspectives in the text and as a result acknowledges that it unsettles any seamless account of the past.[55] Writing of Hogg's *Brownie*, Ian Duncan concludes that it is grounded in collective memory rather than history and that as a consequence it 'fail[s] or refuse[s] to cohere into the grand dialectical form of this historical novel'.[56] Galt's text is also compiled of the interplay between different accounts and stories, and it is similarly disruptive. Collective memory is called upon to produce not a coherent narrative but a *site of memory* where the experience of several generations produces an artefact that prompts reflection upon the shared experiences of the Scottish reformers. While for Ringan and his fellow Covenanters there is an intrinsic connection between the concerns of the Reformation and those of the Covenant, Galt allows his reader to question (in part because of the overt discontinuities between them) the ways in which the account has been stitched together.[57] As a consequence, the idea of history as process, and especially as progress, is undermined so that the act of reading becomes not one of watching history seamlessly move forward, but one of observing the fissures within it and its continual re-enactment or repetition.

Indeed, the concept of history as progress is finally what is challenged in this text for, rather than operating by process and development, it is structured around recurring tropes and repetition. In the first chapter of the novel, for example, Ringan recounts the series of events that led to his grandfather's commitment to the Covenanting cause:

> The persecutions which from that day the monks waged, in their conclaves of sloth and sosherie, against the children of the town, denouncing them to their parents as worms of the great serpent and heirs of perdition, only served to make their young spirits burn fiercer. As their joints hardened and their sinews were knit, their hearts grew manful, and yearned, as my grandfather said, with the zealous longings of a righteous revenge, to sweep them away from the land as with a whirlwind.[58]

The novel ends, famously, with the words 'Thus was my avenging vow fulfilled' (322) and is, as has been often acknowledged, an account of how Ringan slips from a moderate position towards one of 'zealous longings of a righteous revenge'. The structure of Galt's novel is therefore repetitive rather than teleological (and this is all the more marked for the reader who can only read Ringan's comment that 'the fortunes of the papistical Stuarts are foundered forever' in the light of subsequent events in Scottish history).[59] This suggests a model of history that is not about progress or dialectical process, but which is, rather, structured around repetition and a sense that Providence (the will of God to act out his work in the world) cannot be escaped in the way that 'history', in the Enlightenment stadial sense, allows. As a consequence, however, it also produces a text that does not move on from the Covenanting cause but, rather, invites perpetual re-engagement with it.

It is, perhaps, as Bardsley argues, the trauma of the events surrounding Covenanting history that prompts Galt to look for an alternative model in *Ringan Gilhaize*. But, while this results in a novel that articulates what cannot be said by history rather than what can be articulated, it does not, perhaps ironically, mean that it has nothing to say to the present about Scotland's Covenanting past. Bardsley questions why Galt writes Ringan as a character with whom we cannot sympathise. She suggests that by this act Galt negates the possibility that an act of witness can ever be inscribed within literature since *Ringan Gilhaize* 'forecloses any lingering possibility of ordinary readerly identification' with its central character.[60] However, such an account of the text overlooks the fact that in the place of witness – or even because of its lack – Galt may have offered what we may recognise as an act of commemoration. By resisting process and narrative coherence and by drawing attention to the fissures that lie between memory and witness, the novel puts in their place a text that does not aim to narrate that history in conventional terms but, through its own methods, seeks to forestall the act of forgetting and prompt engagement with the Covenanting cause in imaginative ways. Thus it offers a space where sympathy for that cause can be captured by, rather than narrated to, the reader. Perhaps against all odds, modern readers do sympathise with Ringan and with the Covenanting cause, seeing in it resonances for our own troubled times.[61] The text may not resolve this painful episode in Scottish history but it does something that is in the end perhaps more appropriate. It forces us to engage with it imaginatively, reflect upon it, and, as a consequence, like Old Mortality, 'repair the emblems of the past' as we read the novel so that forgetting the Covenanters becomes an impossibility.

CHAPTER SEVEN

The Insider's Eye in the Age of Improvement, Urbanisation, and Revolution[1]

Christopher A. Whatley

The more I read John Galt the more I become even more convinced than I was in 1979 that Galt has been shamefully neglected in Scotland.[2] Galt is worth reading and celebrating as a major Scottish writer. From the historian's perspective he is one of the most perceptive observers of Scottish society during the golden age of Scottish literary production. It was also in this period that Scotland's industrial or industrious revolution took place, when rural Scotland was undergoing the transformation that would create the orderly landscape we see nowadays in the Lowland countryside. Improvement is the catchall term for the process that was under way. It had an impact on Scotland's towns, which grew at an unprecedented rate. They too saw substantial alterations in their shape and appearance, which in many places are still evident. Much of this change – the move to modernity – was influenced too by that phenomenon we sometimes compress into the term Enlightenment. Manifestations of this include the slow and uneven demise of the influence of custom (and prejudice) and the adoption of new ways of understanding and acting, based on observation and reason. Ordinary people became consumers, as opposed to being mainly producers living on the margins of subsistence, and began to be more aware of, and become actors in, movements for political change rather than defenders of the status quo.[3]

There are many kinds of primary sources that allow historians to identify and describe the main features of what was an extraordinary period in Scotland's history. But most of the time the sources are fragmentary. Necessarily, historians are writing from the outside, constrained by shifts in historiographical fashions and the perceptions and concerns of the present, and applying the benefits of hindsight. Significance and meaning are arrived at through deduction, in accordance with our own understanding of the topic or issue being investigated. This raises the question of how much convergence there is between what contemporaries thought was happening and how historians understand the past. Or is history, as Voltaire asserted, 'nothing more than a pack of tricks that we play upon the dead'?[4] Would those people from the past that historians confidently portray recognise as authentic what has been written many decades or even centuries later about their experiences, lifestyles, values, or motivations?

What Galt offers the historian of the late eighteenth and early nineteenth centuries is a voice from within, the insights of an insider's eye. This is important. There were other witnesses who described aspects of the period, such as the authors of the county agricultural reports that were written at the turn of the nineteenth century. These, though, were deliberately quasi-scientific, and deal largely with land organisation, cultivation methods, crops, and markets, but with people only in passing. The *Statistical Accounts* provide full records of parish life in Scotland at the end of the eighteenth century, but again there is often a distance between the ministers who compiled the reports and what they could know about the lives and mind-sets of their parishioners. Many visitors left comments, but necessarily these are impressionistic. There are testimonies written by working people at the sharp end of the new, more intensified manufacturing economy. But their focus is restricted, even if what they wrote could also be compelling.[5] There are chroniclers of the period, men like George Penny of Perth who, as an eye-witness, left a closely observed account of life in that county town from around 1760 to 1830 – the period Galt covers.[6] But Penny deals with only one place; Galt's canvas is much wider. Galt also has a finer eye for detail, is more perceptive, and understands human beings and what they stood for and their foibles better than most of his contemporaries. He saw at first hand and perhaps above all engaged with some of the big challenges – and opportunities – of his time.[7] These included the rapid and fundamental changes in rural and urban Scotland alluded to above. He was fully conscious of their social consequences. Amongst these were the potentially destabilising effects of new ways of organising work and space on social relations and indeed the social order itself. Adding to the mix were influences and ideas emanating from overseas, not least the revolutions in America, France, and elsewhere in Europe. Population growth too was occurring at higher rates than earlier, as was emigration, not least to North America – the attractions of which drew many enterprising Scots, including Galt himself. There were threats to Scotland's identity as a component part of the British union state, as well as to core elements of Scottish identity from within Scotland – for Galt primarily in the form of Walter Scott's writing, which he feared might undermine Scotland's Presbyterian tradition and values, including the right of individuals to resist tyranny. Galt's response on this front – as someone whose west-coast background was staunchly Presbyterian – was to write *Ringan Gilhaize*.[8]

Galt is usually described as a novelist, albeit one whose best-known 'novels' are firmly grounded in the social life of the countryside and small towns of later eighteenth- and early nineteenth-century Scotland – 'Provincial Scotland'.[9] Literary critics have found much of merit in relation to Galt's capacities as a creative writer. Well known is that Galt was less keen to promote himself in this way. His earlier works were biographies, travelogues, and provincial tales and sketches.[10] It was with some trepidation that he added a fictional dimension to the documentary material with which he felt more secure.[11] He readily admitted that neither *Annals of the Parish* nor *The Provost* had a plot, explaining instead that the two books were better understood as exemplars of 'a kind of local theoretical history'. Galt's interest was in the agencies and processes of improvement, and how this manifested itself in town and country.[12] Yet notwithstanding Galt's reservations about these works, critically they were a success and achieved substantial sales.[13]

But clearly both *Annals* and *The Provost* are, to different degrees, works of imagination. Galt explained in his autobiographical *Literary Life* that some of the characters and incidents are almost entirely fictional. Rightly, in 1979, the late Ken Simpson went as far as to commend *Annals* as a 'major work of fiction […] a consummate psychological study […and] a masterpiece of ironic writing'.[14] In fact, in the same volume (which I edited), I cast some doubt on the extent to which Galt could be relied upon as an historical source, notwithstanding the many critics who had credited Galt for just this quality in his work, and still do.[15] With the arrogance of youth (I had just finished my PhD, on Ayrshire's industrialisation), I pointed out the inaccuracies in Galt's chronicle of his parish of Dalmailing, concluding that 'one could not better understand the development of any single parish through reading Galt's work'. Rather, I suggested, a mark of Galt's achievement was that he had created a world that readers were prepared to believe in.[16] I was wrong, not because Galt had created a credible fictional world, but because *Annals* and *The Provost* are a brilliant representation of semi-rural, small town, provincial Scotland in the context of a growing industrious economy and Britain's expanding global empire, which Galt by his artistry brings to life. In fact, his art intensifies their realism, much as a modern-day television drama-documentary or (from a different perspective) a Ken Loach film can do.

Until relatively recently, the dominant paradigm for urban Scotland during the period Galt was writing about has been Glasgow and, to a lesser extent, other larger towns.[17] Yet Glasgow is not Scotland and it certainly was not typical of most Scots' experience of urban life in Galt's lifetime. In 1801 almost twice as many people (around 156,600) lived in the ten Scottish towns that ranked immediately below Edinburgh and Glasgow than resided in Glasgow (with 84,100 inhabitants).[18] The other model has been Edinburgh. Edinburgh, it has generally been assumed, was unique because of its role as Scotland's Enlightenment 'hotbed of genius', even if we now know that Glasgow shared in the Enlightenment ethos, as did Aberdeen.[19] But what about Scotland's other towns – the smaller places? Urban historians know more about early modern Dundee now than a decade ago, but what about Alloa, Brechin, Dunfermline, Falkirk, Inverness, or Perth?[20] The larger of these places were consistently amongst the country's top twelve towns in the eighteenth and early nineteenth centuries. When Galt was active, urban Scotland was typified by manufacturing villages in country parishes (like Dalmailing) and small burghs (like Gudetown). In 1821 just over eighteen per cent of Scots lived in towns that housed between 2,500 and 9,999 people, compared to marginally under eighteen per cent who resided either in the capital or other towns with populations over 10,000. Indeed, not always appreciated is that more people lived in municipalities with fewer than 5,000 inhabitants than in places twice this size and over.[21] Thirty-three towns had populations of between 2,000 and 5,000. In other words, many more Scots were familiar with places such as those that Galt drew his material from (Irvine and Greenock), than Edinburgh or Glasgow. What nowadays is categorised as provincial Scotland was in Galt's lifetime mainstream Scotland.

The deficiency in our understanding of provincial Scotland began to be addressed in 2009 by a small team of historians led by Professor Bob Harris, supported by the late Professor Charles McKean, the architectural historian, and myself, with funds from the AHRC. In this project, 'Scotland's Smaller Towns in the Era of the Enlightenment, 1745–1820', we looked at around thirty of Scotland's smaller towns – a cross-section, by size, location, type, and function. Many of the findings have appeared in print already, in article and chapter form.[22] What this investigation revealed is how accurate and perceptive Galt was on the nature of urban improvement and its material and social impact. Despite being dependent in large part on what he knew about or gleaned from Irvine and to a lesser extent Greenock, his fictional parish of Dalmailing and burgh of Gudetown are nowhere specific. But this is Galt's achievement; they are everywhere. They are the ubiquitous smaller centres described in the previous paragraph. Galt, in *Annals* and *The Provost*, and in his other works also, managed to capture the zeitgeist of rural and provincial Scotland in the era of improvement and Enlightenment. More so in Scotland than in England, Bob Harris has remarked, there was a 'shared urban consciousness', a common – national – sense of purpose and a fairly uniform direction of travel, born of a perception in elite circles that post-Union Scotland was lagging behind England and other parts of Europe.[23] The inspiration for change probably came from south of the border as well as those parts of Europe achieving Scots knew best and sought to emulate – the Netherlands for example. The impetus however came from within, led by Whig improvers like Archibald Campbell, 3rd duke of Argyll, whose influence over Scottish affairs from the 1720s until his death in 1761 was immense, and backed by national improving agencies such as the Board of Trustees for Fisheries and Manufactures and the Bank of Scotland.[24]

The blueprint for urban improvement may well have been the grandiose plan for Edinburgh's new town that was published in 1752 and disseminated by the Convention of Royal Burghs. The Convention had long acted as a vehicle for the exchange of ideas and mutual support for Scotland's burgh oligarchies, and certainly across the country's urban sector there emerged a kind of Whig-informed civic code of modernisation along with a widespread rejection of the 'feudal' past that was identified as one cause of Scotland's 'backwardness'.[25] Also around the time of the publication of the plans for Edinburgh in the mid eighteenth century, there can be discerned a new optimism amongst the middle-ranking elites of Scotland's smaller towns and a self-conscious engagement with what historians have defined as improvement.[26] Telling in relation to Galt and how he might have understood the contemporary urban environment, we have a report from his hometown, Greenock, that some time prior to 1800 William Sibbald, an architect, had produced a plan for the Clydeside town that was 'similar to that carried out in the New Town of Edinburgh by the same man in conjunction with Robert Reid'.[27]

Another feature of the improvement 'movement' in later eighteenth century Scotland was a remarkable degree of self-conscious competition between towns. This included copycat behaviour in terms of the design of town houses, churches, and even the pervasive use of sash and case windows and slate roofs. The importance of emulation is well exemplified in *The Provost* when provost Pawkie reflects on his campaign for street lamps, a new innovation in Gudetown as in most places. These would serve for the 'ornament and edification of the burgh' (a phrase commonly used at the time), but what had motivated Pawkie was that such lamps were to be seen 'in all well regulated cities and towns of any degree'.[28] But Galt goes further than this by highlighting real world examples of such inter-town rivalry. So in *The Ayrshire Legatees*, for example, Miss Rachel Pringle writes in glowing terms about Ardrossan, the earl of Eglinton's new town, a 'monument [...] left there of his public spirit' which in due course would become 'a grand emporium'.[29] But, Miss Pringle reports, this is not the view of the people of the neighbouring town of Saltcoats, a 'sordid race' who complain that Ardrossan's rise will be their ruin – a comment that reflects contemporary views on the comparative characteristics of the two places: one an aristocrat's visionary planned town, the other a coal port and former salt-manufacturing centre that had grown in fits and starts under the control of the Cunninghames of Auchenharvie.

Such competitiveness is conveyed too in some of the dialogue in *The Gathering of the West*, Galt's account of the expedition of a party from the west of Scotland to Edinburgh for the visit of King George IV in 1822. Another marker of an improved town was that it should have pavements, usually made with flagstones, along the sides of the buildings and apart from the central carriageway – an innovation that required town councils to dissuade householders from tipping waste matter from their windows onto the street below, a long-established practice the stopping of which in turn removed the necessity for pedestrians to walk down the centre of the street. So in *The Provost* Galt devotes chapter 27 to the issue of the plainstones, with Gudetown emulating Glasgow by paving the sides of the streets in this way, by which means the town, in provost Pawkie's words, 'has been greatly improved and convenienced'.[30] The sometimes snide and sharp-tongued narrator in *The Gathering of the West*, who has one of his main characters, Mrs M'Auslan, visit a Greenock dressmaker, Miss Menie M'Neil, develops the theme further:

> Whether there is any truth in the allegation of the Glasgow people, that nothing walks in the middle of the street but cows and Greenock folk, we shall for the present suppress our natural inclination to investigate the causes of a subject so interesting to philosophy and to state the important fact, that soon after breakfast Mrs M'Auslan was seen picking her steps along the crown of the causeway [... and notwithstanding the

efforts of the town clerk in urging town councillors to improve the walkways], the side-pavements of Greenock seem still to have a natural predilection to continue in the same state [...]³¹

But Galt is aware too that fashionable innovations had their downsides. The lamps provost Pawkie had erected 'might reasonably have been thought [...] a terror to evil-doers'. In fact the reverse was true. Servant girls could now go out at night without the lanterns they carried by hand formerly; these were 'kenspeckle commodities, and of course a check on every kind of gavaulling [carousing]'. Consequently, 'out of the lamps sprung no little irregularity in the conduct of the servants', much to the displeasure of those of their mistresses who would have preferred them not to have gone out, 'when they could be more profitably employed at home'.³²

Although Galt was obviously fond of Greenock, and preferred it to nearby Port Glasgow, 'an insignificant town, with a steeple', it was Glasgow – 'that opulent metropolis of the muslin manufacturers' – that astonished him, while what impressed him about Edinburgh (if we can assume that the Rev Dr Pringle in the *Ayrshire Legatees* represented his thinking) was the orderly development of the New Town, 'the houses grown up as if they were sown in the seed-time with the corn by a drilling machine, or dibbled in rigs and furrows like beans and potatoes'.³³ By Galt's metaphors we are taken deep into the mentality of his age and by inference learn – or to use that expressive Scottish word, *jalouse* – what for contemporaries was new and meaningful. And what was desirable: which, above all, was orderliness. Thus, even a ladies' slipper maker from Perth, Thomas Murie, on a recruiting mission with his volunteer regiment, the Royal Perthshire Militia, late in 1799, knew what to look for as he journeyed through the Lowland towns. Kilmarnock he thought little of, as it was 'very irregular built [...] the streets narrow except at the Cross'. By contrast was Ayr, with its 'regular built' new town and 'very handsome' new bridge, its 'several streets well paved & lighted', the main one from the bridge being 'the most public part [...] the best inhabitants dwell in it & the most of the merchants has their shops there.' As with Galt, it was Glasgow that most impressed Murie. The capital of the west of Scotland was 'elegantly built upon a regular plan', with wide streets 'paved & lighted on both sides & straight'.³⁴

What Galt provides us with, based on his own first-hand knowledge as an observer but also as a participant in the business and associational life of Greenock, are unique insights into the thought processes of his characters. Galt understood that the main driver behind urban improvement was commerce and the prospect of gain.[35] Scotland's towns were, above all else, a locus for making money. For towns as collective bodies a governing principle was 'to do whatever was necessary to sustain economic progress'.[36] Accordingly, when narrows or closes were widened, streets straightened, and market crosses moved (all of which measures Galt describes and explores), the primary motive was to ease the flow of traffic and transport, to facilitate access to and from markets, within and beyond the respective towns. This is not to say that elegance and ornamentation were of no consequence. If the economic and commercial ethic of the age led the change process, there was a place too for 'visual aggrandisement'.[37] Enlightenment values and culture incorporated a concern for 'ornament' alongside utility and the requirement for order and regularity. That is, towns organised along rational lines: industrious places that were also sociable, humane, and urbane,[38] Galt's ideal.

Improvement was in the hands of private individuals – in *The Provost* represented initially by the aptly named Baillie Andrew McLucre, 'a greedy body' according to our narrator. McLucre had his counterparts in the real world of Scotland's later eighteenth-century towns: the entrepreneurial middling sort. For anyone who cares to look, they readily spring from the voluminous archives of Scotland's burgh councils. Most funding for improvement projects came not from the public purse, but from the purses of the public.[39] Several town councils in Scotland were, by the early nineteenth century, bankrupt.[40] Burgh indebtedness too was commonplace, often the result of over-ambitious or, more often, ill-planned improvement schemes. Corruption and jobbery contributed too, along with long-term financial mismanagement and downright incompetence on the part of burgh magistrates and councils. Indeed, burgh reform and effective financial management were important items on the improvement agenda.[41] Entirely believable, therefore, despite sounding far-fetched, is Provost Pawkie's account of how he increased town revenues by building a new toll bridge, but then created enormous difficulties for his successors as they were unable to pay the five per cent interest on the capital after road traffic declined with the arrival of peace after the war with France ended in 1815.[42] Again the example is revealing: bridge building was a regular feature of the improvement process, the older medieval structures being too weak or narrow for the increase in wheeled traffic that occurred in the later eighteenth century.

Another pressing issue for townspeople was the proprietorship and use of common land. Prior to the seventeenth and eighteenth centuries, numerous Scottish burghs had portions of common ground, either owned by the town itself or granted for the use of the inhabitants by a neighbouring landowner. Such land was utilised for a variety of purposes – as a source of kindling for their fires or of peat, and somewhere town dwellers could acquire turf and stone for building. It could be used by favoured burgesses to graze their sheep and cattle, and sometimes for sports and games and urban ceremonials.[43] In the eighteenth century, however, town councils became increasingly aware of the commercial value of their holdings, and of the need to generate additional revenue to support their civic ambitions. Consequently, they discouraged customary usage of the towns' commons and either sold it or leased it out to rent-paying tenants – often in the face of fierce opposition from those townspeople who had formerly had access to the common land and valued its advantages. In Gudetown in *The Provost* we find provost Pawkie and his fellow civic governor, the aforementioned baillie McLucre, enclosing and improving fifty acres of the town's moor, with McLucre subsequently obtaining at an 'easy rate' a lease of the ground for 999 years. Carried out in the name of improvement, and in Pawkie's eyes a demonstrable success, there was, however, a counter-reaction. Galt's text runs as follows: 'But to the best of actions there will be adverse and discontented spirits; and, on this occasion, there were not wanting persons naturally of a disloyal opposition temper, who complained of the enclosure as a usurpation of the rights and property of the poorer burghers.'[44] We now know, from looking at historical evidence such as council minutes and court records that this was how such measures were viewed, and received by the 'people below', throughout much of urban Scotland. In Irvine, Ayr, and Hawick, there were objections as well as appeals to the Court of Session on just the grounds that Galt describes. In Irvine, the divide lay between the commercially ambitious merchants whose wish was to lease the land for industrial and other revenue-generating purposes (something which also benefited the town council), and on the other hand the more conservative trades incorporations, whose inclination was to protect the interests of their small master members, journeymen, and the burgh's poorer inhabitants.[45]

Galt also casts light on improvement as an attitude of mind, which had cultural ramifications. Linked with this were ideas of acceptable social behaviour and what constituted polite society. In part this required civic leaders and the more affluent inhabitants of towns to withdraw from older, traditional activities and behaviours, for instance, their involvement in certain sorts of the more rumbustious civic ceremonials that had punctuated the town's annual cycle – fairs, sports, or, most spectacularly, the king's birthday celebrations. Instead, urban elites were expected – and sought – to engage in more sober pursuits, like genteel balls, and literary and debating societies, associational activity we know that Galt himself pursued. Indeed, social life was overwhelmingly associational; clubs and societies abounded, even in the smaller places. Most towns had at least one Masonic lodge; many had several.[46] Numerous too, more so it seems than England, were subscription and circulating libraries – which added to the towns' serious character, but were also the principal means by which Enlightenment ideas and cultural values percolated through to provincial Scotland. It is no surprise, then, that John Galt was a member of Greenock's subscription library. And, of course, in some places, especially the weaving centres (including new cotton mill settlements like Galt's Cayenneville – or real world Catrine in Ayrshire), bookshops and newspapers were the route-way to radicalism, as the nervous, Tory-inclined Galt makes clear in *The Provost*. Pawkie declared himself 'exceedingly troubled' that a newspaper was to be published in Gudetown. That its ethos was to be liberal was no comfort; promoted by 'hands not altogether clean of the coom of jacobinical democracy', Pawkie felt it necessary to intervene and turn the paper into a loyalist organ.[47] The prevailing fear that the unchecked flow of ideas might in some way challenge the existing establishment during the era of the French Revolution is something that, once more, recent historical research has confirmed; it explains, for example, the series of steep increases in taxes on newspapers in the 1790s.[48] Anxiety about threats to the social order in general – which we see throughout provost Pawkie's career but which was also a recurring concern for Galt – was why in addition to their interest in efficiency, urban authorities attempted to reduce the number of fairs and, where possible, relocate them to the fringes of the town, as well as to remove other opportunities for large-scale disorder.

The presumption might be that Galt included a chapter on the king's birthday proceedings simply for literary effect. Indeed, until the 1990s, when historians began to look more closely at the king's birthday in Scotland, Galt's account, to which he devotes one of his longer chapters, could well be seen in this light. Perhaps even more picaresque are the opening pages of *Annals* where Mr Balwhidder was met with an angry mob as he tried to answer the call from his new charge, and had to endure the humiliation of crawling into his church through a window. A few years ago readers might be excused for concluding that Galt had included this incident as an instance of mildly comic relief, and certainly it has the effect of 'diminishing the authority readers might be tempted to [...] attribute to the figure of a minister'.[49] Yet we know now – following Callum Brown's work on protest over church patronage in Scotland –that riots directed against unpopular new ministers, notably those who were appointed by landed patrons (in the case of Dalmailing the Laird of Breadlands) and against the wishes of the local heritors, elders, and above all the ordinary parishioners, were the most common form of popular protest in rural Scotland in the eighteenth century.[50]

Similarly, Galt's narration of the meal riot in Gudetown might seem exaggerated. After all, the price of a peck of meal had only been increased by one penny. However, what modern research has shown is that it was just such a variance from the norm that sparked meal riots. Work I have published elsewhere has shown that in the mid-1790s rioting broke out in many parts of Scotland when the price of a peck of meal rose much above a shilling or a shilling and a penny, the price that had been paid for several decades.[51] In 1796, during a period of shortage in Peterhead, the town's volunteers issued a warning to the magistrates not to admit soldiers as they would force up the price of meal. The volunteers' written demand to this effect ends with the words, 'Meal at one Shilling per peck, God Save the King'. Similarly, in Macduff, rioters there would only allow grain to be shipped from the port if the burgh's magistrates could obtain meal for the inhabitants at the same price, that is one shilling.[52] What Galt offers are vivid fictional constructions, drawn from close observation, of Edward Thompson's historical conception of the early modern crowd's or populace's 'moral economy'.[53] Thompson's seminal essay on this subject was published in 1971; *The Provost* in 1822, around 150 years earlier. In fact, in every other detail Galt's account of food rioting, in which each carefully chosen word and phrase adds meaning, matches what we learn from more traditional and usually much less colourful sources.

If we turn now to the measures the town authorities adopted to pre-empt disturbances of this kind, again what is revealed is the pinpoint accuracy of Galt's portrayals. Thus, in Chapter 39 of *Annals of the Parish*, which deals with the year 1798, we learn that owing to the poor spring a scanty harvest is likely. This in turn persuaded Mr Cayenne, a leading merchant, to buy and import to Irville from America and the Baltic additional supplies of grain from which, when the time came, he made a substantial profit by selling this to the better-off inhabitants of Dalmailing at inflated prices. Slipped into the text (and easily skipped over) is the remark: 'Some of the neighbouring parishes, however, were angry that he [Mr Cayenne] would not serve them likewise, and called him a wicked and extortionate forestaller; but he made it plain to the Meanest capacity, that if he did not circumscribe his dispensation to our own bounds it would be as nothing.'[54] A minor matter apparently, yet what Galt is alluding to here is actually one of the most controversial issues in Scotland at the end of the eighteenth century. This was the centuries-old right that burghs, parishes, and counties had to block the movement of grain and meal out of their own vicinity in times of shortage, the aim being to secure the supply of staple foodstuffs for their own inhabitants. Indeed, so important was this matter that it went to the Court of Session, where in 1801 Lord Meadowbank ruled that the ancient custom should be swept away. To do otherwise and to allow burgh magistrates to retain meal exclusively for the use of their own people, the pursuer in the case argued, threatened the commercial system itself. Drawing on the work of the late economic theorist and moral philosopher Adam Smith in his plea, what epithet, he asked rhetorically, would Smith have applied 'to the interference of a magistrate, whose limited and local knowledge but ill qualifies him for regulating the affairs of a great nation'.[55] The paper (see endnote 51) that drew attention to this enormously significant but largely overlooked legal case and judgement was published in 2012; Galt was onto the vexed subject long before that.

In theory, the king's birthday was the occasion when the urban community united to demonstrate its loyalty to the reigning monarch. For most of Galt's lifetime this was King George III, whose birthday was celebrated on June 4. Usually the celebrations began with a formal procession, with the great and the good leading the way, not only a town's provost and magistrates but also other authority figures such as the minister or ministers, senior army officers, supervisors of the customs and excise, lawyers, and leading citizens such as merchants and physicians. Anyone who was particularly unpopular was therefore in a highly exposed position as the procession walked in front of, or even through, a large crowd of the town's inhabitants.[56] In provost Pawkie's Gudetown, the objects of the crowd's wrath are the aptly named Mr Firlot, a profiteering grain merchant, and Mr Stoup, an overly zealous and again tellingly named customs officer. The cause of the general unease that culminated in the Gudetown riot was the town council's decision to stop the time-honoured distribution of free coals for the bonfire. This action was considered, as reported by Pawkie, to be 'a heinous trespass on the liberties and privileges of the people' – in other words an unwarranted attack on popular custom. Yet what happened in fictional Gudetown was by no means exceptional; throughout urban Scotland the fourth of June was becoming a major problem for civic heads. There follows a quotation from the minutes of Montrose town council in June 1786, a week or so after that year's proceedings: 'The council, considering that the practice on the King's birthday of drinking his Majesty's health at the cross is attended with much inconvenience, and that the custom is given up in most other burghs [emulation again] the Council abolish that practice in time coming and resolve that for the future the company shall meet at the Provost's house and proceed directly to the Town Hall to celebrate the anniversary.'[57] Notwithstanding such declarations of good intent, several decades were to pass before the social confrontations and violence associated with the monarch's birthday holiday were eliminated.

Galt's selection of a grain merchant and a customs officer is deliberate and astute: across Lowland Scotland in the eighteenth century it was men from these two occupations who were most commonly resented and most often the object of verbal abuse and physical assault.[58] Both carried the risk – especially when communities were under stress – of transgressing the mainly unspoken but popularly understood rules of the moral economy and suffering the consequences of so doing. The targeting of men like Firlot and Stoup was unfair according to Galt's narrator in *Annals*, who made clear that he saw nothing wrong with the fact that a merchant-manufacturer such as Mr Cayenne made a profit from his business activities, which included job creation and ensuring a decent supply of meal. In this respect, Galt highlights the very real tension still prevalent during his lifetime that was caused by the competing pulls of commercialising, modernising Scotland, and the sheet-anchor of tradition.

The point is reinforced if we return to the king's birthday. Not only were the crowd's passions fuelled by copious quantities of free drink. Those present also had access to the weapons of the weak: fire and fireworks, burning tar barrels, and also the flotsam and jetsam of the street, stones and mud. Stray animals, mainly cats and dogs, could also be employed, stretched grotesquely as they were thrown around, finishing round the neck of a hapless magistrate. The world was turned upside down and, for a time anyway, disorder – and the people below – reigned supreme.[59] In capturing all this, but also describing the circumstances that resulted in disorder, Galt has his finger on a pulse that was beating across urban Scotland. In words he describes what the artist David Octavius Hill captured visually in his closely observed and finely detailed engraving of the king's birthday in Perth in 1819.[60]

PERTH—CELEBRATION OF THE KING'S BIRTHDAY (GEORGE III.) 1819.
This cartoon is a reproduction of a pencil sketch by a well-known contemporary artist.

How right, therefore, was the anonymous editor of the edition of *Annals* and *The Ayrshire Legatees*, published by MacLaren and Company late in the nineteenth century, when he concluded that in his earlier works Galt had 'bequeathed to posterity a faithful record [... of] those national manners, habits of thought and modes of expression' that existed a century earlier; their merit, the same writer went on, lay not in 'ingenious intricacy of incident, or evolvement of story', but 'in reflecting realities as nearly and truthfully as possible'.[61]

Galt's fictional writing is more, though, than an accurately observed record of his times, his main focus, invaluable as this is for historians and other students of the period. By applying a series of literary devices, from the choice of names he gives to his characters – 'name types' – to the way the thoughts and words of his characters reveal contemporary attitudes, Galt immerses us more deeply into his world than is possible for most historians to do.[62] But also buried within his writing is to be found Galt the political activist, a man whose purpose was to guide behaviour. He was also a social theorist.[63] Along with Sir Walter Scott and many of his conservative contemporaries, Galt was, as we have seen already, alarmed by the activities of Scotland's radicals. His responses are to be found not only in *Annals* and *The Provost* but also *Lawrie Todd* and *The Gathering of the West*. *The Gathering* was first published in *Blackwood's Magazine* in 1823, not long after the shock for the authorities of the so-called Radical War of 1820. The reverberations from this, including popular disturbances, continued to cause alarm for some time afterwards. Working-class resentment over the radicals' defeat was intense, and manifested as rioting in places with which Galt was familiar: Glasgow,

Paisley, Port Glasgow, and Greenock.[64] Of all this Galt seems to have been acutely aware; hence his attempts to counter what many feared was the prelude to revolution. In the *Gathering*, ostensibly about the king's visit to Edinburgh although underlain by concerns about the Radical challenge, Galt cleverly uses a variety of devices, both overt and subtle, to drive home his message.

There is direct attack, with the condemnation of Paisley's weavers as members of a sedentary occupation who like all other 'indoor artizans' were 'particularly subject to the moral flatulency of hypothetical ideas'.[65] Galt then goes on to contrast the radical weavers' response to the news of the king's imminent arrival in Scotland with the 'lively excitement' and 'impulses of loyal curiosity' that moved the 'bustling, ruddy, maritime Greenock folks' to contribute to the festivities being planned to greet the king. Then there are the names given to some of the more prominent of them, like Clattering Tam, a 'thorough and engrained radical' who was 'an eminent member of the Radical Association', and the wonderfully evoked 'auld gash-gabbit Jamie o' the Sneddon', that is, Paisley's well-known weaving suburb. There are sly descriptions too, as when just after his reference to the 'ruddy' inhabitants of Greenock, we come upon the 'pale-faced' Paisley weavers. Unhealthy bodies, unhealthy minds?

He resorts too to ridicule, which was more effective for readers at the time as it was directed towards a practice that had its roots in a type of protest British radicals in the 1820s (and Chartists in the 1830s) adopted: abstention from taxed goods, including alcohol, tea, coffee, and sugar.[66] Galt describes a 'patriotic' band of weavers' wives, who around 1820 stopped drinking tea and other excisable commodities in order to deny the government a source of revenue, 'in conformity to which, and actuated by the frenzy of the time, they seized their teapots, and marching with them in procession to a bridge, sacrificed them to the Goddess of Reform, by dashing them, with uplifted arms and an intrepid energy, over into the river' – before then ratifying their 'solemn vows' with 'copious libations of smuggled whisky'.[67] To abjure tea-drinking then is no hardship for Paisley's wild and lawless whisky-drinking women.

There is ridicule too in the manner with which Galt treats the weavers' demands for the king to come to Paisley and perhaps even settle in Scotland. The text points to the recognition by some of the shrewder weavers that such a visit, even if short, would be good for trade. The narrator refers also to the 'recent process of their ingenuity', that is the notion, obviously mistaken, that somehow the fluctuations in trade were caused by 'the ancient and unaltered institutions of King, Lords and

Commons'. Although Galt is not unsympathetic to some of the weavers' criticisms – of Parliament, for instance, as 'the rotten carcase o' British liberty' – the delusions of the weaver hot-heads are contrasted with the wiser words of one of their more reasonable brethren, Peter Gauze. Compared with the others, Gauze was 'one of those clever and shrewd fellows who, by the exercise of their natural sagacity, rise from the loom into the warehouse, and ultimately animate the vast machinery of the cotton-mills'.[68] Representative of the emerging Scottish ideal of the hard-working, self-made man, it is through Gauze that the voice of reason is heard. Neatly dressed (unlike the others), Gauze advises his fellow weavers – using language and metaphors Galt's intended audience would readily understand – to abandon their plan to go and see the king in Edinburgh as a deputation. This would hardly entice the king to Paisley: 'it wouldna look weel', says Gauze, 'considering the natural objection of the government to committees among the people for political purposes'. Better to travel to Edinburgh as individuals, and as members of the community at large. After crushing Tam in argument, and watching him slope off, mocked by his erstwhile weaver brothers, Gauze continues his critique of the radicals' methods. Thus, he flatters his audience by acknowledging their craft skills, but then turns this to advantage by arguing that

> it's as necessary for a man to serve an apprenticeship in the art of law-making, as in the weaving o' muslin. For though the King and his Lords and Commons aiblins ken the uses and the ways o' the shuttle and the tredles, just as we do councils and parliaments, they would make a poor hand in the practice; and I doubt we would ravel the yairn, and spoil the pirns o' government, were we to meddle wi' them.

Common folk should know their place, and win favour from the king by being respectful; good behaviour will induce good legislation.

There is no more compelling or more humane – by which I mean empathetic – writer on the towns and townspeople of Scotland during the dramatic period about which he writes, than John Galt.

CHAPTER EIGHT

Pioneering the Political Novel in English

Gordon Millar

Writers on political fiction have not been helpful in establishing Galt's reputation. Christopher Harvie is an exception and comes close to paying appropriate tribute to Galt when he describes *The Member* (1832) as 'the first political novel *tout court*.'[1] *The Provost* (1822) he sees imprecisely as 'set in more debatable land'. Galt is, in fact, vital to any discussion of political fiction because he made a pioneering, sustained contribution that drew on pre-Reform politics. *The Provost*, about local politics, and *The Member*, about a Westminster political career, are landmark works that have the most political content in Galt's fiction, although this chapter will conclude by offering other examples of his engagement with political fiction.

Galt writes of himself as 'a Tory, as much as a man could be with whom politics have ever been secondary'.[2] The proof that politics was anything but secondary to Galt is suggested in his pride at George Canning's reaction to *The Provost*.[3] Non-political contemporary reaction to *The Provost* was also appreciative of creative skill that could be put to good purpose in writing about politics:

> This work [*The Provost*] is not for the Many; but in the unconscious, perfectly natural, Irony of Self-delusion, in all parts intelligible to the intelligent Reader, without the slightest suspicion on the part of the Autobiographer, I know of no equal in our Literature.[4]

Samuel Coleridge's singling out of unconscious irony is praise for Galt's preference for using an autobiographical form. In *The Provost* and *The Member* this takes the form of a fictional political memoir.

Galt's comments on his own work show that he was consciously developing what he believed to be a new approach that may appear particularly suited to writing political fiction, which requires a verisimilar framework of historical, ideological, and personal references. In his *Autobiography* (1833), Galt writes:

> Merely because the incidents are supposed to be fictitious, they have been all considered as novels, and yet, as such, the best of them are certainly deficient in the peculiarity of the novel. They would be more properly characterised in several instances as theoretical histories, than either as novels or romances.[5]

For Galt the novel is more fictional than what he is writing. He writes in his *Literary Life* (1834) that, in composing, he followed the rule of bringing 'impressions on the memory harmoniously together' and states that 'no ingenuity can make an entirely new thing'.[6] This approach included the intention to teach the reader:

> I considered the novel as a vehicle of instruction, or philosophy, teaching by example, parables, in which the moral was more valuable than the incidents were impressive.[7]

It is useful to see Galt's theoretical histories as his experiment with the novel. There is confirmation of this explanation in the pattern of his writing. Forced after 1829 to make money to pay off his debt after the collapse of his Canadian projects, it was only in 1831, as soon as his financial fortunes had revived sufficiently, that he was able to write something to better please himself and of which he hoped that 'what was lost in popularity, would have been made up in durability'.[8] The result was *The Member*, written in a similar form to *The Provost*.

The Provost achieves completeness in its portrayal of a political life in a way that, among Galt's other works, only *The Member* approaches. Whereas the latter describes only part of a career, *The Provost* has an entirety about it.[9] It covers the years from James Pawkie's apprenticeship as a young man in about 1760 to his retirement after a long commercial and political career shortly after the end of the wars with France in 1815. The story is ostensibly told with a disarming, if at times infuriating, candour by Pawkie himself. It is about the earning, exercise, and giving up of political power, and includes Pawkie's experience of many of the elements that make up political life. Elections, lobbying, local government finance, the temptations of corruption, defeat on individual issues, maintaining public order, and the press and news manipulation all play a role, and in each of these areas, from an early point in the novel, the effects of Reform begin to be felt.

The Provost is a novel dominated by one man because James Pawkie reveals himself, as Coleridge says, unknowingly and ironically, with all the strengths and weaknesses associated with politicians. His very name is an indicator of character. The *Concise Scots Dictionary* defines 'pawkie' as 'wily, crafty', but also as 'shrewd, astute'.[10] This suggests a character somewhere between worldly-wise and street-smart. Indeed, it is part of Galt's representation of the politician to fuse the two, the engaging, attractive cleverness of a public performer who can also get things done: politics as the art of the possible. Pawkie relies on cunning and dissembling to hide his real motives, but his urbane view of his milieu, and often of himself, means that the wiliness is not off-putting, but rather something to be savoured.[11]

Galt gives *The Provost* its form by building it round the arc of Pawkie's personal, commercial, and, most importantly, political career. Having started a business, Pawkie sets about building up a reputation as a useful pillar of the community in Gudetown. The policy he adopts is 'rather to be entreated than to ask' for a public role.[12] Once on the town council, he is initially the astute novice who believes it is best 'to rule without being felt, which is the great mystery of policy'.[13] This is not a demagogue exploiting volatile popular opinion, but someone who, through patience, persuasiveness, even code switching in his use of Scots and English, is naturally suited to the milieu he is entering.[14]

The next stage of Pawkie's career shows him benefiting from the swing of the political pendulum away from his rivals in leading public positions. He re-enters office as provost for a second time with a free hand and an extended tenure of two years as against the normal one. During this part of the novel we see the politician in his prime, wielding power with experience and with a programme to accomplish.[15] This is a leader whose colleagues need him and who can, without real opposition, set in train a full programme, with improvements in the town's infrastructure, repairs to the church, and suppression, also in his own commercial interests, of the traditional fairs.

The final part of the novel deals with Pawkie's third provostship. Ruth Aldrich's comment on Pawkie that, 'at the close it is difficult to decide whether Pawkie has actually become a better man or merely a slyer one' is an expression of the novel's achievement.[16] His reflections at the time of his colleague Bailie McLucre's death show that it was not so much McLucre's corruption he objected to: 'the thing was not so far wrong in principle, as in the hugger-muggering way in which it was done'.[17] There is also room for doubt about his sincerity when he later compares himself to a caterpillar that has been transformed: 'I became conscious of being raised into public life for a better purpose than to prey upon the leaves and flourishes of the commonwealth'.[18] Do we take him at his word and see the butterfly as a symbol of his improvement, or do wings simply give him the means to range more widely, albeit circumspectly, in the application of his old ways?[19] The answer may be that Pawkie is both better and slyer, a conclusion that is supported by Pawkie's own point that he was forced by the changing nature of the times to become a less venal politician. At the time of his resignation Pawkie acknowledges the 'reforming spirit abroad among men'.[20] In his view people expect their politicians to behave as politicians always have, and the slow improvement promised by Reform is just that, slow.

Within the framework of Pawkie's career, Galt portrays a number of political phenomena specific to the pre-Reform period. Pawkie's desire to control the levers of patronage associated with the office of dean of guild is an early example. His suggestion to the incumbent, Bailie McLucre, that he take on the role of delegate at the forthcoming parliamentary election, in order to get him out of the way, is a case of moving a political opponent up and out.[21] McLucre's subsequent use of his position in order to get the candidates for the Westminster seat to bid for his crop of potatoes, and thereby secure his delegate's vote, is an example of corrupt 'jookerie' associated with the narrow franchise in pre-Reform Scotland.[22]

Pawkie's occasional references to council finance are a key element in his self-propaganda. At the time of the repair of the kirk, the funds raised are mentioned as 'the first public debt ever contracted by the corporation'.[23] At the end of Pawkie's career, Gudetown is described as 'in great credit' and as raising money for public projects from people 'ready and willing to lend'. After his departure from office, Pawkie can claim that 'had things gone on in the way they were in my time, there can be no doubt that the borough would have been in very flourishing circumstances'.[24] He conveniently ignores in this projected version of events the effects of the post-Napoleonic-war slump, which he mentions at the start of the next chapter, and takes in the context of finance, as so often in the memoir, the credit for what has gone right. In positioning Pawkie in this way, Galt made use of a historical context in which the effects of a poor post-war economy and bad management were to lead Scottish burghs into insolvency and to pressure for municipal reform.[25]

To patronage and finance can be added lobbying and the manipulation of public opinion. Pawkie initially opposes the setting up of a Gudetown newspaper. This is one of a number of occasions in the memoir when Pawkie shows himself to be an exponent of what historically has come to be called 'management' in Scotland, the government of the country based on the political and commercial Union of 1707, and the authority of the Hanoverian monarchy and of their ministers in London.[26] If Pawkie sees himself as anyone's representative, it is in the role of the local face of royal and government authority in Gudetown. Amusingly, however, the upshot of this episode is Pawkie himself being manipulated, unable to resist the flattery of seeing his own name in print in the form of reports on speeches given and dinners attended.

The Provost has been hindered from being seen as a landmark novel by misleading critical categorisation as provincial literature.[27] Christopher Harvie restricts political fiction to a metropolitan parliamentary setting, and *The Provost* refers to Parliament only in the constituency context of the election of members. In fact, *The Provost*, in its unity, its comprehensiveness, its detail, and its subtle, humorous quality, is the first novel in which politics forms the backbone. That alone would entitle it to a far more prominent place than it has enjoyed outside Scotland.

The Member is also a fictional autobiography. Like *The Provost*, it gives a view of politics from the practitioner's standpoint and is unblushing in its description of political venality. As in Pawkie's case, *The Member* describes the political career of the fictional author, Archibald Jobbry. This falls into three phases, an echo of Pawkie's three provostships, at the beginning of each of which there is an election, the latter two contested. The progression from the experiences of a parliamentary novice, to the memoirs of an MP's struggle to maintain his independence of party, to his explanation of his adherence as a moderate Tory to a failing government, describes Jobbry's development as a political operator. As such, at least initially, Jobbry, like Pawkie, is certainly worthy of his name, with its connotation of dealing corruptly for private gain or advantage.[28]

There are, however, differences between the two novels. *The Member* describes only a part of Archibald Jobbry's life. It is the fictional memoir of a man who enters Parliament in later years after spending a long period in India. Furthermore, Jobbry eventually becomes actively concerned with national and even international political issues and ideas in a way that Pawkie, the passive observer or beneficiary of such outside events, never does. Central to *The Member* are the effects of the Reform controversy and discussion of related political issues, such as Roman Catholic Relief and the Corn Laws. Perhaps reflecting the fact that it was written after three less-than-easy years for Galt, *The Member* is also less polished.[29] Its chapters are numbered, but not titled. Its secondary characters are less rounded than in the earlier work.

The Member is prefaced by a dedication to William Holmes, dated 1 January 1832. Holmes was a Tory whip and dispenser of patronage and, therefore, someone with whom a non-fictional Jobbry would have been likely to come into contact.[30] The date signals the book's relevance to parliamentary reform. The dedication provides an overture to the book's main theme, namely that Jobbry and Holmes are politicians whose useful careers are about to be overcome by 'the sharp, dogged persons likely to be returned under the schedules'.[31] Jobbry sees Reform as being about to sweep away an easy-going system that works. Not least among the things to be swept away are Jobbry's and Holmes's seats. Under the redistribution schedules of the Reform Act these were to be given to underrepresented areas, such as the greater manufacturing cities. *The Member* shows Jobbry's drift from calculating independence to 'Toryish inclination', although he does not count himself as one of the sixty diehard Tories he identifies in his third parliament.[32] Holmes would certainly have been among the sixty, and therefore the irony of claiming in the dedication a place as Holmes's 'old friend and pupil' works because those in the know realise it is misleading.[33]

In fact, the whole work is potentially misleading. Seeking to refute an inquiry as to the grounds for Galt's perceived fictional admission of defeat and failure on the part of Jobbry, an anti-Reform Tory, a *Fraser's Magazine* review observed:

> We could not deny that the stupid Whigs had been deceived by playful irony, or that the wicked Radicals had, like the toad of eastern allegory, extracted venom from the sunbeam of Galt's wit, but we endeavoured to assure our friend of his unshaken allegiance to the old institutions of the country.[34]

Galt's artistic intention was to create Jobbry with special attention to those aspects of the character's political life that his opponents would take exception to, but of which Galt deep down approves. Galt intends

Jobbry to be positively likeable, worthy of respect, and even deserving of admiration for his down-to-earth political pragmatism, especially when contrasted with the portrayal of Nathan Butt in *The Radical*. The fact that Whig critics were taken in indicates the success of Galt's irony in this work, and led to Coleridge's remarks on *The Provost* being echoed by the *Fraser's* reviewer:

> The *Member* is too clever – its very excellence is faulty! Irony is at all times hard to be understood by the multitude; but the irony is here so exquisite, as to mislead even the more discerning.[35]

By the 'discerning' are surely meant those with enough political experience to know better.

A further example of Galt's intentional, ironic humour comes quickly in the work with Jobbry's explanation of his reasons for becoming involved in public life. Parliament is the ultimate source of patronage for his brood of relatives.[36] Jobbry's openness about his venality – that it is not just for his own self-enrichment – makes him more likeably roguish than his Gudetown counterpart.

Galt includes episodes and themes in Jobbry's parliamentary career that give the novel its character as a 'theoretical history'. The details of Jobbry's negotiations for the purchase of a Commons seat are an early example. The price of the Frailtown constituency, calculated pro rata on how much of a septennial parliament is left to run, comes down from two thousand pounds per session to six hundred, which, at about half the historical going rate, is a bargain and a fictional continuation of a trend of such returned Anglo-Indian nabobs entering Parliament this way that first started in the 1750s.[37]

The fictional comedy based on historical reality is continued when Galt begins to explain the constituency Jobbry has purchased. Only after his election does Jobbry ask Mr Spicer, a constituent, 'by the by, in what county is Frailtown'.[38] This provides a humorous perspective on the relationship an MP for a bought seat was likely to have with his constituents. John Ward has identified Frailtown as modelled on Higham Ferrers in Northamptonshire, Galt's 'Vamptonshire'.[39] In the pre-Reform Parliament, by one account, Higham Ferrers had an electorate of about forty voters, one hundred and twenty-five houses and just over seven hundred inhabitants.[40] As Jobbry's later experience at his two contested elections shows, the electorate in Galt's Frailtown was five, six if the mayor is included, which would have made it just tinier than the notoriously small Old

Sarum in Wiltshire.[41] Frailtown's five or six electors makes the contested elections more nerve-wracking. This is especially the case in the first such election, when one elector, trapped in a music case, is released at the vital moment and ensures Jobbry's election.[42]

Unlike James Pawkie, who always strives to represent himself as able to manage events and people, Archibald Jobbry is often at their mercy, moved by the demands or circumstances of others, whether it be grasping relatives, desperate supplicants like Mr Selby later in his career, or in this case unreliable electors. At both his contested elections Jobbry's parliamentary career is at risk. In *The Member* elections happen 'live'. Bribery, use of mob tactics – the players who 'throw squibs and jibes' against Jobbry's first opponent, Mr Gabblon – the last-minute note from the borough's patron that causes the mayor, Mr Spicer, to take unwell, thereby removing one of Jobbry's opponents: all these were not uncommon at parliamentary elections of the time.[43]

Frankness about venality is an aspect of Jobbry's character with which more modern critics have difficulty. Charles Snodgrass writes that 'Archibald Jobbry's behaviour as an "independent" reveals his slippery nature'.[44] Carla Sassi approvingly expands on this point about slipperiness: 'Snodgrass, in one of the few studies on this novel, deals with Jobbry's "slippery nature", his Machiavellian ability to lobby both sides of the House – notwithstanding his proclaimed moderate Tory stance – and still keep his seat'.[45] Both critics surely apply inappropriate ethical standards to the politics of the 1820s and 1830s when they describe Jobbry as 'slippery' and 'unfit'. Ethically there was nothing slippery about being an independent in pre-Reform parliaments, or about refusing to become attached to a ministry, as Jobbry does. On the contrary, independents were held in higher esteem than ministry placemen. In any case, a member's loyalty was perforce often not primarily to party but to a local patron, something of which Mr Tough unsuccessfully advises Jobbry to avoid even the impression in accepting Lord Dilldam's invitation to dinner after his first contested election.[46] The Snodgrass and Sassi interpretations arguably apply an ahistorical political paradigm in their implied disapproval of Jobbry for not having a clear party allegiance. Lobbying both sides of the House while proclaiming a moderate Tory stance would have been no bar to a member keeping his seat, provided he had the support of his patron or of the leading influence wielders in a constituency, or was rich enough to buy his election on his own account. Disciplined two-party politics, with clearly definable sides in the House of Commons, was not a situation a non-fictional Jobbry would have recognised; indeed, he contrasts a party man 'with my own notions of what a plain member should be, who has the real good of his country at heart'.[47]

Even allowing for this anachronism, however, there is a further inaccuracy in that Jobbry's moderate Toryism is not proclaimed, but is something he develops reluctantly in the course of his experiences, a process that is central to understanding *The Member*. This new development starts with his encounter with Mr Selby, who is a victim of government's repeated failure to pay promised compensation for losses sustained during an invasion of one of the colonies – something that eventually leaves both him and his family 'utterly undone'.[48] Jobbry is responsible for Selby making another application to the government for justice, and the failure of this leads to the change in Jobbry: 'I yet saw that there was some jarring and jangling in the working of the State, that was not just agreeable.'[49]

Until this encounter with Mr Selby, in chapter 28, exactly half-way through the memoir, it is Jobbry the operator that predominates and the humour, especially in his obtaining and passing on patronage, is unclouded. Jobbry's approach to patronage becomes a system, in the operation of which he describes himself as growing 'more dextrous'.[50] After his failed attempt to help Selby, Jobbry is less jaunty and more introspective. His change of spirit gives depth to the portrait of a politician developing as his career progresses. This is no caricature. In a scene that gives a vibrant sense of his changing sentiments, Jobbry reflects on his 'sheer weariness of spirit', on Westminster, which is described as 'jangling' and 'foul', and the feeling he expresses of being drawn towards the good and the non-worldly.[51] There are references here to Moses in the desert and to the spirituality of the Ganges. His description of Westminster at midnight has an emotional and visual quality to it that would have been quite out of character had Galt given it to Pawkie.

Into the space left by loss of interest in being the political fixer and operator comes a greater concern for issues. Chapters 29 to 31 each deal in succession with a major issue of the day, respectively the Holy Alliance, Roman Catholic Emancipation, and repeal of the Corn Laws. Jobbry's views on these issues support his analysis of his position in the breakdown of the composition of the Commons he makes at the start of his third parliament. He identifies an equal number of about sixty rigid Tories and Whigs on opposite wings. Jobbry says he belongs to neither group. A Whig would not have expressed support for the Holy Alliance, a union of autocratic powers that was anathema to Whig notions of civil and religious liberty.[52] A diehard Tory would never have voted against his conscience, as Jobbry does, on Roman Catholic Emancipation.[53] A pragmatic, moderate Tory could argue, as Jobbry does, that the Corn Laws were necessary to regulate the trade in corn, but only so far as fair trade did not exist with other countries.[54]

Further confirmation that Galt is portraying a moderate Tory is found in the closing chapters of *The Member*, in which Jobbry accepts an invitation from Boldero Blount to visit the latter's country estate and see for himself the effects of Reform fever. Galt places this historically between the death of George IV, which occurred in June 1830, and the fall of the Wellington ministry, which happened in November of the same year. During this autumn, agricultural revolts, known as the Swing Riots after their mythical leader, Captain Swing, took place in the corn-growing areas of southeastern and southern England.[55] Galt sets Blount's estate in this region and Jobbry, while conducting an investigation into the riots, hears the suggestion of a local schoolmaster, Mr Diphthong, for creating a local employment fund as an alternative to paying labourers out of the poor-rates and thereby pauperising them. Diphthong's solution involves raising property taxes, which Jobbry objects would cause the downfall of great estates. Diphthong's response goes to the heart of the Reform issue: "'I think not,' said he; "the great properties have had their day: they are the relics of the feudal system, when the land bore all public burdens. That system is in principle overthrown".[56] Jobbry's memory of this is revealing: 'I cannot get the better of what he propounded about the feudal system being at an end, and of the system by which he thinks it is to be succeeded.'[57] He cannot out-of-hand reject Diphthong as a simpleton, levelling democrat, and he tacitly admits the force of the argument that the feudal system is at an end by his inability to answer Diphthong's analysis. The extent of parliamentary reform achieved in the 1830s may have been modest, but the landmark lay in the establishment of a principle of representation based on a generally applicable franchise at the expense of a mixed system that included representatives who were essentially the vassals of political patrons.

The Member is about a moderate and, for his time, perceptive politician who has the courage to be affected by the views of political opponents, but yet is also brave enough to say that some abuses are, if not worth preserving, then at least worth reforming wisely.[58] Galt increasingly demands respect for his character's opinions. Jobbry justifies his antipathy to what he views as the heresy of savings in government by way of a coherent critique of 'the new-fangled doctrines of the Utilitarians'.[59] These ideas, he argues, may actually increase 'high crimes and misdemeanours' among political leaders because, if savings deprive them of the 'candle-ends and cheese-parings' necessary to enable them to associate with the otherwise powerful and wealthy in society, then they will be exposed to temptation and corruption.[60] Jobbry may believe that with the Reform Act 'the axe will have been laid to the root of the British Oak', by which is presumably meant the country's ancient constitution, but, by the end of the novel, he appreciates why the axe will fall.[61] Jobbry, if he had been in Parliament some fourteen years later, might well have stayed loyal to Robert Peel, and would have been an unlikely die-hard Protectionist.

In comparison with Pawkie in *The Provost*, Jobbry's adjustment takes place on the level of ideas rather than of tactics. Perhaps this accounts for the fact that even Ian Gordon, Galt's biographer, accepts the argument that '*The Member* is the first political novel in English'.[62] Politics, though, is about ideas *and* tactics. Giving *The Provost* its due place takes nothing away from Galt's achievement in *The Member*. It simply allows political fiction to deal with more than ideas and to take place outside the confines of metropolitan Westminster.

Moreover, the best of Galt's work in this field, as seen in these two novels, should be seen in the context of his other writing which, with various degrees of success, included politics. Galt provided breadth, as well as depth and quality, in his contribution to political fiction. *The Radical* (1832), for example, is a wry portrait of a hypocritical political extremist, and is the fullest political characterisation, from boy to MP, after those of Pawkie and Jobbry. As Nathan Butt's name – Nothing But; Naethin But in Scots – suggests, he is an uncompromising Radical, who professes to love mankind in general. He cannot, however, treat those close to him with kindness, and he is flexible enough with his principles that, when it comes to his own political prospects in an election, he decides to be 'all things to all men; for it is necessary, on such occasions, to swerve a little from the straightforwardness of principles'.[63] Butt's Radicalism is based not on extending the franchise as far as possible, but on rule by the wise few, of whom he thinks he is naturally a member, a point which is driven home in the form of a hostile newspaper report that, to his annoyance, corrects his views on what might be expected of a Radical.[64]

Another earlier political example, complementing that of Pawkie in the previous year, is Peter Gauze in *The Gathering of the West* (1823), a Paisley weaver who refuses to be overawed by the great. In discussion with fellow weavers he argues for going to Edinburgh to pay their respects to George IV when he visits Scotland in 1822.[65] Galt depicts Gauze's

Radicalism more sympathetically than Nathan Butt's in that it is rational, moderate, and based on a willingness to persuade others. The king is only a magistrate and deserves respect because of the position he holds in the community of which they are all members. In Peter Gauze, Galt represents Radicalism as moving on from the rioting and strikes of 1819 and 1820 in the west of Scotland and Paisley in particular.[66] Galt's favourable comparison of Scottish loyalty with Irish rebelliousness is an unusual example of outspoken patriotism.[67]

Galt's political fiction includes, among others, the manipulative local councillor, the independent turned critical party-loyalist MP, the inflexible extremist, and the reformed and moderate Radical. Galt's political fiction stands out not only because it is pioneering, but also because of the intensity and breadth of its political subject matter. Far more than Disraeli or Trollope, for example, Galt concentrates on politicians at work, rather than in love, in debt, or on the sports field.

CHAPTER NINE

Reading for Something Other than the Plot in Galt's 'Tales of the West'

Anthony Jarrells

> [...] but firstly there was no plot, and secondly there was no sequence of events, and no coherence, everything came at you higgledy-piggledy, and that was fine per se, but what was it that was higgledy-piggledy?
> Karl Ove Knausgaard, *My Struggle*, volume 5 (2016)

Although John Galt is perhaps best remembered for his fictional account of a Scottish country minister in *Annals of the Parish* (1821), it was two previously published works, both of them also about regional communities in the west of Scotland, that established Galt as a first-rate writer of Scottish stories – a peer, some thought, to the great Walter Scott. *The Ayrshire Legatees* was published in *Blackwood's Edinburgh Magazine* starting in 1820 and *The Steam-Boat* followed immediately on its heels, beginning its serial run in 1821. Indeed, their success led William Blackwood to reissue each as a single-volume novel and to agree to publish a work that Galt had been calling *The Pastor* (later renamed *Annals of the Parish*). Galt had tried to publish *The Pastor* with Archibald Constable a few years before. But Constable rejected it, feeling – it seems – that there would be little interest from the public, pre-Walter Scott, in reading fiction set in Scotland.

For Galt, *The Ayrshire Legatees*, *The Steam-Boat*, and *Annals of the Parish* were parts of a more general but still 'coherent' work that he thought of as his 'Tales of the West'.[1] It was not only a shared regional setting that made for such coherence, but also resistance to novelistic plotting that runs through all three works. Blackwood rejected Galt's proposed title, 'Tales of the West', and strongly encouraged him to write something more along the lines of a three-volume novel – something with 'a good and striking story' (the result was *Sir Andrew Wylie of that Ilk*, published in 1822).[2] But it is worth considering these three 'tales' together, both for the ways that they resist novelistic plotting, or what

Galt would call 'fable', and for what they might be said to offer in place of plot: something Galt characterised as 'theoretical history'. Galt's fictions were experiments written in an age when the novel was only just becoming the recognisable and dominant genre that we know it as today, an age, too, when the short story proper had yet to shape itself around the thematic consistency and sense of closure that readers were coming to expect from novels. The tale was well suited for Galt's experimentation – first, because it was a genre known for its distinctive mix of fact and fiction and, second, because the tale's two major associations were with regional history and the oral tradition. Both were disappearing in the Romantic period, and Galt's fiction of these years can be said to offer an account of the various threats he saw to these twin pillars of community. The tales may read now like failed experiments, especially in the case of *The Steam-Boat*, but together they suggest the possibility of reading for something other than plot – or, more specifically, for experiencing both the potential for community that storytelling affords and the kinds of obstacles to such telling that modern, commercial life puts in the way. Galt's 'Tales of the West' are proto-modernist in the ways they foreground the act of telling.[3] What they tell is time: not so much at the level of content or character development, but rather in the curious form of the tale itself, a doomed genre in an age of constant interruption.

Constant interruption was, ironically, a regular feature of the Romantic tale, as were lengthy digressions and confusing chronologies. In October 1824, for example, Galt's friend and fellow *Blackwood's* writer, David Macbeth Moir, published the first instalment of his 'Wonderful Passage in the Life of Mansie Wauch, Tailor', a tale that recounts a humorous episode involving an obliging but somewhat obtuse resident of the town of Dalkeith who has to take a turn guarding the local cemetery against 'resurrection' men. 'About this time there arose a great sough and surmise,' the tale begins, 'that some loons were playing false with the kirkyard, howking up bones from their damp graves, and hauling them away to the college.'[4] The next instalment in the series, 'Farther Portions of the Autobiography of Mansie Wauch, Tailor', published in June 1825, jumps back in time to Mansie's origins. 'I have no distinct recollection of the thing myself,' Mansie states, 'but I have every reason to believe that I was born on the 15th of October, 1765'.[5] The second instalment contains four 'portions': the first two follow a roughly chronological order, from birth to schooling and apprenticeship, then the latter two return to various other 'wonderful' things and 'remarkable' incidents experienced by Mansie. As a bracketed note prefacing 'portion fourth' explains, '[t]he reader may observe, that Mansie does not *stitch* on regularly, and that he is a little partial to *vandikes*; but we cannot *twist* him, and allow him to resume the *threads* of his discourse, at his good will and pleasure'.[6]

Moir penned ten instalments of Mansie's adventures before issuing them together as a single-volume novel, published by Blackwood, in 1828. What is perhaps most remarkable about the novel version, *Life of Mansie Wauch, Tailor in Dalkeith*, is that in it Mansie does in fact stitch on regularly and that, despite his partiality to 'vandikes' (or zigzagging narration), his story has been twisted in such a way as to bring the different threads of his discourse together. *Life of Mansie Wauch* begins with some 'preliminaries' in which Mansie, still telling his story in the first person, talks about the '[...] trade of committing to paper all the surprising occurrences and remarkable events that chanced to happen to [him] in the course of Providence'.[7] Chapter one then starts with Mansie's grandfather. Chapter two moves on to the life of his father. And in chapter three we find Mansie's 'coming into the world', including portions published in the *Blackwood's* instalment of June 1825. It is not until chapter ten that we come to the wonderful passage recounted in the original article of October 1824. And while the first sentence remains the same – '[a]bout this time there arose a great sough and surmise [...]' – the meaning and effect of the phrase, 'this time', have changed considerably.[8] What could 'this time' refer to in the original version, given that there is no context – no before or after – and no historical or personal markers to situate the episode in a bigger picture or development? The effect is disorienting; the reader can have no idea of what time it is that is in question.

But the effect in the novel version is quite the opposite. In this version, the 'this time' of the grave scene refers to a specific moment in the unfolding of Mansie's life: it has been placed, that is, in the kind of meaningful 'textual and temporal succession' that Peter Brooks describes, simply, as 'plot'.[9] What at first feels random, floating, cut off from sequence, is now particular, ordered, and part of 'the logic and dynamic of narrative'.[10] According to Brooks, this logic should be satisfying. 'Plot', he suggests, 'is the principle of interconnectedness and intention which we cannot do without in moving through the discrete elements – incidents, episodes, actions – of a narrative'.[11] In Mansie's case, however, it is not as satisfying as it should be, at least not compared to the original. The novel version of Mansie's life, while filling in the gaps and providing the befores and afters, lacks the vitality and open-endedness of the magazine instalments. Something has been lost in the exchange Moir makes for plot. Indeed, were *Life of Mansie Wauch* to be put back into periodical form, this time following the chronological reordering provided by the novel, it would read like the literal translation – from French back into English – of Mark Twain's 'Celebrated Jumping Frog of Calaveras County' (1865), a translation that demonstrated to Twain only that the French had no sense of humour.

Moir's 'Mansie' series was directly inspired by Galt's tales of small-town life in the west of Scotland, something Moir acknowledged when he dedicated his *Life of Mansie Wauch* to Galt in 1828. Galt not only helped to establish *Blackwood's Magazine* as a serious venue for humorous, regional fiction, but he, too, worked between the registers of the magazine and the novel – single-volume and triple-decker. When Galt published his tales in book-form, however, after finding initial success with them in the pages of *Blackwood's*, he did not reorder and connect the individual instalments to nearly the same extent as Moir. Galt's first series, *The Ayrshire Legatees*, for instance, appeared in the June 1820 issue and ran for eight instalments through February 1821. Each instalment contains letters written by various members of the Pringle family, who are travelling to London to collect a legacy left by a deceased relative in India, and responses to the letters from friends and parishioners back in Garnock, a fictional village situated between Irvine and Kilwinning, in Ayrshire. The organisation of the series, reminiscent of Tobias Smollett's *Expedition of Humphry Clinker* (1771), allowed Galt to create a large cast of character types and to compare, often humorously, the provincial pieties of rural life with the confusions and conceits of the great metropolis. The first instalment in the series begins with Mr M'Gruel, a surgeon and 'correspondent in Kilwinning' who sends the magazine 'several letters from the different members of Dr Pringle's family, during their present visit to London'.[12] The novel version, published in 1821, gets rid of the fictional correspondent and starts instead with the second paragraph of the original instalment: 'On last New Year's day Dr Pringle received a letter from India [...]' – though it removes that second word, 'last', untethering the action from any specific year. The rest of the novel stays mostly true to the magazine version, eliminating only the later references to the correspondent, M'Gruel, and several 'Responsive notices to correspondents' that began to appear in the fifth instalment of the *Blackwood's* series. The novel also groups the letters into chapters and adds short titles for each, ranging from the literal ('The Departure', 'The Voyage', 'The Legacy') to the more ponderous ('Philosophy and Religion', 'Discoveries and Rebellions'). No additional context or back-story is given. As in the magazine instalments, Galt's narrator is content to let 'the parties speak for themselves'.[13]

The first instalment of Galt's next series, 'The Steam-Boat; or the Voyages and Travels of Thomas Duffle, Cloth-Merchant in the Salt-Market of Glasgow', appeared in the same issue as the final instalment of 'The Ayrshire Legatees', so eager was Blackwood to capitalise on the success of his new recruit. Arguably, one of the strangest works of fiction published in the period, *The Steam-Boat* recounts three voyages taken by Duffle: two between Glasgow and Greenock, and a third, via Leith, to London. Duffle meets a variety of people during his travels and many of them – from Scotland, North America, Norway, Russia, and elsewhere – are invited to share a tale. Recording the 'most remarkable' of these, Duffle groups the tales under the headings of 'voyage first', 'voyage second', and 'voyage third', numbers each one, and provides a brief account of how he 'compiled this book'.[14] The contents of the tales range from the comic and the pathetic to the historical and the absurd. But what is most striking about the series is that Duffle often leaves off in the middle of a story and never returns to fill in the gaps. Steam boats stop and start, passengers get on and off, and stories begun often are left unfinished. As Duffle himself states, 'I could not but [...] liken travelling in a steam-boat to the life of temporal man, where our joys are cut off in fruition, and adversity comes upon us like a cloud'.[15] The suggestion here is of a kind of verisimilitude at the level of form, or telling: the incompleteness of the narrative mirrors the life of 'temporal man' and, in doing so, highlights the ways that commercial society has, in a sense, interrupted the plot.

In the middle of the first tale, 'The Russian', for instance, Duffle breaks in with the following:

> —Just at this passage of the gentleman's story the engine of the boat was stopped, and the captain told him that they were forenent Erskine Ferry, where he was to be landed; by which I was greatly disappointed, having been vastly entertained with what he had related, and making no manner of doubt that the rest of the tale would be equally edifying. – But it was not to be expected that he would sail onward with me [...].[16]

In 'The Hurricane', another tale that was included in the second instalment of the series, Galt's narrator – a sailor – stops his tale at the very moment that his ship has gone down in the storm. He has just made his way to land, miraculously, when Duffle again breaks in to explain that, 'as we drew near to the shore, the sailor had forgotten all the earnest solemnity of his tale'. 'I was left in a kind of an unsatisfied state,' he continues, 'with the image of the broken ship in my mind, with her riven planks and timbers, grinning like the jaws of death amidst the raging waters'.[17] Many more instances of stories broken up by the motions of travel and commerce followed in future instalments. Whatever hopes readers had of finding a conclusion, perhaps in a later instalment, were left hanging. None ever came – not in the series and not in the book version published by Blackwood in 1822.

Galt made few substantial changes to *The Steam-Boat* when it appeared in book form. As in *The Ayrshire Legatees*, he removed the 'responsive notices to correspondents' and added chapter designations. The only major change was the addition of three tales. Where 'The Steam-Boat. No. VIII', the final instalment in *Blackwood's*, ended with 'The Covenanter', a rejoinder to Walter Scott's negative portrayal of the Covenanters in *Old Mortality* (1816), the book version features two additional tales that had been published separately in *Blackwood's*, 'The Buried Alive' and 'Mrs Ogle of Balbogle', along with a new tale, 'The Beef Barrel; or the Mortification to the Parish of Cardross'. The addition of the three tales allowed Galt to end the book on a less sombre note than the one afforded by 'The Covenanter'. It also gave him the opportunity to bring his account full circle, with Duffle arriving back in Glasgow 'after seeing such uncos, and undergoing such very uncommon adventures'.[18]

If anything, the results of publishing the two *Blackwood's* series in book form were even less satisfying than they were with Moir's 'Mansie' – especially in the case of *The Steam-Boat*. While *Mansie Wauch* sacrifices some of the playfulness of the original series in order to arrange its individual episodes in a more sequential and conventional narrative order, Galt's two series seem to fail as novels precisely to the extent that they do not undergo the same kind of narrative reordering. It is as if they are a kind of literary species out of its natural habitat – a tale or sketch being passed off as a novel. As Francis Jeffrey exclaimed of 'the thing called "The Steam-Boat" [it] has really no merit at all; and should never have been transplanted from the magazine in which we are informed it first made its appearance'.[19] Jeffrey admired *Annals of the Parish* (1821), another of Galt's Blackwood-published works, though this one did not originate in serial form. But the 'series of vulgar stories' (as Jeffrey called them) that comprised *The Steam-Boat* simply made no sense in book form, despite the fact that Galt's narrator, Thomas Duffle, mentions on three occasions in the first number alone that he is 'venturing to come before the public in the book-making line'.[20]

Partly, the negative effect of reading the two series in book form can be attributed to the change in format from magazine series to single-volume 'novel'. As Robert Morrison points out, Galt's work in this period 'deftly exploits the *Blackwood's* context'.[21] '[C]ertainly the *Legatees* never reads so well as when it is read in *Blackwood's*', he explains: 'The articles that surround its eight instalments – written by Maginn, Wilson, Lockhart, Cunningham, Moir, De Quincey, and several others – cast striking lights and shadows over the novel, and extend, qualify, and deepen its observations on a host of issues [...].'[22] Such lights and shadows disappeared in the novelised version and with them went a host of powerful associations with topics such as Scottish identity, political economy, and local history. A second explanation for the negative effect, related to the first but more specific to Galt's particular style, is the way the works in question 'eschew' – in Ian Duncan's words – plot.[23] Such eschewal proved fitting for the magazine format: as Duncan has argued more recently, 'serialization provided a dynamic framework for the effects of fragmentation and heterogeneity' such as those that characterised Galt's 'clishmaclaver' style in these years.[24] But it was less than ideal for publication in volume form, breaking as it did a very different but equally powerful association between the novel and plot.

This association was one of which Galt was well aware. It was also something he deliberately resisted in his fiction, at least until the publication of *Sir Andrew Wylie* (1822). 'It may be necessary to explain', Galt writes in his *Autobiography* (1833),

> that I do not think the character of my own productions has been altogether rightly regarded. Merely because the incidents are supposed to be fictitious, they have been all considered as novels, and yet, as such, the best of them are certainly deficient in the peculiarity of the novel. They would be more properly characterised, in several instances, as theoretical histories, than either as novels or romances. A consistent fable is as essential to a novel as a plot is to a drama, and yet those, which are deemed my best productions, are deficient in this essential ingredient.[25]

A 'consistent fable' is the same thing as a 'plot', what Galt elsewhere calls 'the most material feature of the novel'.[26] But his 'best' productions of the period, he says, lack this material feature. *Annals of the Parish*, for instance, is 'void of anything like a plot'.[27] And *The Ayrshire Legatees* 'is also a work that cannot be justly appreciated as a novel' because, as Galt says, it lacks a clearly defined plot.[28] Such works are better characterised as 'theoretical histories', Galt explains, referring to 'a species of philosophical investigation', as Dugald Stewart described it, by which a historian shows how a given event or phenomenon 'may have been produced by natural causes'.[29] Theoretical, or 'conjectural', history is speculative: it aims to fill in the gaps where no written record is available to supply evidence of how a particular institution or practice – such as language – might have come to be. In its own way, then, theoretical history is 'a licensed kind of fiction', as Duncan argues.[30] But it is one that Galt distinguishes from the novel because, like his own early fictions, it is deficient in that essential ingredient: plot.

The distinction is somewhat curious given that theoretical history has become nearly synonymous with what Regina Hewitt calls the 'progress plot'. 'Conjectural histories', she writes, 'use the idea of progress to chart the rise and development of human institutions and behaviors through distinct stages over time'.[31] But as Hewitt also suggests, scholarship on conjectural history has shifted its focus, of late, 'from documenting the progress plot to analyzing how community is imagined', and discussions of Galt's fiction, not least Hewitt's own, have followed suit.[32] The work of Adam Ferguson in particular has become useful, Hewitt says, for accounting for those moments in Galt where a certain scepticism or unease in the face of commercial modernity can be detected – in, say, the gradual erosion of traditional communities, as documented in *Annals of the Parish*, or in those new conditions imposed upon 'temporal man', which, in *The Steam-Boat* at least, appear to be ill-conducive to storytelling. Ferguson, of course, did not reject the idea that commercial society brought with it many advances and improvements. But he wondered about the losses that attended such progress: of character and independence, for instance, and of the subject of his greatest work, what he described as 'the bands of society'.[33]

That Galt offers such a critique of progress in *Annals of the Parish* is now well understood by scholars.[34] Much less, however, has been said about his other productions of the period, including *The Ayrshire Legatees* and *The Steam-Boat*. Yet these works, too, combine an account of progress – in manners, fashion, access to information, transportation, and international finance – with a more sceptical view of the advances brought about by commercial society. In *The Ayrshire Legatees*, for instance, what Rachel Pringle – the daughter – describes as 'the primitive simplicities of my native scenes' are invoked not only so that Galt might highlight a certain provincial pettiness on the part of many a Garnock parishioner, but also so he can throw the 'going and coming' of the inhabitants of the modern metropolis – on the Sabbath, no less – into starker relief.[35] In the fourth letter of the series, written by Andrew Pringle, the son, we are told of the Reverend Dr Pringle's 'admiration of the increasing signs of what he called civilization' as the family makes its way into London.[36] 'I felt touched with reverence', Andrew writes, 'as if I was indeed approaching the city of THE HUMAN POWERS'.[37] As he continues with his description, though, comparing the view entering London with that of the approach into Edinburgh, he exclaims, 'but, in coming to this Babylon, there is an eager haste and a hurrying on from all quarters, towards that stupendous pile of gloom, through which no eye can penetrate, an unceasing sound, like the enginery of an earthquake at work, rolls from the heart of that profound and indefinable obscurity'.[38] The city goes from being the embodiment of human powers to a picture of Miltonic sin in less than a few sentences, as if Adam Smith suddenly gave way to William Blake and England's green and pleasant lands were transformed – like some early articulation of Theodor Adorno's dialectic of Enlightenment – into a modern Babylon or a manufactured natural disaster.

A few letters later, Andrew, landing on a topic that Adam Ferguson also found much to comment upon, ponders the connection between economic modernity and warfare. After settling with his agent some matters regarding the inheritance that the family has come to collect, Andrew is invited to dine with the man and reflects on this new acquaintance and on the experience of the transaction. 'The incidents, indeed, of this day, have been all highly gratifying', he writes,

> and the new and brighter phase in which I have seen the mercantile character, as it is connected with the greatness and glory of my country – is in itself equivalent to an accession of useful knowledge. I can no longer wonder at the vast power which the British government wielded during the late war, when I reflect that the method and promptitude of the house of Messrs Argent and Company is common to all the great commercial concerns from which the statesmen derived, as from so many reservoirs, those immense pecuniary supplies, which enabled them to beggar all the resources of a political despotism, the most unbounded, both in power and principle, of any tyranny that ever existed so long.[39]

The tone here, on the surface, is positive and elevated with a sense of epiphany, not unlike the scene in Scott's *Rob Roy* when Frank Osbaldistone suddenly realises that the affairs of his father's counting house in London are somehow connected to a Highland rebellion happening hundreds of miles away to the north. Andrew, described in the series as a reader of *The Edinburgh Review*, would be understood by *Blackwood's* readers to be sympathetic to the increasingly 'mercantile character' of national affairs and to the political economic outlook that *Blackwood's* was founded, in certain respects, to oppose (the same might be said of Galt, a businessman – though Galt took some pains in his *Literary Life* to explain that Andrew Pringle was not a stand-in for his own political views and that he was, himself, a Tory).[40] Thus one cannot but feel that, as elsewhere in the series, Galt uses Andrew's optimistic sense of wonder both to highlight a fact or connection and to undercut that same fact or connection, as when, later, he has Miss Mally, a parishioner, respond to acting minister Snodgrass's claim that 'the Londoners, with all their advantages of information, are neither purer nor better than their fellow subjects in the country'.[41] 'As to their betterness', she quips, 'I have a notion that they are far waur; and I hope you do not think that earthly knowledge of any sort has a tendency to make mankind, or womankind either, any better'.[42] There is a subtle irony in Galt's letting his parties speak for themselves, an irony he exploits in order to complicate a more general account of the progress, literal and philosophical, from Garnock to London.

In *The Steam-Boat*, too, Galt lets his parties speak for themselves, although it is not the device of the letter than enables this. Duffle's interest is in 'the manner of the different narrations' rather than merely the 'matter', or content, of the individual stories.[43] In attempting to write out the tales he has heard, Duffle says that, 'I was transported out of my natural body, and put into the minds of the narrators, so as to think their thoughts and to speak with their words'.[44] This is what the tales really record: a certain style of telling, sometimes national (as in Harriet Lee's *Canterbury Tales*, first published in 1797), sometimes regional. Duffle does not retell stories, then, so much as repeat, or aim to repeat, the original telling, inhabiting the thoughts and words of the tellers and making that mode of telling a character, of sorts, in his own story of steam travel. This is one reason, in addition to the starting and stopping of the steamboat, why stories are broken off prior to being finished. When Duffle does try to 'write out a sequel' to the first tale, 'The Russian', he says that, 'it was not at all in the same fine style of language that the traveller employed'.[45] He is thus willing to sacrifice the 'moral reflections' that the original narrator surely would have provided because completing the story constitutes a different kind of interruption: in this case, not of the matter of the story, as in the failure to provide an ending, but of the manner of telling it – a failure, in other words, to allow the parties to speak for themselves. Duffle's being transported into the minds of narrators is not quite the same thing as Adam Smith's sympathy, in which a person imagines what she might feel were she in the place of another. Still, it suggests the limits of community and even of sympathy – in imagining how far one might go in speaking for another – even as the steamboat seems to make possible new communities and new possibilities for sympathy. As Caroline McCracken-Flesher puts it, 'travel increases the opportunities for and interruptions to tale telling, and throws into relief the human difficulty, striving, and sympathy that is communication'.[46]

This is not to say that the matter of the stories, told and half-told, does not also engage questions of progress and loss in modern society. As in *The Ayrshire Legatees*, Galt's approach can be described as comparative – though where in that series he effectively juxtaposed the rural and the urban, playing the advances of civilisation off against the primitive simplicities of the parish, in *The Steam-Boat*, he compares past and present, balancing accounts of 'barbarous' Russians and 'inhabitants before the present race' with Duffle's of-the-moment views of prosperity both in the centre and at the edges of the modern nation. The 'Steam-Boat. No. IV', for example, includes a tale called 'The Deucalion of Kentucky', told by a man of the same name, 'in consequence of being the sole survivor of a town that was washed away by a deluge'.[47] The deluge is of modern making, like that engineered earthquake that Andrew Pringle describes as London, but in leading up to his account of the flood the narrator mentions ancient Indian war tracks and burial mounds and wonders of the American Indians, whom he characterises as 'inhabitants before the present race', if they perhaps were 'antediluvian', referring to an older, more famous, deluge.[48] 'Sometimes I think America is the old world that was destroyed', he exclaims, echoing a sentiment that can be found in any number of eighteenth-century conjectural histories.[49] Duffle is relieved when the steamer lands at Port Glasgow, as he can move on from this 'tale of desolation'. From here we get Duffle's own remarks on the steeple of Port Glasgow and the comparative prosperity of neighbouring Greenock, where the 'enterprising spirit of the place' is evident 'not only in a steeple,'

> but likewise a bottle-cone, and a bell – also a new harbour; besides the place they call the tail of the bank, and that stately edificial pile, the Custom House, with diverse churches, schools, and places of worship; a Tontine Inn, a Play-house, and Assembly Rooms, built at a great cost of thousands of pounds [...].[50]

The instalment does not resolve the differences between the desolation of the tale and the prosperity of the town, though the former, too, was initiated by 'the bold and enterprising character' of the Deucalion of Kentucky's father, who was working to improve industry by enlarging the supply of water to power his mill.[51] The two accounts sit side-by-side and ask the reader to think for herself about the bigger story of progress and loss implied in the account.

Other tales are much more direct in their indictment of modern society, though these, too, are equally averse to supplying a clear moral – the very thing cut off in the opening tale of 'The Russian'. The seventh number of the series reverses the order of the example above, moving from an account of the gardens and opera and assemblies of London to a tale of desolation – two tales, in fact. But the effect of the juxtaposition is the same, leaving Duffle – and the reader – to 'guess and ponder anent the sad and mournful issue' of the society the tale describes. After touring Vauxhall and the opera, Duffle sits down at a coffeehouse to have his dinner and meets a 'hard-favoured stranger' whose responses to Duffle's attempts at conversation seem aimed at forestalling any possibility of communication.[52] But when Duffle, still marveling at 'the great apparition of wealth that seemed to abound everywhere', remarks that 'it is only in London a man can see the happiness of the British nation', the stranger finally responds with, 'and the misery'.[53] The 'preeminence' of London, he continues, exists not in its buildings or outward displays of wealth, but rather, at least for the man 'who looks deeper than the packing-case of society', in 'the possession of a race of beings that I call the Effigies'.[54] Effigies resemble man and do things that men do but they do them 'without reason, imagination, or heart'.[55] They are described as 'foundlings of fortune' and as growing rich 'by the expedients and necessities of the unfortunate'; 'their element', says the stranger, 'consists of the necessities of commercial community, which embraces all the other vicissitudes to which mankind are ordinarily liable'.[56] These effigies, we come to understand, are moneylenders. They are the grease that lubricates the gears of society, but they are not likely to be seen in any of the places where society seeks gaiety and leisure, such as Vauxhall or the opera. Dickensian misers *avant la lettre*, the effigies are very rich but also very unhappy.

Duffle wonders if his coffeehouse companion simply has 'a sour heart towards the sons and daughters of success and prosperity'.[57] But the stranger says, no, he does not, for the effigies can hardly be considered as the same species of sons and daughters: they are inhuman. Even more remarkable, though, is another class of Londoners, he continues. And after ordering a bottle of wine the stranger proceeds to a second tale, 'The Broken Heart', about the outward face of wealth and prosperity. Although the tale begins by mentioning 'two kinds of adventurers who succeed in London' – those like the Effigies, who, though penniless achieve success through industry, and those 'who have friends of power and influence' – the subject, the broken heart, is in fact yet 'another class of beings', those brought up as gentlemen in the country but who 'rarely prosper in London'.[58] In this tale, a young man from a genteel family but brought up with 'acquired notions of elegance inconsistent' with his family's fortune makes his way to London where at first he positively revels in the lifestyle of the well-to-do.[59] He continues like this until he is required to provide support for his brothers and sisters. From then on he becomes a man living a double life, keeping up appearances on one side and slowly disintegrating on the other, until, in the end, he appears to lose all contact with humanity. 'I am excommunicated', he exclaims, before the story is cut off due to the emotional state of the narrator, and Duffle is left once again to ponder the import of what he has just heard. Such moments of irresolution, moments when thinking about how the state of modern society might be one way or another, are tied from the very first instance of tale-telling in the series – 'The Russian' – to interruptions of the plot.

McCracken-Flesher suggests that such interruptions highlight the limitations of community – or what she terms 'narrow definitions' of community – as imagined in the period.[60] Duncan characterises them as 'an experiment in participatory narration'.[61] As in Wordsworth and Coleridge's *Lyrical Ballads* (1798), an earlier and more famous experiment that aimed to elevate feeling over action, Galt's interruptions seem to say to his readers, as Simon Lee says to his, 'perhaps a tale you'll make it'. Whatever the case – and the two readings are not necessarily incompatible – *The Steam-Boat* can be said to lack *fable* both in the sense of a well-defined plot and, given the explicit connection between interrupted plots and absent morals in the series, a lesson (in addition to 'plot', 'fable' can also refer to a short story devised to convey some useful lesson (*OED*)). *The Steam-Boat* is what we might call a theoretical history of the present, supplying the 'constituents of narrative', as Duncan says, but in a way that makes them the materials for a future account of society, circa 1821, one that might be able to better say whether or how far things had progressed.[62] As Mary Poovey notes, for the conjectural historian 'the perspective that mattered was the retrospective gaze cast back from the future'.⁶³ Thus the materials are still raw; they have not yet been assimilated into a coherent plot or bound by temporal succession. Like the film actor described in Walter Benjamin's 'Work of Art in the Age of Mechanical Reproduction', who shoots a scene one week even though the succeeding scene had already been shot a couple of weeks before, the creation is 'by no means all of a piece' and is 'composed of many separate performances'.⁶⁴ Yet it is precisely the out-of-time-ness of each episode, and the disorienting effect of such, that makes the series feel true to experience.

Keith Costain argues that '*Annals of the Parish* is the only theoretical history which Galt ever wrote', although he also suggests that other, non-fiction works by Galt – such as his *Voyages and Travels* of 1812 – demonstrate the same commitment to the 'underlying principles, laws, [and] causes of progress' that comprise theoretical history.⁶⁵ But Galt, seeing his early Scottish fictions as part of a general work, probably thought otherwise. *The Steam-Boat*, too, for instance, is made up of voyages and travels, as is indicated in the subtitle and in the dedication; what Galt says by way of justifying his approach to the 1812 *Voyages and Travels* could just as easily be said of his fictional series of 1821: 'the treatment which strangers receive, in any country, furnishes a topic connected with its domestic economy, and that kind of knowledge is useful to the merchant and politician, as well as amusing to the general reader.'⁶⁶ Whatever the degree of plottedness that features in Enlightenment conjectural history, Galt seems to have recognised other possibilities in the form, possibilities that enabled him to document the contours of small town and big city alike, and to organise his illustrative episodes in ways that did not require the bounded logic of plot to make them meaningful or satisfying or useful.

So, first, then, there is no plot, no sequence of events, and no coherence. Everything comes at you higgledy-piggledy, as Karl Ove Knausgaard, another, more recent writer, who has experimented with mixing fact and fiction under the title of a 'novel', puts it in the epigraph to this essay. But what is it that is higgledy-piggledy, asks Knausgaard? We would do well to ask the same. How are we to be satisfied without the interconnectedness and temporal succession of plot, without what Brooks calls 'the anticipated structuring force of the ending'?⁶⁷ What do we get instead? One answer might be character: the many, often humorous, types that Galt's clever experiments with voice allow to come to the fore. Another answer might be 'facts', as in the empirical data collected by travellers and prized by conjectural historians but also facts about local life on which so many of the tales and ballads of the period – by James Hogg, for instance – are founded. A final answer, one that Knausgaard himself might give, is life itself, or – to use Galt's words – the life of temporal man. This is an answer that we who live on the later end of commercial society, with our smartphones and web connections, our ceaseless work hours and ever-increasing pace of life, are well situated to understand. Galt's series tell us about such a society in part by telling us different stories about it and in part by highlighting the very conditions that have come to make telling a compromised – and as Benjamin would add, a solitary – activity.[68]

CHAPTER TEN

Gender and the Short Story in the Twilight Years

Gerard Carruthers

By the 1830s, the short story was emerging in recognisably modern form. In Scotland, as elsewhere, novelists such as John Galt and James Hogg were turning their hands to shorter, more episodic fiction often with a focus on exotic subject-matter garnered from either home or abroad. Along with Galt and Hogg, Walter Scott is one of the three main figures these days identified in 'The "Blackwood" Group' named after William Blackwood, one of Scott's publishers, who also published novels and short stories by Galt and Hogg. Originally there was a wider grouping – engaged sometimes in multi-authored fictional projects – around Blackwood's *Edinburgh Monthly Magazine* (founded in 1817), later *Blackwood's Edinburgh Magazine* (and colloquially in time known more simply as the 'Maga').[1] Scott, Galt, and Hogg, however, are by far the three greatest Scottish talents associated with this publisher and this magazine in the early nineteenth century, and all are broadly to be associated with the Tory mindset of 'The Maga'. The periodical published a great deal of gothic short fiction, demonstrating the roots of the genre in *fin de siècle* horror tales which abounded in the 1790s, the age of 'revolutionary terror'.[2] The horror fiction of *Blackwood's*, the alarmist 'tales of terror', might be seen as of a piece with the fearful conservative mentality of the magazine. However, Blackwood and *Blackwood's* also contribute to fictional phenomena much less garish, more progressive, including a strong regionalist turn (part of the sensibility of the Romantic movement at large).

Among *Blackwood's* writers – albeit as often writing material for other magazines following and influenced by the 'Maga' – Galt and Hogg became especially adept at purveying short fiction associated with their own localities: Ayrshire/Renfrewshire and the Borders, respectively. Arguably, less amenable to the short story was Walter Scott. Today, 'The Two Drovers' (1827) is often seen as a Scottian best effort in the genre, but qualifications might be made. The text is much longer than Galt's shorter short stories, and it is published as the second of three pieces linked loosely but artfully by the one editor-narrator, Chrystal Croftangry in *Chronicles of the Canongate*. Scott's metier, then, remained the longer, more continuous volume.³ Shorter novels, though, had very much been the metier of John Galt more or less from the beginning of his career as a fiction-writer, with tightly economical texts such as *Annals of the Parish* (1821) or *The Steam-Boat* (1822) at least as prevalent as the extended 'triple-decker' productions, *The Entail* (1823) or *Ringan Gilhaize* (1823). Arguably, then, in this predisposition Galt was very well primed to become one of Scotland's earliest purveyors of the short story. In the twilight of his life, from 1829 in London, and attempting to recuperate from serious illness in Greenock from 1834, Galt produced a series of short stories quite as remarkable as his earlier run of novels and novellas, and very radical in their formal and social reach. Galt's collection, *Stories of the Study*, was published in three volumes in London in 1833, and the fourteen texts range in length from 'The Magos' at eleven pages to 'The Lutherans' at four hundred and sixty-nine pages. Both Galt's preface to *Stories of the Study* and the 'Introduction' which might clearly be identified with the writer himself, alluding as it does to authorial confinement late in life, express sheer delight in fiction and go some way towards cheerfully apologising for the miscellanea (more miscellaneous we might say than any gathering that Scott ever published) which Galt presents in these three volumes. The introduction begins:

> Being necessarily obliged to make a world of my study, I found it expedient to divide it into compartments, and thus it happened that, without any pre-disposition on my part, it naturally assumed a curious arrangement, in which the difficulty of locomotion in myself was in some measure compensated by the distribution into which the volumes and papers were placed for ease of access.⁴

Here we find an interesting confession of subjectivity, apparently necessary on the part of the ailing and sedentary writer. However, that seeming randomness of what occurrences the eye took in, his intimate observational style, had always been Galt's stock-in-trade. One of the finest Galt scholars, Ian A. Gordon, refers to *Stories of the Study*, 'with a few outstanding exceptions [as] an undistinguished gathering in the various genres that he had been turning out in the past few years for *Fraser's Magazine*'.⁵ Galt himself might seem in the preface to give support to

Gordon's view as he muses over the necessity of spinning out a publication to three volumes for commercial reasons, but a critical eye in the early twenty-first century might discern in Galt's anthology an honest (and cunning) recognition of the multifariousness and the subjectivity of both chronicler and subject-matter in the whirl of life in the early decades of the nineteenth century. The title itself, *Stories of the Study*, recognises a limited (somewhat, whimsical antiquarian) perspective put out and abroad in good black print. In this modesty topos applied to ambitiously diffuse material, however, we see a typical Galtian manoeuvre: the writer, the human being, generally, who is someone with the chutzpah to attempt rendering a world he or she can never completely control, whether 'stuck' in the study or while more at large in and observing the world. The collection, *Stories of the Study*, including its preliminaries, can be claimed as a foundational document in the establishment of short story anthologies – one of the earliest, albeit in its triple-decker format still inhabiting the frame of earlier, novelistic book-form.

Like 'The Mem, or Schoolmistress' (1834), which appeared in *Fraser's Magazine*, 'The Seamstress' (1833) from *Stories of the Study* was originally an episode for *Annals of the Parish* that Galt did not incorporate in that novel. It reads all the more poignantly separated from the novel's narrative, and rebooted with a more detached narrator, not encumbered with Micah Balwhidder's ironicised character in the *Annals*. In the main protagonist, Miss Peggy Pingle, we find a most unremarkable character through whom flow the large possibilities of quotidian life. Peggy lives alone in a flat in the town of Stourie (or 'dusty') in an unremarkable dwelling: 'The only thing for which it was remarkable was a hospitable-looking roasting-jack, which for many years had been in a state of widowhood' (p. 22).[6] Its owner, our spinster, has not achieved even what her cooking facility metaphorically has done: having never married. Such is the rather excruciating miniaturist technique of Galt here that we squirm even as we are amused. Peggy's is a life of routine with the static dust in Stourie, not literally in the tidy spinster's home but metaphorically in an exquisite contradiction. Peggy's routine is detailed:

> Day after day was with Miss Pingle as the to-day is like the yesterday – twins could not more resemble each other. The only difference perceptible in her condition was produced by the season. She had heard from her father that, on the 10th October, fires were lit for the winter in the Excise-office, and extinguished there, for the summer, on the 5th April, without consulting the weather; and the routine of office was as faithfully observed

by the frugal Seamstress, as if it had been ordained, and as unavoidable as the four-and-twenty hours are separated into day and night (p. 23).

This rather unattractive individual, inattentive to nature and desensitised to her real environment, nonetheless has, or had, another potential in her. Again, we are aware of this in Galt's tragi-comical metaphoric technique: 'In the coldest days, after the 5th of April, Miss Peggy was seen plying her needle with a blue beak and a pellucid jewel at it' (p. 23). This must be one of the most hyperbolic descriptions of a runny nose in literature, with the commonplace rebarbative elevated into an object of great purity and preciousness. Hyperbolic in a kind reverse engineering of the bathetic, the comparison of malfunctioning proboscis with precious stone serves not merely to ridicule but also to point to larger possibilities never grasped in this life. Indeed, Peggy never sees what is at the end of her nose. Defined by her narrow status in life, losing her father when young and accompanying her mother in steady industry (or in 'eydancy', the word that Galt's narrator draws attention to in a prefatory note to what the author labels 'The Tale' proper), Peggy remains in this ordained state for the rest of her life, functional and largely unperturbed by anything. The one possible piece of excitement in her life is the brief courtship of Dominie Loofie (or 'Schoolteacher Strap', referring to the schoolroom instrument of corporal punishment). Loofie woos Peggy with a Latin passage from Ovid's *Art of Love*. We never know precisely what this extract is and it may be gentlemanly romantic or more slyly sexual (the possibilities are there in Ovid for both), but Peggy, acting on advice from a male cousin, responds to Loofie's overtures by enquiring how they are to be financially settled once in wedlock. Loofie goes off offended by this materialism, and ever after Peggy is content in her life of 'single blessedness' (p. 25) looking askance, particularly, at young widows attempting to resume their former married state with a new husband. This registers Peggy's contented, sometimes arrogant, stability taken to its zenith. There are signs though, as Peggy grows older, that she is at least unconsciously aware of something lacking in her life as she seeks out the company of younger folk and even takes to reading the runes via spent candles and fires. This slow warping of her habitual nature, however, never becomes overly febrile, so that at last she 'took to bed, and departed this life, as she had lived, in the most methodical and quiet manner, her dead clothes being found in one corner of her drawers tied up together, with the will [...] pinned in such a manner to the parcel that it could not be missed' (p. 27). At the funeral the minister compares Peggy to the equally eydant

Martha (in the Gospel of Luke, 10.38–42) who had gone on, uninterrupted and prepared food while her sister, Mary, had stopped all else to listen to the wisdom of Jesus who had come to visit. The whole story is obvious enough in its detailing of the life not wrongly lived but rather not entirely lived. There is both excruciation and a degree of tenderness in the portrait of Peggy. She is – perhaps – an extreme exemplar, but her 'tale' or her non-tale of the opportunity missed is something with which all readers can identify on some level. The text also sees the beginnings of a remarkable sequence of stories where the short form and female subject-matter intimately and artistically come together.

In the same year as 'The Seamstress', Galt published 'The Howdie' (anonymously) across two issues of *Tait's Edinburgh Magazine*. Its editor, William Tait, was self-avowedly 'radical' in politics and Galt's appearance in the journal represents something of a break from the 'Blackwood' Group in which Galt is perhaps too often glibly located. William Blackwood, who had a great deal of faith in Galt, was to die a year later in 1834, and his sons who took over the firm were not keen on the writer, sometimes rejecting his submissions. Galt may have been pre-emptive in offering material to *Tait's*, and this situation was no doubt aided and abetted by the presence around the magazine of William Tait's great friend Christian Isobel Johnstone (1781–1857), the early feminist, who was a great admirer of Galt's work. The admiration of Tait and Johnstone (who would eventually take over the editorship of *Tait's*) represents a proto-feminist context for reading 'The Howdie', especially with regard to its layered irony. The full title of the text, 'The Howdie: An Autobiography', might give rise in the reader to discernment of the presumptuousness of its author-protagonist. As with *Annals of the Parish* we have the nice problem of how to deal with self-reflexive irony. Is this humble character to be laughed at in believing that she has anything of importance to commend to print, or is the laughter on us if we are too quick to be condescending toward her supposed pretension? We might suggest here also that Galt is playing with the form of serialisation, as across September and October 1833 the unaware readership of *Tait's* was perhaps being led to believe that this was a true story from horse's, or rather howdie's, mouth. It was not before William Roughhead's six-volume edition of Galt in 1923 that 'The Howdie' was attributed explicitly to its author. Roughhead (1870–1952), that connoisseur of real-life mysteries and one of the fathers of the true-crime genre, utilised letters between Galt and Tait to settle the authorship matter definitively.[7] Seasoned readers of Galt who read the story in *Tait's*, though, were probably in little doubt as to who had written the piece, but for others the clearly literal names for characters in the text such as 'Mrs Forceps', the Howdie or midwife's predecessor, might actually pass for a veil to protect the identity of real people. Johnstone could admire in 'The Howdie' the tale of a self-sufficient professional woman, widowed (and so no Peggy Pingle) from a dearly loved husband. Our midwife's husband is 'identified' as 'James Blithe' adding to the delineation of her happy, even physically joyous, marriage. She is forced to become her own sole breadwinner, though she also has a Christian sense of forbearance and vocation, contemplating her deceased spouse, 'I have often, since his death, thought, in calling him to mind, that it was by his natural sweet nature that the Lord was pleased, when He took him to Himself, to awaken the sympathy of others for me and the bairns, in our utmost distress' (p. 73).

The howdie is tender, resourceful and sympathetic but also at times stubborn and stuck-up, such as when she refuses to help deliver the child of a woman outwith wedlock and from a family tainted with Jacobitism. The pregnant woman's grandmother is affronted by the refusal and threatens consequences, which arrive when the howdie is visited by the minister. His report is that grandmother has accused the midwife of suggesting to the mother that she strangle the newborn as soon as it arrives. In a typical Galt moment we are eloquently taken inside the fear and rage of the midwife as she tells us, 'I was speechless; blue sterns danced before my sight, my knees trembled, and the steadfast earth grew as it were coggly aneath my chair' (p. 85). Galt is a master of conjuring up the personal tremors, more than the large-scale historical tremors, in the life he paints. However, infanticide, the condition of women (both the howdie and the pregnant girl), respectable Presbyterianism, and the spectre of Jacobitism are all marshalled here towards this one woman's emotional climax. The howdie agrees to render her professional services as the safest course of action and:

> Thus it came to pass, that, after the bastard brat was born, the old wife made a brag of how she had spirited the worthy minister to terrify me. Everybody laughed at her souple trick: but to me it was, for many a day, a heartburning; though to the laive of the parish, it was a great mean, as I have said, of daffin and merriment. (p. 86)

Other women are as resourceful as she is and this is part of the irony of her situation – in not consciously recognising the grandmother as a sister. Perhaps, even in recording the incident, however, there is an unconscious recognition by the howdie of her kinship and of an embryonic feminism within her.

In the same year as 'The Seamstress' and 'The Howdie', 'The Gudewife' also appeared, the latter in *Fraser's Magazine*. It is interesting that for this new journal Galt did not simply recycle a female protagonist's tale from *Stories of the Study* or from *Tait's*, but was guided, if not necessarily by a predetermined plan, at least by an unfolding artistic pattern concerning his female subject-matter. Where we have the old maid's eidancy in 'The Seamstress' and the widow's resourcefulness in 'The Howdie', we have the sheer guile of the married woman in 'The Gudewife'. Each of the female characters in these stories begins, in a certain sense, as a stereotype, but the sheer life in each, across the experiential range of poignancy, comedy, sincerity, pomposity, and many other things besides, represents a project in painting the female condition with the same sophistication that Galt employs in regard to male ministers, politicians, and businessmen elsewhere in his larger-scale fiction. Like the howdie, the gudewife has pretension enough to write an autobiography. 'The Gudewife' begins, 'I am inditing the good matter of this book for the instruction of our only daughter when she comes to years of discretion' (p. 10).

As with 'The Howdie', if we are tempted to laugh at a supposed gaucheness in the printing of a life of a housewife, we ought to realise that something radical rather than merely comical is afoot. For a start, Galt's story clearly mimics and then subverts the female conduct manuals of the eighteenth and nineteenth centuries that appeared in Britain and elsewhere (not least in featuring such a strident female 'author'). Such manuals, however, were not completely conservative but contained within them the seeds of feminism, recommending as they sometimes did female intellectual improvement.[8] We are told by our housewife that she has developed good writing and other academic skills because she is the offspring of intelligent stock, her father having been the teacher, Mr Desker, from whom she has inherited her genes and from whose presence she has acquired a stock of learning. This is a woman, then, who is operative only in the limited domestic space simply because of her gender. This is the context for the strong anti-romance element of her situation, even though the lazy reader might read this merely as connected to her seemingly sour, pragmatic personality: 'It fell out, when I was in my twenties, that Mr Thrifter came, in the words of the song of Auld Robin Gray, "a-courting to me"; and, to speak a plain matter of fact, in some points he was like that bald-headed carle. For he was a man, considering my juvenility, well stricken in years' (p. 10). Marriage, as Robert Burns's song acknowledges, is often about economic security for the woman rather than love. Mr Thrifter may be attracted to the young woman, but, for her, pleasures of the flesh are to be put to one side.

For her, sense rather than sensuality is the context for the match and this 'practicality' is gradually subverted according to a proto-feminist programme. Yet again we find that our main character has read the Scottish bard for 'female instruction' when she quotes the song, 'Green Grow the Rashes' about nature's creation of humans where, 'Her 'prentice hand she tried on man, / And syne she made the lassies oh!' (p. 11). These are words she takes at face value as she sets out to demonstrate her superiority to her husband. Not only Burns, but Shakespeare too is appropriated within her determined plans. This well-read woman replays *The Taming of the Shrew*, with the man rather than the woman being broken in to adopt effective subordinate status within the marriage. This involves a delicious episode where, after the manner of Shakespeare's play, the weather in its beneficence is denied. Our pregnant protagonist claims to her husband that the weather has wiled away their servant girl so that this is why he has had to endure a poorly prepared dinner, for which his wife has been in no state to compensate. Mr Thrifter's ordinary, inoffensive behaviour, including any polite conversation with his wife, is all to be stripped away in the process of his indoctrination. His wife even uses the stereotype of female irrationality, especially in her certain condition, to deny to Mr Thrifter any platform for equanimity or rational converse whatsoever. She declaims to him:

'Oh, Mr Thrifter, if ye were like me, ye would say any thing; for I am no in a condition to be spoken to. I'll not say that ye're far wrong, but till my time is bygone ye should not contradict me so; for I am in no state to be contradicted: it may go hard with me if I am. So I beg of you to think, for the sake of the baby unborn, to let me have my own way in all things for a season.' (p. 15)

For this well-read woman then, the collapsing of words and of (male) rationality becomes her modus operandi. Denied a full voice because of her gender, she is going to visit the same fate on Mr Thrifter. And needless to say, even after the birth of their daughter, the wife's manipulation of her husband continues. In a closing moment (in the 'action' of the autobiography), the gudewife seems to be in a fit, so that her husband fetches her a glass of water, which she promptly throws in his face. She warns Mr Thrifter that 'while I live, and the iron tongs are by the chumly lug, never expect to get the upper hand of me' (p. 21). The gudewife in the end is the cunning wife in a text of poetic justice (full of literary allusion) as satisfying as any feminist could wish.

Galt's female short stories are particularly well-formed and see his wry wit suitably, explosively compressed within this genre. Short stories on male identity follow on from the female productions, and these also include some of Galt's finest writing, but in their length they reach again towards novella-form. Appearing in *Tait's* in 1835, 'Tribulations of the Rev. Cowal Kilmun' is perhaps the most gnomic text its author ever produced. It iterates and interacts several versions of maleness, each of which perhaps reflects something of the author's personality/autobiography. Another story in the first person, the text has at its outset a contemplative clergyman 'pondering on the uncertainties of worldly things' (p. 96). This phraseology, as the story's unfolding makes plain, refers to the whole material world being difficult to understand, its clergyman protagonist's undoubted belief in Providence notwithstanding. Kilmun encounters Mr Ettles ('ettles' meaning 'strives'), and we have an immediate opposition between this worldly individual who eventually goes overseas to try his fortune, just as Galt himself had done in North America, and our clergyman both of whose names are more 'settled', referring as they do to sites in Argyllshire: the Cowal peninsula on Loch Fyne and the Firth of Clyde, and Kilmun, a parish on that peninsula beside the Holy Loch. Mr Ettles appears at the manse with Miss Graham, and the two young, particularly beautiful people request an urgent wedding as the groom is leaving to go overseas very soon. Kilmun performs the ceremony and the pair go off not to the marriage bed but their separate ways, no time being available for consummation.

Kilmun has a bad apprehension: 'Why was I dismayed, and boded no good of this mystical marriage has never been in my power to explain; but the thoughts of it settled down on my heart, and I was sad, and given to meditation concerning it for many days' (p. 97). In one sense, yet again we have an old man's story. The twilight of life has taught both Galt and Kilmun that nothing lasts; his is the wisdom of retrospection. With Ettles and his bride, however, things disintegrate with uncommon speed. Their beauty or perfection and also, somewhat superstitiously on Kilmun's part, their failure to consummate the marriage (its 'mystical', or spiritual nature then) both contribute, we might suggest, to his forebodings. Mr Ettles, of course, might be expected to be in a number of kinds of danger going off on his voyage to America, but it is Miss Graham who becomes consumptive and who dies before her husband returns. Cowal Kilmun's name signals to some extent an older vision, a Celtic or Highland second sight, and, implicitly, this has not been legislated away in his Calvinist rationalism; indeed, Calvinism's sense of stories being written at the beginning of time in God's mind (or predestination not only in the afterlife but in the earthly world) might merely complement this older sense of the future already being mapped out. We might also ask, then, if it is Kilmun's morbid Calvinist worldview that sees the inevitability of corruption when confronted by the beauty and virtue of the young couple? Causality in this story is never easily apprehended.

'Providence' is a watchword in the story, a concept to the fore in orthodox Calvinism and mainstream Christianity generally, which sees God's benign plan in all events, however inscrutable that purpose might be to human eyes. Kilmun has the standard, understandable doubts of the believer, seeing bad things in the world, but comes to the conclusion that Ettles' life, which he observes for many years after, is 'an instrument' (p. 103), a means of instruction, or Providence in some way, in his own life. Throughout the story, Kilmun is torn between the pain he sees in the human world and the perfection of God's creation. On one occasion:

> It was a blessed night; and the calm air as holy as if the breath of the spirit of peace had been shed abroad in its serenity. The heavens I thought higher and vaster than common; and the numberless stars as the lamps of the new Jerusalem, and lights in the dwellings of the angels. A religious solemnity was spread over the whole earth, and my thoughts were lifted up (p. 103).

This appreciation of earthly accord with universal plans is soon interrupted by the reappearance of Mr Ettles, the reader by now attuned to read this as an unsettling presence. Ettles is accompanied by a third individual who might physically be modelled on his author, John Galt: 'an elderly man, with a bald head, a contented countenance, and peering eyes, that denoted an inquisitive spirit' (p. 104). Roslin has a particular interest in Ettles, which makes Kilmun somewhat suspicious, oblivious of the irony of his own fascination with Ettles.

Two subsequent events are of particular note in the story. First, Mr Roslin dies suddenly at Greenock, after having summoned Kilmun to his aid, and the minister is then left with the elderly man's funeral arrangements. Kilmun finds that he has been left one hundred dollars for a ring to wear in memorial of Roslin. Second, Ettles meets Kilmun again in Edinburgh and takes the clergyman in search of a mysterious Archibald

Junor. Finding the business and squalor of Edinburgh rebarbative, Kilmun is at last in the presence of a dying pauper whom Ettles claims to be Junor for whom they attempt to do what they can. In fact, afterwards Ettles admits that there was no such person as Junor and the individual they have 'found' represents a common, random occurrence. The story is rounded out, then, with a final example of the many contingencies 'Tribulations of the Rev. Cowal Kilmun' has brought us. Brilliant in its atmosphere of foreboding and, indeed, providential, causal events, the whole thing is a sleight of hand. This is true both for the seemingly connected, resonant events in the narrative and in the brooding playfulness Galt has in distributing part of his own nature through the three male main protagonists: the man of adventure (Ettles), the careful observer (Roslin), and the believing Presbyterian (Kilmun). Kilmun is also by the end of the story writing it all up, seeking meaning and order but never able as we follow through the entire first-person narrative to locate satisfactorily any such qualities. Two things might be noticed. First, this compelling tale, packed with incident, tension, and human feeling, shows Galt laying bare or deconstructing the elements of plot and counterpointing and collapsing the notion of it all, adding up to an explanation of life's events that we can take away from it. Second, in distributing elements of his own identity in his characters, including maleness, Galt has presented us with a text that yet again, as with his female stories, radically challenges our sense of the centre of reality (or the classic realist narrative in fictional terms) as well as authority in life and in the text.

It is not overstating the case to assert that something was happening in Galt's mind and creative practice in his later years, as subjectivity and gender collide amusingly and disturbingly in his short stories. Under these conditions, not only heightened subjectivity but also a radical scepticism was to the fore in an author so often identified as an objective realist. Among his later fictions, we also, though, have vintage Galt: for instance, a tour de force in Scots (even by Galtian standards), 'A Rich Man; Or, he has great Merit', subtitled 'being the Autobiography of Archibald Plack, Esq., Late Lord Mayor of London'. This 'short story' is an epistolary performance where our eponymous character dispenses advice in twenty-eight letters to his university grandson who has written pleading for money. It appeared attributed across three issues of *Tait's* in 1836 and is Galt's last great fictional hurrah. However, it is also the kind of old-fashioned novella to whose obsolescence Galt himself had contributed in the leaner, altogether more unsettling type of short story he had produced in the 1830s.

Endnotes

Introduction

1. See the granting to Galt of a discrete chapter, Angela Esterhammer, 'John Galt's Fictional and Performative Worlds' in Murray Pittock (ed.), *The Edinburgh Companion to Scottish Romanticism* (Edinburgh: Edinburgh University Press, 2011), pp. 166–77.
2. John Galt, *Literary Life and Miscellanies*, 3 vols (Edinburgh: Blackwood, 1834), I, 226.
3. George Douglas Brown, *The House with the Green Shutters*, ed. Dorothy Porter (London: Penguin, 1985), p. 98.
4. See Andrew Nash, *Kailyard and Scottish Literature* (Amsterdam & New York: Rodopi, 2007), p. 115.
5. For more on this issue as well as Galt's deficient 'iconicity', generally, see Gerard Carruthers, 'Remembering John Galt' in Regina Hewitt (ed.), *John Galt: Observations and Conjectures on Literature, History and Society* (Lewisburg: Bucknell University Press, 2012), pp. 33–51.
6. For a very useful survey of Galt's critical reception in the first one hundred and fifty years, see P. H. Scott, *John Galt* (Edinburgh: Scottish Academic Press, 1985), pp. 110–26.
7. See Sir George Douglas, *The Blackwood Group* (Edinburgh & London: Oliphant, Anderson & Ferrier, 1897), p. 88.
8. See Ian A. Gordon, *John Galt, The Life of a Writer* (Edinburgh: Oliver & Boyd, 1972), p. 128.
9. Ibid., p. 129.
10. W. E. K. Anderson (ed.), *The Journal of Sir Walter Scott* (Edinburgh: Canongate, 1998), p. 113.
11. David Craig, *Scottish Literature and the Scottish People, 1680–1830* (London: Chatto & Windus, 1961), p. 219.

12　Ibid., p. 197.
13　See David Daiches, *The Paradox of Scottish Culture* (London: Oxford University Press, 1964).
14　F. R. Hart, *The Scottish Novel from Smollett to Spark* (Cambridge, Massachusetts: Harvard University Press, 1978), p. 31.
15　Ibid, p. 49.
16　John MacQueen, *The Rise of the Historical Novel* (Edinburgh: Scottish Academic Press, 1989), p. 189.
17　Katie Trumpener, *Bardic Nationalism: The Romantic Novel and the British Empire* (Princeton: Princeton University Press, 1997), pp. 16, 17.
18　Ian Duncan, *Scott's Shadow: The Novel in Romantic Edinburgh* (Princeton: Princeton University Press, 2007), p. 237.
19　Esterhammer, 'John Galt's Fictional and Performative Worlds' in Pittock (ed.), *The Edinburgh Companion to Scottish Romanticism*, p. 169.
20　For a detailed discussion of Galt's plays see Frederick Burwick, 'Galt and the Theater', in Hewitt (ed.), *John Galt: Observations and Conjectures*, pp. 229–56.
21　See www.gla.ac.uk/schools/critical/research/researchcentresandnetworks/robertburnsstudies/johngaltsociety/
22　Hewitt (ed.), *John Galt, Observations and Conjectures.*

1. John Galt's Ayrshire

1　Ian A. Gordon (ed.), *John Galt: Selected Short Stories* (Edinburgh: Scottish Academic Press, 1978), p. 7.
2　Although not published until 1834 in *Fraser's Magazine*, 'The Mem' may have been written as 'a postscript to the *Annals*' (Gordon, *John Galt: Selected Short Stories*, p. 197).
3　Gordon, *John Galt: Selected Short Stories*, p. 8.
4　Ibid., p. 21.
5　S. R. Crockett, Introduction to *Annals of the Parish* and *The Ayrshire Legatees* (Edinburgh & London, William Blackwood, 1895), p. xviii.
6　Ibid.
7　Ibid.
8　Henry James, *The Art of the Novel* (New York: Scribner's, 1934) p. 45.
9　John Galt, *Literary Life and Miscellanies*, 3 vols (Edinburgh: Blackwood, 1834), p. 226.
10　Ibid.

11 Ibid., p. 231.
12 *The Autobiography of John Galt* (London: Cochrane and McCrone, 1833), p. 232.
13 Jennie W. Aberdein, *John Galt* (Oxford: Oxford University Press, 1936), p. xxi.
14 Ibid., p. 7.

2. Satire, Hypocrisy, and the Ayrshire-Renfrewshire Enlightenment

1 John Galt, *Annals of the Parish* (Oxford: Oxford World's Classics, 1986 [1821]); Galt, *The Member* (Edinburgh: Scottish Academic Press, 1985 [1831]); Galt, *The Provost* (Oxford: Oxford World's Classics, 1982 [1822]).
2 Kazuo Ishiguro, *An Artist of the Floating World* (London: Faber & Faber, 1986); Ishiguro, *The Remains of the Day* (London: Faber & Faber, 1989).
3 J. MacQueen, 'John Galt and the Analysis of Social History', in A. S. Bell (ed.), *Scott Bicentenary Essays* (Edinburgh: Scottish Academic Press, 1973), pp. 332-44; K. Costain, 'Theoretical History and the Novel: the Scottish Fiction of John Galt', *English Literary History*, 43 (1976), pp. 342-65.
4 Galt, *Literary Life and Miscellanies*, 3 vols (Edinburgh: Blackwood, 1834), I, 226.
5 K. Costain, 'The Community of Man: Galt and eighteenth-century Scottish Realism', *Scottish Literary Journal*, 8 (1981), 10-29.
6 Cf. K. Simpson, 'Ironic Self-Revelation in *Annals of the Parish*', in C. A. Whatley (ed.), *John Galt 1779-1979* (Edinburgh: Ramsay Head Press, 1979).
7 Galt, *Literary Life*, I, 152.
8 Galt, *The Ayrshire Legatees* (Edinburgh: James Thin, 1978 [1820-21]); Tobias Smollett, *The Expedition of Humphry Clinker* (Harmondsworth: Penguin, 1967 [1771]).
9 John Mullan, 'How Jane Austen's Emma changed the face of fiction', *Guardian*, 5 December 2015.
10 Jonathan Swift, *Gulliver's Travels* (Penguin: Harmondsworth, 1967 [1726]); Swift, *A Modest Proposal* (1729), in J. McMinn (ed.), *Swift's Irish Pamphlets* (Gerrards Cross: Colin Smythe, 1991), pp. 141-50.
11 J. Kinsley (ed.), *Burns: Poems and Songs* (Oxford: Clarendon Press, 1969), pp. 56-59.

12 William Shakespeare, *Twelfth Night* (Harmondsworth: Penguin, 1980).
13 Molière, *Tartuffe* (1664), which soon appeared in English translation as *Tartuffe, or, The French Puritan* (London, 1670).
14 Samuel Butler, *Hudibras*, 2 vols, (Glasgow, 1761 [1663–80]); Kidd, 'Enlightenment and Ecclesiastical Satire before Burns', in R. McLean, R. Young and K. Simpson (eds.), *The Scottish Enlightenment and Literary Culture* (Lewisburg: Bucknell University Press, 2016), pp. 95–114.
15 C. Kidd, 'The Fergusson Affair: Calvinism and dissimulation in the Scottish Enlightenment', *Intellectual History Review*, 26 (2016), 339–54; L. McIlvanney, *Burns the Radical* (East Linton: Tuckwell, 2002), pp. 134–37
16 W. Ferguson, *Scotland 1689 to the Present* (Edinburgh: Oliver & Boyd, 1968), p. 13.
17 *Acts of the Parliament of Scotland 1124–1707*, 12 vols (Edinburgh, 1814–1875), XI, 402–03, 413–14.
18 *Acts of the General Assembly 1638–1842* (Edinburgh, 1843), pp. 453–56 (p. 455).
19 Francis Hutcheson, *An Inquiry into the Original of our Ideas of Beauty and Virtue* (Indianapolis: Liberty Fund, 2008 [1725]).
20 G. Mailer, 'Anglo-Scottish Union and John Witherspoon's American Revolution', *William and Mary Quarterly*, 3rd ser., 67 (2010), 709–46; Mailer, *John Witherspoon's American Revolution* (Chapel Hill: University of North Carolina Press, 2017).
21 John Witherspoon, *Ecclesiastical Characteristics* (1753), in Witherspoon, *Works*, 9 vols (Edinburgh, 1804–05), VI, 162–63.
22 Ibid., VI, 162.
23 Ibid., VI, 185.
24 John Witherspoon, *The trial of religious truth by its moral influence. A sermon preached at the opening of the Synod of Glasgow and Air [Ayr], October 9th, 1753* (Glasgow, 1759), pp. 40–41, 45.
25 John Witherspoon, *The History of a Corporation of Servants* (Glasgow, 1765), pp. 31, 66.
26 Swift, *Gulliver's Travels*, p. 223.
27 John Adam, *How a Minister should approve himself unto God. A sermon preached at the opening of the Synod in the High Church of Glasgow, on Tuesday, April 9, 1765* (Glasgow, 1765), p. 34.
28 Galt, *Annals*, pp. 59, 66, 88, 133, 173–74.
29 *Scots Magazine*, 29 (Apr. 1767), 171–75 (p. 172).
30 F, 'To the Author of the *Scots Magazine*', 15 Jan. 1767, in *The Grounds of the Process set on foot by the Synod of Glasgow and Ayr, against*

    Mr Alexander Fergusson, Minister at Kilwinning (Glasgow, 1769), p. 19.
31 Ibid., *Letter from Aberdeen*, 9 Feb. 1767, p. 30.
32 National Records of Scotland [NRS], *Records of the Synod of Glasgow and Ayr*, CH 2/464/4/54.
33 NRS CH 2/464/4/71; *Scots Magazine*, 31 (Apr. 1769), 222.
34 *Scots Magazine*, 30 (Jan. 1768), 10.
35 Philorthodoxus, *Kilwinning Divinity Weighed and Found Wanting* (Glasgow, 1768), pp. 13, 15, 17.
36 *Grounds of Process*, 'Introduction', p. 1; *Scots Magazine* 31 (March, 1769), 151–52.
37 John Graham, *The Religious Establishment in Scotland examined upon Protestant principles* (London, 1771); John Graham, *Subscription to Human Articles of Faith, examined* (London, 1775).
38 F. Voges, 'Moderate and Evangelical Thinking in the Later Eighteenth Century: Differences and Shared Attitudes', *Records of the Scottish Church History Society*, 22 (1985), 141–57.
39 William McGill, *Christian Unity Illustrated* (Glasgow, 1766), p. 35.
40 William McGill, *A Practical Essay on the Death of Christ* (Edinburgh, 1786); John Russel, *The Reasons of Lord's Agony in the Garden* (Kilmarnock, 1787); James Moir, *The Scripture-Doctrine of Redemption by the Death of Our Lord Jesus Christ* (Glasgow, 1787).
41 William McGill, *The Benefits of the Revolution, A sermon, preached at Ayr, On the 5th of November, 1788. To which are added, Remarks on a Sermon, Preached on the same day, at Newton upon Ayr* (Kilmarnock, 1789).
42 Kinsley (ed.), *Burns: Poems and Songs*, pp. 373–76.
43 C. Kidd, 'Enlightenment and Anti-Enlightenment in Eighteenth-century Scotland: an Ayrshire–Renfrewshire Microclimate', in J-F. Dunyach and A. Thomson (eds.), *The Enlightenment in Scotland: National and international perspectives* (Voltaire Foundation, Oxford: Oxford University Press, 2015), pp. 59–84, esp. pp. 77–81.
44 Gavin Struthers, *The history of the rise, progress and principles of the Relief Church* (Glasgow, 1843), pp. 360–67.
45 Kinsley (ed.), *Burns: Poems and Songs*, pp. 37–39.
46 Ibid., pp. 56–59.
47 P. Scott, 'The first publication of "Holy Willie's Prayer"', *Scottish Literary Review*, 7 (2015), 1–18.
48 James Maxwell, 'Subscription to Creeds, or Confessions of Faith', in Maxwell, *Scheme of Redemption* (n.p., 1790), p. 62.

49 James Hogg, *The Private Memoirs and Confessions of a Justified Sinner* (Oxford: Oxford World Classics, 1995 [1824]).
50 Galt, *Provost*, pp. 22–27, 94, 138.
51 Galt, *Annals*, pp. 117, 132.
52 Ibid., p. 129.
53 Ibid., pp. 98–100.
54 Galt, *Legatees*, p. 6.
55 Ibid., p. 55.
56 Ibid., p. 42.
57 Ibid., p. 46.
58 E.g. Ibid., pp. 106–10, 122.
59 Galt, *Legatees*, p. 30.
60 Ibid., p. 43.
61 Ibid., p. 80.
62 Ibid., p. 139.
63 Ibid., p. 80.
64 Ibid., p. 81.
65 Ibid., p. 96.
66 Ibid., p. 116.
67 Ibid., p. 142.
68 E.g. Galt, *Annals*, p. 152.
69 Ibid., p. 42.
70 Ibid., pp. 63–65.
71 Cf. Henry Mackenzie, *The Man of Feeling* (Oxford: Oxford World Classics, 2001 [1771]).
72 See e.g. Hutcheson, *Inquiry*; Adam Smith, *Theory of Moral Sentiments* (Indianapolis: Liberty Fund, 1982 [1759]); J. Dwyer, *Virtuous Discourse: Sensibility and community in late eighteenth-century Scotland* (Edinburgh: John Donald, 1987).
73 Galt, *Annals*, p. 170.
74 Ibid., p. 175.
75 Ibid., pp. 184–85.
76 Ibid., p. 185.
77 Ibid., p. 202.
78 Galt, *Ringan Gilhaize* (Edinburgh: Canongate Classics, 1995 [1823]).
79 Ibid., pp. 445–47; C. Kidd, 'Assassination Principles in Scottish Political Culture: Buchanan to Hogg', in C. Erskine and R. Mason (eds.), *George Buchanan* (Farnham: Ashgate, 2012), pp. 284–86.
80 Galt, *The Radical* [together with *The Member*] (Edinburgh: Canongate Classics, 1996 [1832]).

3. Finding Galt in Glasgow

1   John Galt, *Literary Life and Miscellanies*, 3 vols (Edinburgh: Blackwood, 1834), II, 114.
2   Ian Duncan, *Scott's Shadow: The Novel in Romantic Edinburgh* (Princeton: Princeton University Press, 2007), p. 39.
3   See e.g. David Daiches, *The Paradox of Scottish Culture* (London: Oxford University Press, 1964); Anand C. Chitnis, *The Scottish Enlightenment* (London: Croom Helm, 1976); Richard Sher, *Church and University in the Scottish Enlightenment* (Edinburgh: Edinburgh University Press, 1985); and Daiches et al., *A Hotbed of Genius: The Scottish Enlightenment, 1730–90* (Edinburgh: Edinburgh University Press, 1986), which, despite their diverse approaches and styles, all portray Edinburgh as the chief city in the Scottish Enlightenment.
4   N. T. Phillipson, 'Towards a Definition of the Scottish Enlightenment', in P. Fritz and D. Williams (eds), *City and Society in the Eighteenth Century* (Toronto: Hakkert, 1973), pp. 125–47 (p. 125).
5   R. H. Campbell, 'Scotland's Neglected Enlightenment', *History Today*, 40 (May 1990), pp. 22–28 (p. 24).
6   A. Hook and R. Sher (eds), *The Glasgow Enlightenment* (East Linton: Tuckwell Press and Eighteenth-century Scottish Studies Society, 1995).
7   There are very good chapters and essays taking note of the Foulis brothers, but the only book-length text on the brothers remains David Murray's *Robert & Andrew Foulis and the Glasgow Press, with some account of the Glasgow Academy of the Fine Arts* (Glasgow: James Maclehose & Sons, 1913).
8   Although Tobias Smollett is included in George Eyre-Todd's *The Glasgow Poets* (Glasgow: William Hodge, 1903), there were few Glasgow poets of note in the early- to mid-eighteenth century. Later, Thomas Campbell became Glasgow's most celebrated poet.
9   James A. Kilpatrick, *Literary Landmarks of Glasgow* (Glasgow: Saint Mungo Press, 1989), p. 94.
10 Henry L. Fulton, 'Smollett's Apprenticeship in Glasgow, 1736–1739', *Studies in Scottish Literature*, 15:1 (1980), pp. 175–86 (p. 175).
11 Tobias Smollett, *The Expedition of Humphry Clinker* (London: Penguin, 1985 [1771]), p. 274.
12 Ibid., p. 283.
13 R. K. Gordon, *John Galt* (Toronto: Oxford University Press, Canadian Branch, 1920), p. 25.

14 Ibid., p. 33.
15 Keith M. Costain, 'Theoretical History and the Novel: The Scottish Fiction of John Galt', *English Literary History*, 43:3 (1976), pp. 342–65 (p. 344).
16 Galt, *Literary Life and Miscellanies*, II, 198.
17 Ian Duncan, 'Scott and the Historical Novel: A Scottish Rise of the Novel', in Gerard Carruthers and Liam McIlvanney (eds), *The Cambridge Companion to Scottish Literature* (Cambridge: Cambridge University Press, 2012), pp. 103–16 (p. 113).
18 Chitnis, 'The Scottish Enlightenment in the Age of Galt', p. 34.
19 Liam McIlvanney, 'The Glasgow Novel', in Gerard Carruthers and Liam McIlvanney (eds), *The Cambridge Companion to Scottish Literature*, pp. 217–32 (p. 221).
20 John Galt, *Annals of the Parish and The Ayrshire Legatees* (London: Macmillan and Co., 1903), p. 20.
21 Ibid., pp. 29–30.
22 Ibid., p. 118.
23 Ibid., p. 180.
24 John Galt, *The Ayrshire Legatees; or, The Pringle Family* (New York: W. B. Gilley, 1823), p. 14.
25 John Galt, 'The Gathering of the West; or, We're Come to See the King', *Blackwood's Magazine*, September 1822 (Edinburgh: William Blackwood, 1822), p. 314.
26 Ibid., p. 317.
27 Thomas Hamilton, *The Youth and Manhood of Cyril Thornton*, ed. Maurice Lindsay (Aberdeen: Association for Scottish Literary Studies, 1990 [1827]), p. 73.
28 Ibid., p. 28.
29 Ibid., pp. 88–89.
30 Ibid., p. 403.
31 Robert Crawford, *On Glasgow and Edinburgh* (Cambridge, Mass.: Belknap Press of Harvard University Press, 2013), p. 73.
32 Thomas A. Markus, 'Domes of Enlightenment: Two Scottish University Museums', *The International Journal of Museum Management and Curatorship*, 4:3 (1985), pp. 215–42 (p. 224).
33 Hamilton, *Cyril Thornton*, p. 426.
34 T. H. Bryce, 'The Hunterian Museum', *Glasgow University Students' Handbook* (Glasgow; Glasgow University, 1935), pp. 50–52 (p. 51).
35 Galt, *Annals of the Parish*, p. 108.
36 Ibid, p. 173.

37 Galt, *Literary Life*, II, 264.
38 Ibid.
39 John Galt, 'Memoir of Galt', from *The Annals of the Parish and The Ayrshire Legatees* (Edinburgh: Blackwood and Sons, 1850), pp. lxxxix–xc.
40 John Galt, *Bogle Corbet; or, The Emigrants*, 3 vols (London: Henry Colburn & Richard Bentley, 1831), II, 34–35.
41 Michael Scott, *Tom Cringle's Log* (New York and London: Macmillan and Co., 1895 [1829–1834]), p. 314.
42 Ibid., p. 109.
43 Ibid., p. 116.
44 As far as a Glasgow school is concerned, we may also consider the same sense of discovery in the early drafts of John Mayne's poem 'Glasgow' (1783).
45 Galt, *Bogle Corbet*, I, 28.
46 Ibid., p. 69. It is possible that Galt, having acknowledged Hamilton's *Cyril Thornton*, pays homage here to his friend's 'canopy of smoke' line.
47 Galt, *Bogle Corbet*, I, 71.
48 Gilbert Stelter, 'John Galt: The writer as town booster and builder', in Elizabeth Waterston (ed.), *John Galt: Reappraisals* (Guelph: University of Guelph, 1985), pp. 17–43, (p. 21–22).
49 Galt, *Bogle Corbet*, III, 38.
50 Galt, *The Literary Life*, II, 39.

4. Galt the Speculator: *Sir Andrew Wylie*, *The Entail*, and *Lawrie Todd*

1 Paul Johnson, for instance, claims that '[t]he rapid expansion of the world economy in the early 1820s marked the upswing of the first modern trade cycle', which was followed by 'the beginning of the first world financial crisis': *The Birth of the Modern: World Society 1815–1830* (London: Weidenfeld and Nicolson, 1991), pp. 862, 889. Similarly, historian S. G. Checkland writes: 'The much increased role played by the capital market in the financing of trade and industry has caused some scholars to regard the excitement of 1825 as the first cyclical boom of the modern sort': *The Rise of Industrial Society in England 1815–1885* (London: Longmans, 1964), p. 13.
2 See the economic approaches to nineteenth-century literature by Patrick Brantlinger, *Fictions of State: Culture and Credit in Britain, 1694–1994* (Ithaca: Cornell University Press, 1996); Mary Poovey, *Genres of the Credit Economy: Mediating Value in Eighteenth- and*

Nineteenth-Century Britain (Chicago: University of Chicago Press, 2008); Tamara S. Wagner, *Financial Speculation in Victorian Fiction: Plotting Money and the Novel Genre, 1815–1901* (Columbus: Ohio State University Press, 2010); and Alex J. Dick, 'Walter Scott and the Financial Crash of 1825: Fiction, Speculation, and the Standard of Value' in *Romantic Circles Praxis Series*, vol. title: *Romanticism, Forgery and the Credit Crunch*, February 2012, www.rc.umd.edu/praxis/forgery/index.html. Two other especially relevant articles are Lisa Heiserman Perkins' 'Keats's Mere Speculations', *Keats-Shelley Journal*, 43 (1994), 56–74; and Fiona Robertson's 'Of Speculation and Return: Scott's Jacobites, John Law, and the Company of the West', *Scottish Literary Journal*, 24 (1997), 5–24. With reference to Keats and Scott (respectively), Perkins and Robertson discuss financial, imaginative, and philosophical forms of speculation, and writing itself as speculation, similarly to the ways in which the present chapter analyses these interrelated forms of speculation in Galt's work.

3   John Galt, 'Essay on Commercial Policy', *Philosophical Magazine*, 23:90 (November 1805), 104–12. Part of the treatise appeared as Galt's 'The Ancient Commerce of England, Prior and to the Reign of Edward III. Inclusive' in *Fraser's Magazine*, 4 (November 1831), 403–21. The continuation, entitled 'History of English Commerce from the Reign of Edward III to the Accession of James,' remains as an unpublished manuscript in the Archives of Ontario, Toronto.

4   Emily Apter, 'Speculation and Economic Xenophobia as Literary World Systems: The Nineteenth-Century Business Novel' in Christie McDonald and Susan Rubin Suleiman (eds), *French Global: A New Approach to Literary History* (New York: Columbia University Press, 2010), pp. 388–403 (p. 390).

5   John Galt, *Sir Andrew Wylie, of that Ilk*, 3 vols (Edinburgh: Blackwood and London: Cadell, 1822), I, 130.

6   Ibid., II, 237.

7   Ibid., I, 93; II, 170.

8   Jerome Christensen, *Lord Byron's Strength: Romantic Writing and Commercial Society* (Baltimore: Johns Hopkins University Press, 1993), pp. 158–59.

9   Galt, *Wylie*, III, 310.

10 Ibid., I, 285.

11 Ibid., I, 287.

12 Ibid., III, 99.

13 John Galt, *The Entail, or, The Lairds of Grippy*, ed. Ian A. Gordon (Oxford: Oxford University Press, 1984), p. 3.
14 Ibid.
15 Galt's short 'Biographical Sketch of William Paterson' appeared in the *New Monthly Magazine*, 35 (1832), 168–76; the longer (and even more laudatory) unpublished manuscript entitled 'Some account of William Paterson by whom the Banks of England and Scotland were established and the Scottish colony at the Darien projected' is in the Archives of Ontario.
16 Galt, 'Biographical Sketch of William Paterson', p. 176.
17 Ibid., p. 171.
18 For a discussion of the Poyais affair in relation to literature of the 1820s, including a reading of *Sir Andrew Wylie* similar to the one in this chapter but in a different context, see Angela Esterhammer, 'Speculation in the Late-Romantic Literary Marketplace' in *Victoriographies*, 7:1 (2017), pp. 7–24.
19 Galt, *Entail*, p. 3.
20 Ibid., p. 368.
21 Ibid., p. 100.
22 Ibid., p. 3.
23 Ibid., p. 42.
24 Mark Schoenfield, 'The Family Plots: Land and Law in John Galt's *The Entail*', *Scottish Literary Journal*, 24:1 (1997), 60–65 (p. 61).
25 Galt, *Entail*, p. 36.
26 Ibid., p. 137.
27 Ibid., p. 251.
28 Ibid.
29 See Jennie W. Aberdein, *John Galt* (London: Oxford University Press, 1936) for an account of the uncertainties of the Canada Company in 1825–26 (pp. 142–43) and its near failure at the end of the decade (p. 164).
30 John Galt, *Lawrie Todd; or, The Settlers in the Woods* (London: Bentley, 1832), p. 185.
31 Ibid., p. 187.
32 Ibid., p. 42.
33 Ibid., p. 108.
34 Ibid., p. 364.
35 Ibid., p. 79.
36 Ibid.

37 Ibid., p. 121.
38 John Galt, 'The Speculawtor: A Tale Illustrative of the Modern Principles of Commerce', *Tait's Edinburgh Magazine*, n.s., 5 (1838), 39–45 (p. 40).
39 Ibid., p. 43.
40 Ibid.
41 Ibid.
42 Ibid., p. 44.
43 Ibid.
44 Ibid., p. 45.

5. How John Galt Wrote North America

1 John Galt, *The Autobiography* (London: Cochrane and M'Crone, 1833) I, 278.
2 H. B. Timothy, *The Galts: A Canadian Odyssey* (Toronto: McLelland & Stewart, 1977), p. 50.
3 Ian A. Gordon, *John Galt: The Life of a Writer* (Toronto: Toronto University Press, 1972), p. 74.
4 John Galt, *Literary Life and Miscellanies*, 3 vols (Edinburgh: Blackwood, 1834), p. 351.
5 Galt, *The Autobiography*, II, 200.
6 Galt, *Literary Life*, I, 235.
7 Galt, 'The British and Americans', in *The Lady's Magazine and Museum*, February 1833, p. 47.
8 Galt, *Autobiography*, II, 61.
9 Robert C. Lee, *The Canada Company and the Huron Tract* (Toronto: Natural Heritage Books, 2004).
10 J. K. Herreshoff (ed.), *Letters of John Galt: The Canadian Years*, (Ann Arbor: University of Michigan Press, 1990).
11 Gordon, p. 86.
12 Galt, *Lawrie Todd, or, The Settlers in the Woods*, (London: Colburn and Bentley, 1830), and *Bogle Corbet, or, The Emigrants* (London: Colburn and Bentley, 1831).
13 National Library of Scotland, Colburn & Bentley Letter Books, vol. 52, p. 184.
14 Kenneth Simpson, *The Protean Scot* (Aberdeen: Aberdeen University Press, 1988), p. 31.
15 Galt, *Literary Life*, I, 296.
16 Grant Thorburn, *Forty Years Residence in America* (London: James Fraser, 1834).

17 Archives of Ontario, MS 564, Reel 9, vol. 1, Letter from Galt to the Company, 16 December 1826.
18 Galt, 'Scotch and Yankees, A Caricature', in *Blackwood's Magazine,* Edinburgh, Part 1, January 1833, p. 91, Part 2, February 1833, p. 188.
19 *OED Online.* Oxford University Press, March 2014 [www.oed.com].
20 Bernard Shaw, *The Doctor's Dilemma* (London: Constable, 1930), p. 107.
21 Kenneth McNeil, 'Time, Emigration and the Circum-Atlantic World: John Galt's "Bogle Corbet"', in Regina Hewitt (ed.), *John Galt Observations and Conjectures on Literature, History, and Society* (Lewisburg: Bucknell University Press, 2012).
22 Galt, as Agricola, *The Colonial Question,* in *Blackwood's,* March 1830.
23 McNeil, p. 310.
24 Galt, *Literary Life,* I, 312.
25 Timothy, p. 16.
26 Gordon, p. 7.
27 Galt, *The Autobiography,* II, 264.
28 Gordon, p. viii.
29 Paul Scott, *John Galt* (Edinburgh: Scottish Academic Press, 1985), p. 100.
30 Galt, 'Bandana on Colonial Undertakings', in *Blackwood's Edinburgh Magazine,* August 1826, 304.
31 Galt, *Literary Life,* I, 340.

6. Commemorating the Covenanters in *Ringan Gilhaize*

1 Thomas McCrie, Review of *Tales of My Landlord, The Edinburgh Christian Instructor,* Jan. 1817, pp. 41–73 and Feb. 1817, pp. 100–201, p. 61. As has been well documented by Ina Ferris (see below), behind McCrie's criticisms of Scott's novel there lay a larger distrust of historical fiction; McCrie suggests that the 'encroachments of the writers of fiction upon the province of true history' might 'do much mischief' (p. 47).
2 Walter Scott, anonymous review of *Tales of my Landlord, Quarterly Review,* January 1817; reprinted in *The Prose Works of Sir Walter Scott, Bart.,* 28 vols (Edinburgh: Robert Cadell, 1834–36), XIX, 1–86.
3 James Hogg's report of Scott's comments on his own novel of the Covenanting times *The Brownie of Bodsbeck* (1818), published in James Hogg, *Memoirs of the Author's Life* and *Familiar Anecdotes of Scott,* ed. Douglas S. Mack, (Edinburgh: Scottish Academic Press, 1972), pp. 105–06.

4 John Galt, *Ringan Gilhaize* (1823) in D. S. Meldrum and William Roughhead (eds), *The Works of John Galt*, 10 vols (Edinburgh: John Grant, 1936), II, 178. Quoted in Crawford Gribben, 'Religion and Scottish Romanticism' in Murray Pittock (ed.), *The Edinburgh Companion to Scottish Romanticism* (Edinburgh: Edinburgh University Press, 2011), pp. 112–23 (p. 122).
5 Galt, *Literary Life and Miscellanies*, 3 vols (Edinburgh: Blackwoods, 1834), I, 254.
6 Douglas S. Mack, 'Hogg's Politics and the Presbyterian Tradition' in Ian Duncan and Douglas S. Mack (eds), *The Edinburgh Companion to James Hogg* (Edinburgh: Edinburgh University Press, 2012), pp. 64–72 (pp. 68–69).
7 Graham Tulloch, 'Hogg and the Novel' in Ian Duncan and Douglas S. Mack (eds), *The Edinburgh Companion to James Hogg* (Edinburgh: Edinburgh University Press, 2012), pp. 122–31, (p. 127).
8 Gribben, pp. 121–22.
9 Mack, p. 70.
10 Ina Ferris, *The Achievement of Literary Authority: Gender, History and the Waverley Novels* (Ithaca and London: Cornell University Press, 1991), p. 187.
11 Regina Hewitt gives an excellent account of the significance of conjectural history to Galt's work. See 'Introduction: Observations and Conjectures on John Galt's Place in Scottish Enlightenment and Romantic-Era Studies' in Regina Hewitt (ed.), *John Galt: Observations and Conjectures on Literature, History, and Society* (Lewisburg: Bucknell University Press, 2012), pp. 1–29.
12 György Lukács, *The Historical Novel*, trans. Hannah Mitchell and Stanley Mitchell (London: Merlin Press, 1962 [1937]).
13 See Ian Duncan, *Scott's Shadow: The Novel in Romantic Edinburgh* (Princeton: Princeton University Press, 2007) for a full articulation of the ways in which Scott follows this model.
14 Duncan, p. 219. Duncan argues that *Ringan Gilhaize* enters into a 'complex philosophical debate with Scott' and that it undertakes a 'disciplinary reckoning with the Scottish historical novel' (p. 223).
15 Walter Scott, *The Tale of Old Mortality*, ed. Douglas S. Mack, Edinburgh Edition of the Waverley Novels 4b (Edinburgh: Edinburgh University Press, 1993 [1816]), p. 10.
16 Catherine Jones, *Literary Memory: Scott's Waverley Novel and the Psychology of Narrative* (Lewisburg: Bucknell University Press, 2003), p. 21.

17 Ferris, p. 172.
18 Ibid., p. 143.
19 Duncan, p. 141.
20 Ina Ferris, '"On the Borders of Oblivion": Scott's Historical Novel and the Modern Time of the Remnant', *Modern Language Quarterly*, 70:4 (December 2009), 473–95 (p. 474).
21 Tamara Gosta, 'Sir Walter Scott's Palimpsests: Material Imprints and the Trace of the Past', *European Romantic Review*, 22:6, 707–26 (p. 711).
22 See Duncan, p. 144 and p. 225.
23 Ferris, '"Borders of Oblivion"', pp. 487–88.
24 Kerwin Lee Klein, 'On the Emergence of Memory in Historical Discourse' in *Representations*, 69 (Winter 2000), 127–50 (p. 127).
25 Piere Nora, 'Between Memory and History: *Les Lieux de Mémoire*' in *Representations*, 26, Special Issue: Memory and Counter-Memory (Spring, 1989), 7–24 (p. 7).
26 Ibid., p. 7.
27 Ibid., p. 8.
28 Ibid., p. 19.
29 See www.nts.org.uk/Culloden/Home/ for the Culloden visitors' website.
30 Nora, p. 24.
31 Ibid., p. 21.
32 Jerome de Groot, *The Historical Novel* (London: Routledge, 2010), pp. 111–12.
33 Astrid Erll, 'Traumatic pasts, literary afterlives, and transcultural memory: new directions of literary and media memory studies' in *Journal of Aesthetics and Culture*, 3 (2011), 1–5 (p. 2).
34 Alyson Bardsley, 'Trauma and Witness in *Ringan Gilhaize*' in Regina Hewitt (ed.), *John Galt: Observations and Conjectures on Literature, History, and Society* (Lewisburg: Bucknell University Press, 2012), pp. 141–65 (p. 144).
35 John Galt, *Ringan Gilhaize or The Covenanters*, ed. Patricia J. Wilson (Edinburgh: Scottish Academic Press, 1984), p. 168.
36 Ibid., p. 181.
37 Ibid., p. 200.
38 Ibid., p. 201.
39 Ibid., p. 263.
40 Bardsley, p. 153.
41 *Ringan Gilhaize*, p. 297.

42 Chad T. May notes that modern theories of trauma and memory recognise that 'While active memory represents the conscious shaping of past events into a narrative of meaning, a process like the structuring of a historical account around a particular philosophical or abstract notion of historical change, passive memory indicates the fragmentary, unexpected, and unruly associations that emerge from a disordered mind'. Chad T. May '"The Horrors of My Tale": Trauma, the Historical Imagination, and Sir Walter Scott', *Pacific Coast Philology*, 40:1 (2005), 98–116 (p. 100).

43 Duncan, p. 221.

44 Dugald Stewart, 'Theoretical or Conjectural History' in Alexander Broadie (ed.), *The Scottish Enlightenment: An Anthology* (Edinburgh: Canongate Press, 1997), pp. 670–74 (p. 671).

45 *Ringan Gilhaize*, p. 1.

46 Ibid., p. 75.

47 Ibid., p. 146.

48 E.g. at p. 159 the reader is referred to George Buchanan and an appendix containing a translation of the Declaration of Arbroath is attached to the novel, thus stretching the imaginative time of the novel still further.

49 Galt, *Literary Life*, I, 250–51.

50 Charles Swann, 'Past into Present: Scott, Galt and the Historical Novel', *Literature and History*, 3, March 1976.

51 Erll, p. 2.

52 Nora, p. 21.

53 See Ferris, *Authority*, p. 166, p. 183 and p. 185.

54 Bardsley, p. 143.

55 John MacQueen, p. 115.

56 Duncan, p. 188.

57 Duncan reads the novel as a 'single seamless telling' that makes up 'a continuous unified cause in the [tragic] subjectivity of piety'. (p. 256, p. 250) but I am suggesting that the novel's narrating strategies more self-consciously draw attention to the fissures and ruptures in Ringan's account by foregrounding the tensions between memory and narration.

58 *Ringan Gilhaize*, pp. 3–4.

59 Ibid., p. 322.

60 Bardsley, p. 158.

61 John MacQueen suggests that 'Ringan Gilhaize at no point loses the reader's sympathy'. See John MacQueen, '*Ringan Gilhaize* and

Particular Providence' in Christopher A. Whatley (ed.), *John Galt 1779–1979* (Edinburgh: The Ramsay Head Press, 1979), pp. 107–19 (p. 118) and Patricia J. Wilson suggests that the novel 'laid bare the soul' of the Covenanting movement and that Galt is 'intent on making us understand his Covenanters'. See '*Ringan Gilhaize*: A Neglected Masterpiece?' in Whatley, pp. 120–50 (p. 122, p. 140). When teaching the novel in recent years I have always found that students sympathise with Ringan.

7. The Insider's Eye in the Age of Improvement, Urbanisation, and Revolution

1. An earlier version of Christopher Whatley's chapter appeared on the website of the John Galt Society.
2. See Christopher A. Whatley, '*Annals of the Parish and History*' in C. A. Whatley (ed.), *John Galt 1779–1979* (Edinburgh: Ramsay Head Press, 1979), pp. 51–63.
3. See C. J. Berry, *Social Theory of the Scottish Enlightenment* (Edinburgh: Edinburgh University Press, 1997); A. Broadie, *The Scottish Enlightenment: The Historical Age of the Historical Nation* (Edinburgh: Birlinn, 2001); and C. A. Whatley, *Scottish Society, 1707–1830: Beyond Jacobitism, Towards Industrialisation* (Manchester: Manchester University Press, 2000).
4. There is a fascinating discussion on this aspect of the historian's dilemma by A. J. Youngson in his *The Prince and the Pretender: A Study in the Writing of History* (Beckenham: Croom Helm, 1985).
5. Whatley, *Scottish Society*, p. 236.
6. G. Penny, *Traditions of Perth* (Coupar Angus: Culross & Son, 1986).
7. E. Frykman, *John Galt's Scottish Stories, 1820–1823* (Uppsala: A. B. Ludequitska Bokhandeln, 1959), pp. 187–218.
8. D. Mack, *Scottish Fiction and the British Empire* (Edinburgh: Edinburgh University Press, 2006), p. 149.
9. F. R. Hart, *The Scottish Novel: A Critical Survey* (Edinburgh: John Murray, 1978), pp. 31–52.
10. M. Bohrer, 'John Galt's *Annals of the Parish* and the narrative strategies of tales of locale', in Regina Hewitt (ed.), *John Galt, Observations & Conjectures on Literature, History and Society* (Lewisburg: Bucknell University Press, 2012), pp. 95–118.
11. Frykman, *John Galt's Scottish Stories*, p. 220.
12. John Galt, *Literary Life and Miscellanies*, 3 vols (Edinburgh: Blackwood, 1834; General Books ed., 2009), pp. 75–78, 110.

13 I. Gordon, *John Galt: The Life of a Writer* (Edinburgh: Oliver & Boyd, 1972), pp. 42–54.
14 K. G. Simpson, 'Ironic self-revelation in *Annals of the Parish*', in Whatley, *John Galt*, p. 65.
15 See, for example, Gordon, *John Galt*; and I. Duncan, *Scott's Shadow: The Novel in Romantic Edinburgh* (Princeton: Princeton University Press, 1997).
16 C. A. Whatley, '*Annals of the Parish* and history', in Whatley (ed.), *John Galt*, pp. 52–53.
17 For an example of this tendency see T. M. Devine, 'Urbanisation', in T. M. Devine and R. Mitchison (eds), *People and Society in Scotland, volume I, 1760–1830* (Edinburgh: John Donald, 1988), pp. 27–52; and the same author's 'Scotland', in P. Clark (ed.), *The Cambridge Urban History of Britain: Volume II, 1540–1840* (Cambridge: Cambridge University Press, 2000), pp. 151–64.
18 Calculated from data in I. D. Whyte, 'Scottish and Irish urbanization in the seventeenth and eighteenth centuries: a comparative perspective' in S. J. Connolly, R. A. Houston and R. J. Morris (eds), *Conflict, Identity and Economic Development: Ireland and Scotland, 1600–1939* (Preston: Carnegie Publishing, 1995), p. 24.
19 D. Daiches, P. Jones and J. Jones (eds), *A Hotbed of Genius: The Scottish Enlightenment, 1730–1790* (Edinburgh: Edinburgh University Press, 1986); A. Hook and R. Sher (eds), *The Glasgow Enlightenment* (East Linton: Tuckwell Press, 1997); and J. J. Carter (ed.), *Aberdeen and the Enlightenment* (Edinburgh: Mercat Press, 2002).
20 On Dundee see C. McKean, B. Harris, and C. A. Whatley (eds), *Dundee: Renaissance to Enlightenment* (Dundee: Dundee University Press, 2009).
21 I. D. Whyte, 'Urbanisation', in T. M. Devine and J. R. Young (eds), *Eighteenth Century Scotland: New Perspectives* (East Linton: Tuckwell Press, 1999), pp. 176–94.
22 B. Harris and C. McKean, *The Scottish Town in the Age of the Enlightenment, 1740–1820* (Edinburgh: Edinburgh University Press, 2014).
23 Harris and McKean, *Scottish Town*, p. 4.
24 See R. L. Emerson, *An Enlightened Duke: The Life of Archibald Campbell (1682–1761), Earl of Ilay, 3rd Duke of Argyll* (Kilkerran: humming earth, 2013).
25 Harris and McKean, *Scottish Town*, pp. 82–83; C. Kidd, *Subverting Scotland's Past: Scottish Whig historians and the creation of an Anglo-British identity, 1689–c. 1830* (Cambridge: Cambridge University Press, 1993), pp. 129–84.

26 Harris and McKean, *Scottish Town*, pp. 7, 104.
27 T. W. Hamilton, *How Greenock Grew* (Greenock, 1947), p. 19.
28 John Galt, *The Provost and Other Tales* (London: MacLaren and Co., n.d.), p. 78.
29 John Galt, *Annals of the Parish* and *The Ayrshire Legatees* (London: MacLaren and Co., n.d.), pp. 169–70.
30 Galt, *The Provost*, p. 80.
31 John Galt, *The Gathering of the West* (Edinburgh and London: William Blackwood and T. Cadell, 1823), pp. 14–15.
32 Galt, *The Provost*, p. 108.
33 Galt, *Annals of the Parish* and *The Ayrshire Legatees*, p. 173.
34 Perth and Kinross Council Archives, MS 14/16/3, Diary of Thomas Murie, pp. 6–7, 11–12.
35 For an illuminating study of *Annals* as a Whiggish 'manifesto for growth and progress', but tempered by the constraints of community (or 'the Burkean ballast' of the Rev Micah Balwhidder), see Bohrer, 'John Galt's *Annals of the Parish*', esp. pp. 106–18.
36 Harris and McKean, *Scottish Town*, pp. 109, 114.
37 Ibid. *Scottish Town*, p. 104.
38 Ibid., *Scottish Town*, p. 7.
39 Ibid. *Scottish Town*, p. 131.
40 Ibid., *Scottish Town*, pp. 123–7.
41 Ibid., *Scottish Town*, pp. 126–7.
42 Galt, *The Provost*, pp. 136–7.
43 Whatley, *Scottish Society*, p. 76.
44 Galt, *The Provost*, p. 25.
45 Whatley, *Scottish Society*, pp. 155, 159; see too K. R. Bogle, *Scotland's Common Ridings* (Stroud: Tempus, 2002), pp. 87–101.
46 Harris and McKean, *Scottish Town*, pp. 190–91, 442–43.
47 Galt, *The Provost*, pp. 112–5.
48 C. A. Whatley, 'Roots of 1790s Radicalism: Reviewing the Economic and Social Background', in B. Harris (ed.), *Scotland in the Age of the French Revolution* (Edinburgh: John Donald, 2005), pp. 30–36; B. Harris, *The Scottish People and the French Revolution* (London: Pickering & Chatto, 2008), pp. 45–46.
49 Bohrer, 'John Galt's *Annals of the Parish*', p. 104.
50 C. G. Brown, 'Protest in the Pews: Interpreting Presbyterianism and Society in Fracture During the Scottish Economic Revolution', in T. M. Devine (ed.), *Conflict and Stability in Scottish Society 1700–1850* (Edinburgh: John Donald, 1990), pp. 97–99.

51 C. A. Whatley, 'Custom, Commerce and Lord Meadowbank: the Management of the Meal Market in Urban Scotland, c. 1740–c. 1820', *Journal of Scottish Historical Studies*, 32:1 (2012), 1–27.
52 National Records of Scotland, Justiciary Court Records, JC26/287, JC26/297.
53 See E. P. Thompson, 'The Moral Economy of the English Crowd in the Eighteenth Century', in E. P. Thompson, *Customs in Common* (London: Penguin, 1991), pp. 185–258.
54 Galt, *Annals*, p. 131.
55 Whatley, 'Lord Meadowbank', p. 2.
56 C. A. Whatley, 'Royal Day, People's Day: The Monarch's Birthday in Scotland, c. 1660–1860', in R. Mason and N. Macdougall (eds), *People and Power in Scotland: Essays in Honour of T. C. Smout* (Edinburgh: John Donald, 1992), pp. 170–88.
57 Angus Archives, M1/1/9, 14 June 1786.
58 Whatley, *Scottish Society*, pp. 160–64, 170–74.
59 C. A. Whatley, '"The privilege which the rabble have to be riotous": carnivalesque and the monarch's birthday in Scotland, c. 1700–1860', in I. Blanchard (ed.), *Labour and Leisure in Historical Perspective, Thirteenth to Twentieth Centuries* (Stuttgart: Franz Steiner, 1994), pp. 89–100.
60 The picture was published in S. Cowan, *The Ancient Capital of Scotland* (London: Simpkin, Marshall, Hamilton, Kent & Co., 1904).
61 'Biographical Memoir', in J. Galt, *Annals of the Parish and the Ayrshire Legatees* (London: Maclaren & Co., n.d.), pp. xxvi–xxvii.
62 For a helpful if brief discussion of Galt's utilisation of type-names, see H. B. de Groot, 'Public Benefits and Private Gains: The Provost and The Member', in Hewitt (ed.), *John Galt*, pp. 283–87.
63 R. Hewitt, 'John Galt, Harriet Martineau, and the Role of Social Theorist', in Hewitt (ed.), *John Galt*, pp. 345–72.
64 Whatley, *Scottish Society*, pp. 324–27.
65 Galt, *Gathering of the West*, p. 28.
66 M. Chase, *Chartism: A New History* (Manchester: Manchester University Press, 2007), pp. 62, 147.
67 Galt, *Gathering of the West*, p. 27.
68 Ibid., p. 33.

8. Pioneering the Political Novel in English

1 Christopher Harvie, *The Centre of Things: Political Fiction in Britain from Disraeli to the Present* (London: Unwin Hyman, 1991), p. 33.

2   John Galt, *Autobiography* (London: Cochrane and McCrone, 1833), II, 197.
3   Galt, *Autobiography*, II, 231. George Canning (1770-1827), became Leader of the House of Commons and Foreign Secretary in 1822, shortly after The *Provost* was published in the May of that year.
4   A. J. Ashley, 'Correspondence – Coleridge on Galt', *Times Literary Supplement*, 25 September 1930, p. 757.
5   Galt, *Autobiography*, II, 219.
6   John Galt, *Literary Life and Miscellanies*, 3 vols (Edinburgh: Blackwood, 1834), I, 229.
7   Galt, *Autobiography*, II, 210.
8   Galt, *Literary Life*, I, 318. Ian A. Gordon, *John Galt: The Life of a Writer* (Edinburgh: Oliver & Boyd, 1972), p. 104.
9   Sir George Douglas, *The Blackwood Group* (London: Oliphant, Anderson and Ferrar, 1897), p. 67, writes of *The Provost*'s perfection as an artistic whole.
10 *Concise Scots Dictionary* (Edinburgh: Polygon, 1985), p. 479. See also P. H. Scott, *John Galt* (Edinburgh: Scottish Academic Press, 1985), pp. 52-53, for a fuller discussion of this point.
11 Keith M. Costain, 'The Prince and the Provost', *Studies in Scottish Literature*, 6 (1968), pp. 20-35 (p. 26). W. Croft Dickinson, *John Galt: "The Provost" and the Burgh* (Greenock: Papers of the Greenock Philosophical Society, 1954), p. 5.
12 John Galt, *The Provost*, ed. Ian A. Gordon (Oxford: Oxford University Press, 1982), chapter 1.
13 Ibid., chapter 3.
14 J. Derrick McClure, 'Scots and English in *Annals of the Parish* and *The Provost*', in Christopher Whatley (ed.), *John Galt, 1779-1979* (Edinburgh: Ramsay Head Press, 1979), pp. 195-210 (p. 207).
15 *The Provost*, chapter 14.
16 Ruth I. Aldrich, *John Galt* (Boston: Twayne, 1978), p. 62.
17 *The Provost*, chapter 23.
18 Ibid., chapter 47.
19 John MacQueen, *The Rise of the Historical Novel: The Enlightenment and Scottish Literature* (Edinburgh: Scottish Academic Press, 1989), II, 169.
20 *The Provost*, chapter 47.
21 Under the pre-1832 Scottish electoral system, burghs were grouped and the MP chosen by an electorate of delegates, one for each burgh, usually selected by the respective burgh councils.

22 *The Provost*, chapters 4 and 5. 'Jookerie' is Scots for trickery, deceit or roguery. In 1820 the number of electors in Scotland was 4,239 out of a population of just over two million. See W. Ferguson, 'The Reform Act (Scotland) of 1832: intention and effect', *Scottish Historical Review*, 45 (1966), 105–14 (p. 105).
23 *The Provost*, chapter 16.
24 Ibid., chapter 46.
25 See John F. McCaffrey, *Scotland in the Nineteenth Century* (London: Macmillan, 1998), p. 24.
26 See M. Lynch (ed.), *The Oxford Companion to Scottish History* (Oxford: Oxford University Press, 2001), pp. 276–77.
27 Harvie writes, for example, 'Galt's wit works because it is provincial' (Harvie, p. 34).
28 The *OED* also mentions getting a person into some position by jobbery.
29 Galt returned to England in May 1829 after the failure of his mission for the Canada Company. He was confined in an open debtors' prison between July and November of the same year. This ended in his being declared insolvent. See Gordon, *John Galt*, (Edinburgh: Oliver and Boyd, 1972), pp. 85–104.
30 John T. Ward, '*The Member* and Parliamentary Reform', in *John Galt 1779–1979*, pp. 151–63 (pp. 151–53). See also *DNB*, XXVII, 809, which says of Holmes: 'For thirty years "Black Billy" Holmes was the adroit and dextrous whip of the tory party, and his great knowledge of the tastes, wishes, idiosyncrasies, and family connections of all the members on the tory side of the house made him a most skilful party manager and dispenser of patronage'.
31 Galt, *The Member* and *The Radical*, ed. Ian A. Gordon and Paul H. Scott (Edinburgh, Canongate, 1996), *The Member*, Dedication.
32 *The Member*, chapter 26.
33 Holmes by special permission of the Prime Minister, the Duke of Wellington, was allowed to vote against the government's Roman Catholic Relief Bill. Opposition to this measure was a litmus test for die-hard Tories at this time. See *Old DNB*, IX, 1093–94.
34 'The Member: An Autobiography', *Fraser's Magazine*, 4 (1832), 369–75 (p. 369).
35 *Fraser's*, 4 (1832), 369.
36 *The Member*, chapter 1.
37 Edward Porritt, *The Unreformed House of Commons*, 2 vols (Cambridge: Cambridge University Press, 1903), I, 357.

38 *The Member*, chapter 7.
39 Ward, pp. 158–59.
40 T. H. B. Oldfield, *The Representative History of Great Britain and Ireland*, 6 vols (London: Baldwin, Cradock and Joy, 1816), IV, 294.
41 Oldfield, v, 217.
42 *The Member*, chapter 14.
43 Ibid., chapters 13 and 23. See, for example, the account of the Maldon election of 1826 in Peter Jupp (ed.), *British and Irish Elections, 1784-1831* (Newton Abbot: David & Charles, 1973), pp. 114–22.
44 Charles Snodgrass, 'Dismembering *The Member*: Galt's "Pawkie" Political Persona', *Scottish Literary Journal*, 24 (1997), pp. 66–71 (p. 69).
45 Carla Sassi, 'Subverting Britannia's (Precarious) Balance: a Re-reading of John Galt's *The Member: an Autobiography*', *Rivista Di Studi Vittoriani*, 8 (1999), 25–45 (pp. 35–36).
46 *The Member*, chapter 15.
47 Ibid., chapter 25.
48 Ibid., chapter 18. In describing Selby's fate, Galt could draw on his own experiences in Canada, his dismissal by the Canada Company and his ending up in debtors' prison. See Gordon, *John Galt*, pp. 85–89.
49 Ibid., chapter 19.
50 Ibid., chapter 8.
51 Ibid., chapter 27.
52 The Holy Alliance, concluded between the rulers of Russia, Prussia, and Austria in 1815, bound them in a Christian union of 'charity, peace and love'. See David Thomson, *Europe since Napoleon* (Harmondsworth: Penguin, 1966), pp. 96–97.
53 Bruce Coleman, *Conservatism and the Conservative Party in Nineteenth-Century Britain*, (London: Edward Arnold, 1988), pp. 50–51.
54 See Robert Stewart, *Party and Politics 1830–1852* (London: Macmillan, 1989), pp. 87–89.
55 Michael Brock, *The Great Reform Act* (London: Hutchinson, 1973), pp. 123–24; and Derek Fraser, 'The Agitation for Parliamentary Reform', in J. T. Ward (ed.), *Popular Movements c. 1830–1850* (London: Macmillan, 1970), pp. 31–53 (p. 39).
56 *The Member*, chapter 35.
57 Ibid., chapter 35.
58 Regina Hewitt argues that Galt did not accept the 'progress plot' of conjectural history. This is well evidenced by this part of the novel in particular. See Regina Hewitt (ed.), *John Galt: Observations and*

Conjectures on Literature, History and Society (Lewisburg: Bucknell University Press, 2012), p. 8.
59 *The Member*, chapter 9.
60 Ibid., chapters 8 and 9.
61 Ibid., Dedication.
62 Gordon, *John Galt*, pp. 106–107.
63 Galt, *The Member* and *The Radical*, ed. Ian A. Gordon and Paul H. Scott (Edinburgh: Canongate, 1996); *The Radical*, chapter 23.
64 *The Radical*, chapter 22.
65 John Galt, *The Gathering of the West*, ed. by Bradford Allen Booth (Baltimore: Johns Hopkins Press, 1939), pp. 52–53.
66 McCaffrey, p. 22.
67 *The Gathering of the West*, p. 102.

9. Reading for Something Other than the Plot in Galt's 'Tales of the West'

1 Ian A. Gordon, *John Galt: The Life of a Writer* (Edinburgh: Oliver & Boyd, 1972), p. 41.
2 Quoted in Gordon, p. 45. As Gordon goes on to suggest, whether *Sir Andrew Wylie* provided such a story is open to debate. What Blackwood eventually got, Gordon says, was something between a good long story and the more plotless magazine series that Galt had found initial success with.
3 Katie Trumpener also refers to Galt's fiction as proto-modernist, reading his work as a radical critique of the developmental logic of Scott's Waverley Novels. See *Bardic Nationalism: The Romantic Novel and the British Empire* (Princeton: Princeton University Press, 1997), p.156.
4 *Blackwood's Edinburgh Magazine* 16 (October 1824), 456.
5 *Blackwood's* 17 (June 1825), 667.
6 Ibid., p. 669.
7 D. M. Moir, *Life of Mansie Wauch, Tailor in Dalkeith* (London and Edinburgh: T. N. Foulis, 1911), p. vii.
8 Ibid., p. 69.
9 Peter Brooks, *Reading for the Plot: Design and Intention in Narrative* (Cambridge: Harvard University Press, 1984), p. 37.
10 Ibid., p. 10
11 Ibid., p. 5.
12 *Blackwood's* 7 (June 1820), 262.
13 John Galt, *The Ayrshire Legatees* (Edinburgh: The Saltire Society, 2002), p. 160.

14 *Blackwood's*, 8 (February 1821), 517.
15 *Blackwood's*, 9 (May 1821), 168.
16 *Blackwood's*, 8 (February 1821), 524.
17 *Blackwood's*, 8 (March 1821), 645.
18 Galt, *The Steam-Boat* (Edinburgh: William Blackwood, 1822), p. 359.
19 Francis Jeffrey, 'Secondary Scottish Novels', *Edinburgh Review* 39 (1823), 177.
20 Ibid., p. 178. Duffle's mentions of making a book occur on pp. 517–18 in 'The Steam-Boat. No. 1', *Blackwood's*, 8 (February 1821).
21 Robert Morrison, 'John Galt's Angular Magazinity', in Regina Hewitt (ed.), *John Galt: Observations and Conjectures on Literature, History, and Society* (Lewisburg: Bucknell University Press, 2012), p. 268.
22 Ibid., p. 268.
23 Ian Duncan, *Scott's Shadow: The Novel in Romantic Edinburgh* (Princeton: Princeton University Press, 2007), p. 217. For George V. Griffith, this eschewal of plot is a feature of the short fiction series. 'Freed from the temporal rigidity of plot,' he explains, 'the sequence of parts in a series is unimportant and the parts may often be rearranged with a casual freedom'. Griffith, 'John Galt's Short Fiction Series', *Studies in Short Fiction*, 17 (January 1980), 458–59.
24 Ian Duncan, 'Altered States: Galt, Serial Fiction, and the Romantic Miscellany', in Hewitt (ed.), *John Galt: Observations and Conjectures on Literature, History, and Society*, p. 55.
25 John Galt, *The Autobiography of John Galt*, 2 vols (London: Cochrane and M'Crone, 1833), II, 219.
26 Galt, *Literary Life and Miscellanies*, 3 vols (Edinburgh: Blackwood, 1834), p. 155.
27 Ibid., p. 155.
28 Ibid., p. 226.
29 Dugald Stewart, 'Account of the Life and Writings of Adam Smith, LL.D', in W. P. D. Wightman and J. C. Bryce (eds), *Essays on Philosophical Subjects* (Oxford: Clarendon Press, 1980), p. 293. See also Duncan, *Scott's Shadow*, pp. 216–17; Regina Hewitt, 'Introduction: Observations and Conjectures on John Galt's Place in Scottish Enlightenment and Romantic-Era Studies', in Hewitt (ed.), *John Galt: Observations and Conjectures on Literature, History, and Society*, pp. 3–12; and Keith M. Costain, 'Theoretical History and the Novel: The Scottish Fiction of John Galt', *English Literary History*, 43:3 (Autumn 1976), 345–46.
30 Duncan, *Scott's Shadow*, p. 217.

31 Hewitt, 'Introduction', p. 4. The point is echoed by Costain, who suggests that 'theoretical histories were written to trace the progress of British or European society through the respective stages' of hunting, shepherding, agriculture, and commercial society. 'Theoretical History and the Novel', p. 345.
32 Ibid., p. 11. See also Hewitt's 'John Galt, Harriet Martineau, and the Role of the Social Theorist', in Hewitt (ed.), *John Galt: Observations and Conjectures on Literature, History, and Society*, pp. 345–72.
33 Adam Ferguson, *An Essay on the History of Civil Society* (1767), ed. Fania Oz-Salzberger (Cambridge: Cambridge University Press, 1995), p. 207
34 See for example Trumpener, *Bardic Nationalism*, pp. 277–78; Duncan, *Scott's Shadow*, pp. 223–30; and Anthony Jarrells, '"Associations Respect[ing] the Past": Enlightenment and Romantic Historicism', in Jon Klancher (ed.), *A Concise Companion to the Romantic Age* (Oxford: Wiley-Blackwell, 2009), pp. 70–73.
35 *Blackwood's*, 7 (August 1820), 473; *Blackwood's*, 7 (August 1820), 594.
36 *Blackwood's*, 7 (June 1820), 266.
37 Ibid., p. 266.
38 Ibid., pp. 266–67.
39 Ibid., p. 271.
40 Galt, *Literary Life*, p. 227.
41 *Blackwood's*, 8 (October 1820), 18.
42 Ibid., p. 18.
43 *Blackwood's*, 8 (February 1821), 517.
44 Ibid., p. 517.
45 Ibid., p. 524.
46 Caroline McCracken-Flesher, 'The Sense of No Ending: John Galt and the Travels of Commoners and Kings in "The Steam-Boat" and "The Gathering of the West"', in Hewitt (ed.), *John Galt: Observations and Conjectures on Literature, History, and Society*, p. 77.
47 *Blackwood's*, 9 (June 1821), 259.
48 Ibid., p. 260.
49 Ibid., p. 260.
50 Ibid., p. 263.
51 Ibid., p. 260.
52 *Blackwood's*, 10 (September 1821), 168.
53 Ibid.
54 Ibid.
55 Ibid.

56 Ibid.
57 Ibid., p. 170.
58 Ibid.
59 Ibid.
60 McCracken-Flesher, 'The Sense of no Ending', p. 74.
61 Duncan, 'Altered States', p. 61.
62 Ibid.
63 Mary Poovey, *A History of the Modern Fact: Problems of Knowledge in the Sciences of Wealth and Society* (Chicago: University of Chicago Press, 1998), p. 226.
64 Walter Benjamin, 'The Work of Art in the Age of Mechanical Reproduction', *Illuminations*, ed. Hannah Arendt, trans. Harry Zohn (New York: Schocken Books, 1968), p. 230.
65 Costain, 'Theoretical History and the Novel', p. 363, p. 362.
66 John Galt, *Voyages and Travels, in the Years 1809, 1810, and 1811; Containing Statistical, Commercial, and Miscellaneous Observations on Gibraltar, Sardinia, Sicily, Malta, Sergio, and Turkey* (London: T. Cadell, 1812), p. iv.
67 Brooks, *Reading for the Plot*, p. 93.
68 See Benjamin, 'The Storyteller', *Illuminations*, p. 87.

10. Gender and the Short Story in the Twilight Years

1 George Douglas in his *The 'Blackwood' Group* (Edinburgh & London: Oliphant, Anderson & Ferrier, 1897) sees the group more widely as including Galt, John Wilson, D. M. Moir, Susan Ferrier, Michael Scott, and Thomas Hamilton (but not Walter Scott, presumably standing out in his genius as a class of his own). Douglas would also have included in his book James Hogg and John Gibson Lockhart, but for the fact that these writers are to be given separate volumes in the same 'Famous Scots' series for which Douglas is writing.
2 See Robert Morrison and Chris Baldick (eds), *Tales of Terror from Blackwood's Magazine* (Oxford: Oxford World Classics, 1995). Galt's piece selected for this modern anthology is 'The Buried Alive' published anonymously in *Blackwood's* in 1821 and incorporated into his novella *The Steam-Boat* (1822); the text is very probably influential upon Edgar Allan Poe.
3 Although it should be acknowledged that Scott's experiments in writing, including shorter pieces such 'Phantasmagoria' and 'My Aunt Margaret's Mirror,' are most certainly contributing to a flux in fictional form within this period; see Alison Lumsden, 'Walter Scott and

    Blackwood's: Writing for Adventurers' forthcoming in the journal *Romanticism* (I am very grateful to Professor Lumsden for pre-publication sight of this essay).

4 John Galt, *Stories of the Study* (London: Cochrane & McCrone, 1833), p. 1.

5 Ian A. Gordon, *John Galt: The Life of a Writer* (Edinburgh: Oliver & Boyd, 1972), p. 113.

6 For convenience, quotations for Galt's short stories dealt with in this essay are all taken from Ian A. Gordon (ed.), *John Galt: Selected Short Stories* (Edinburgh: Scottish Academic Press, 1978); although this volume is also now out of print it is readily available on the second-hand market.

7 William Roughead (ed.), *The Howdie & Other Tales* (Edinburgh & London: Foulis, 1923).

8 For instance, Jane Austen read Thomas Gisborne's *An Inquiry into the Duties of the Female Sex* (1805) in its sixth edition of that year; although Gisborne's tract was conservative in some of its aspects it also recommended reading and education for middle-class women.

Further Reading

I. John Galt's Writing

'Modern Editions' below shows the scant list of recent editing applied to Galt, which is instructive in itself; the fullest modern bibliography of Galt is an excellent piece of work by Tim Saur, *Descriptive Bibliography of John Galt*, formerly online at the University of Guelph but currently unavailable.

Modern Editions

Annals of the Parish, ed. James Kinsley (Oxford: World Classics, 1986).
The Entail, ed. Ian A. Gordon (London: Oxford University Press, 1970).
The Last of the Lairds, ed. Ian A. Gordon (Edinburgh: Mercat Press, 1976).
The Provost (London: Oxford University Press, 1973).
The Reform: Being The Member and The Radical, ed. Ian A. Gordon (Edinburgh & London: Scottish Academic Press, 1973).
Ringan Gilhaize, ed. Patricia J. Wilson (Edinburgh: Canongate, 1995).

Short Stories

The Howdie & Other Tales, ed. William Roughead (Edinburgh & London: Foulis, 1923).
Selected Short Stories, ed. Ian A. Gordon (Edinburgh: Scottish Academic Press, 1978).
Stories of the Study, 3 vols (London: Cochrane & McCrone, 1833).

Correspondence

Letters of John Galt, The Canadian Years, ed. J. K. Herreshoff (Ann Arbor: University of Michigan Press, 1990).

II. Secondary Sources

Monographs

Aberdein, Jennie W., *John Galt* (London: Oxford University Press, 1936).
Aldrich, Ruth I., *John Galt* (Boston: G. K. Hall, 1978).
Duncan, Ian, *Scott's Shadow: The Novel in Romantic Edinburgh* (Princeton: Princeton University Press, 2007).
Frykman, Erik, *John Galt's Scottish Stories, 1820-1823*. (Uppsala: Lundequistska Bokhandeln, 1959).
Gibault, Henri, *John Galt, Romancier Ecossais* (Grenoble: Université des langues et lettres de Grenoble, 1979).
Gordon, Ian A., *John Galt: The Life of a Writer* (Edinburgh: Oliver & Boyd, 1972).
Lyell, Frank Hallam, *A Study of the Novels of John Galt* (Princeton: Princeton University Press, 1942).
Parker, W. M., *Susan Ferrier and John Galt* (London: Longmans for the British Council, 1965).
Scott, P. H., *John Galt* (Edinburgh: Scottish Academic Press, 1985).
Timothy, H. B., *The Galts: A Canadian Odyssey. John Galt 1779-1839* (Toronto: McClelland and Stewart, 1977).
Trumpener, Katie, *Bardic Nationalism: The Romantic Novel and the British Empire* (Princeton: Princeton University Press, 1997).

Collections of Essays

Hewitt, Regina (ed.), *John Galt, Observations & Conjectures on Literature, History and Society* (Lewisburg PA: Bucknell University Press, 2012).
Waterston, Elizabeth (ed.), *John Galt: Reappraisals* (Guelph: University of Guelph, 1985).
Whatley, C. A. (ed.), *John Galt 1779-1979* (Edinburgh: The Ramsay Head Press, 1979).

Essays and Chapters

Bardsley, Alyson, 'Novel and Nation Come to Grief: The Dead's Part in John Galt's *The Entail*', *Modern Philology*, 99 (2002), 540-63.
Bardsley, Alyson, 'Your Local representative: John Galt's *The Provost*', *Scottish Literary Journal*, 24:1 (1997), 72-76.
Caykent, Ozlem, 'Enlightened Conservatism: John Galt on Law, Morality and Human Nature', *History of European Ideas*, 30 (2004), 183-96.

Cass, Jeffrey, 'John Galt, Happy Colonialist: The Case of the Apostate; or, Atlantis Destroyed', *The Wordsworth Circle*, 41 (2010), 167–70.
Costain, Keith M., 'The Community of Man: Galt and Eighteenth-Century Scottish Realism' *Scottish Literary Journal*, 8:1 (1981), 10–29.
Costain, Keith M., 'Early Remembrances: Pastoral in the Fictional World of John Galt', *University of Toronto Quarterly*, 47 (1978), 283–303.
Costain, Keith M., 'The Prince and the Provost', *Studies in Scottish Literature*, 6 (1968), 20–35.
Costain, Keith M., 'The Scottish Fiction of John Galt', in Douglas Gifford (ed.), *The History of Scottish Literature* vol. 3, *The Nineteenth Century* (Aberdeen: Aberdeen University Press, 1988), pp. 107–23.
Costain, Keith M., 'The Spirit of the Age and the Scottish Fiction of John Galt', *Wordsworth Circle*, 11 (1980), 98–106.
Costain, Keith M., 'Theoretical History and the Novel: The Scottish Fiction of John Galt,' *English Literary History*, 43 (1976), 342–65.
Crawford, Robert, *Scotland's Books: A History of Scottish Literature* (Oxford: Oxford University Press, 2009), pp. 436–44.
De Groot, H. B. 'John Galt' online in the *Literary Encyclopedia* www.litencyc.com
Demata, Massimiliano, 'From Caledonia to Albani: Byron, Galt and the Progress of the Eastern Savage', *Scottish Studies Review*, 2:2 (2001), 61–76.
Douglas, George, 'John Galt', in *The 'Blackwood' Group* (Edinburgh & London: Oliphant, Anderson & Ferrier, 1897), pp. 47–93.
Divine, Ann Roberts, 'The Changing Village: Loss of Community in John Galt's *Annals of the Parish*', *Studies in Scottish Literature*, 25 (1990), 121–33. Available at scholarcommons.sc.edu/ssl/vol25/iss1/9
Duncan, Ian, 'Scott and the Historical Novel: A Scottish Rise of the Novel', in Gerard Carruthers and Liam McIlvanney (eds), *The Cambridge Companion to Scottish Literature* (Cambridge: Cambridge University Press, 2012), pp. 103–16.
Esterhammer, Angela, 'London Periodicals, Scottish Novels and Italian Fabrications: *Andrew of Padua the Improvisatore* Re-membered', *Studies in Romanticism*, 48 (2009), 469–90.
Esterhammer, Angela, 'John Galt's Fictional and Performative Worlds', in Murray Pittock (ed.), *The Edinburgh Companion to Scottish Romanticism* (Edinburgh: Edinburgh University Press, 2011), pp. 166–77.
Esterhammer, Angela, 'Speculation in the Late-Romantic Literary Marketplace', *Victoriographies*, 7 (forthcoming 2017).

Gifford, Douglas, 'Myth, Parody and Dissociation: Scottish Fiction, 1814–1914', in Douglas Gifford (ed.), *The History of Scottish Literature* vol. 3, *The Nineteenth Century* (Aberdeen: Aberdeen University Press, 1988), pp. 217–59.

Gordon, Ian A., 'Galt's *The Ayrshire Legatees*: Genesis and Development', *Scottish Literary Journal*, 16:1 (1989), 35–42.

Griffith, George V., 'John Galt's Short Fiction Series', *Studies in Short Fiction*, 17 (1980), 455–62.

Hall, Louis B., 'Peripety in John Galt's *The Entail*', *Studies in Scottish Literature*, 5 (1967), 176–84. Available at scholarcommons.sc.edu/ssl/vol5/iss3/4

Hart, Francis Russell, 'John Galt' in *The Scottish Novel from Smollett to Spark* (Cambridge, Massachusetts: Harvard University Press, 1978), pp. 31–52. [Published also as *The Scottish Novel: a critical survey* (London: John Murray, 1978)]

Jeffrey, Francis, 'Secondary Scottish Novels', *Edinburgh Review*, 39 (1823), 158–96.

McClure, J. D., 'The Language of *The Entail*', *Scottish Literary Journal*, 8:1 (1981), 30–51.

McCulloch, Margery Palmer, 'The Provost and His Lord: John Galt and Lord Byron', in Angus Calder (ed.), *Byron and Scotland* (Edinburgh: Edinburgh University Press, 1989), pp. 68–79.

McKeever, Gerard Lee, '"With wealth come wants": Scottish Romanticism as improvement in the fiction of John Galt', *Studies in Romanticism*, 55 (2016), 69–94.

MacQueen, John, *The Rise of the Historical Novel* (Edinburgh: Scottish Academic Press, 1989), pp. 110–92.

MacQueen, John, 'John Galt and the Analysis of Social History', in A. S. Bell (ed.), *Scott Bicentenary Essays* (Edinburgh: Scottish Academic Press, 1973), pp. 332–42.

O'Hagan, Andrew, 'You Can Go Home Again', *The Herald*, 28 February 2009.

Sassi, Carla, 'Subverting Britannia's (Precarious) Balance: a Re-reading of John Galt's *The Member: an Autobiography*', *Rivista Di Studi Vittoriani*, 8 (1999), 25–45.

Schoenfield, Mark. 'The Family Plots: Land and Law in John Galt's *The Entail*', *Scottish Literary Journal*, 24:1 (1997), 60–65.

Simmons, Claire, 'John Galt, the Scottish Enlightenment and the Crisis of Genre', *Scottish Literary Journal*, 24:1 (1997), 53–76.

Snodgrass, Charles, 'Dismembering *The Member*: Galt's "Pawkie" Political Persona', *Scottish Literary Journal*, 24:1 (1997), 66–71.

Trumpener, Katie, 'Annals of Ice: Formations of Empire, Place and History in John Galt and Alice Munro', in Michael Gardiner, Graeme Macdonald, Niall O'Gallagher (eds), *Scottish Literature and Postcolonial Literature: Comparative Texts and Critical Perspectives* (Edinburgh: Edinburgh University Press, 2011), pp. 43–56.

Waterston, Elizabeth, 'Galt, Scott, and the Frontiers of Canadian Fiction,' *Journal of Canadian Fiction*, (Summer 1972), 60–65.

Waterston, Elizabeth, 'John Galt and the Canadian Star of Destiny,' *Canadian Literature*, 129 (Summer 1991), 116–27.

Waterston, Elizabeth, 'John Galt's Canadian Experience', *Studies in Scottish Literature* 15 (1980), 257–62.

Wilson, Patricia J. 'John Galt at Work: Comments on the MS. of *Ringan Gilhaize*', *Studies in Scottish Literature*, 20 (1985), 160–76.

Wilson, Patricia J. '*Ringan Gilhaize:* The Product of an Informing Vision', *Scottish Literary Journal*, 8:1 (1981), pp. 52–68.

Notes on Contributors

Gerard Carruthers FRSE is Francis Hutcheson Professor of Scottish Literature at Glasgow University and General Editor of the Oxford University Press edition of the works of Robert Burns. Recent books include the co-edited volumes (with Don Martin) *Thomas Muir of Huntershill: Essays for the Twenty-First Century* (2016) and (with Liam McIlvanney) *The Cambridge Companion to Scottish Literature* (2012).

Angela Esterhammer is Principal of Victoria College and Professor of English at the University of Toronto. General Editor of the *Edinburgh Edition of the Selected Works of John Galt*, her publications include *Romanticism and Improvisation, 1750–1850* (2008). Her current project is entitled 'Speculation, Improvisation, Mediality: The Late-Romantic Information Age'.

Anthony Jarrells teaches in the English Department at the University of South Carolina. Author of *Britain's Bloodless Revolutions: 1688 Romantic Reform of Literature* (2005) and editor of *Blackwood's Magazine,* volume 2: *Selected Prose* (2006), he writes on the novel in English and on Romanticism. He is working to complete a book on Romantic-period short fiction, titled *The Time of the Tale*.

Colin Kidd FBA, FRSE is Wardlaw Professor of Modern History at the University of St Andrews and a Fellow of All Souls College, Oxford. A regular contributor to the *London Review of Books* and the *Guardian*, he is author of several books, most recently *The World of Mr Casaubon: Britain's Wars of Mythography 1700–1870* (2016).

Craig Lamont is a lecturer and teacher of Scottish Literature at Glasgow University. His PhD thesis on Georgian Glasgow won the Universities'

Committee for Scottish Literature 2016 Ross Roy Medal. He has worked as a research assistant on projects funded by the AHRC and the Royal Society of Edinburgh and continues to research new aspects of the work of John Galt, Robert Burns, and Allan Ramsay.

Alison Lumsden is a Professor in English Literature at Aberdeen University. A General Editor for the Edinburgh Edition of the Waverley Novels, she now lead-edits the Edinburgh Edition of Walter Scott's Poetry. Co-director of Aberdeen University's Walter Scott Research Centre and Honorary Librarian at Abbotsford House, and published on many aspects of Scottish literature, she has particular interests in the nineteenth century.

Ian McGhee was a civil servant and pursued his lifelong love of Galt after retirement by studying Scottish Literature at Glasgow University where he obtained an MA and an MPhil based on Galt's relations with North America. He is Secretary of the John Galt Society.

Gordon Millar completed a PhD in mid-nineteenth-century Scottish political history and an MPhil in Scottish Literature, both at Glasgow University, and a post-doctoral habilitation at Fribourg University, Switzerland, on the nineteenth-century political novel in English, publishing in both areas. A Research Associate on the *New DNB* project, he taught English Literature at Fribourg and is now Head of International Relations at the Lucerne School of Business.

Andrew O'Hagan's most recent novel is *The Illuminations*. He has three times been nominated for the Booker Prize and is a Fellow of the Royal Society of Literature. A director of the *London Review of Books*, he serves as Patron of the John Galt Society.

Christopher A. Whatley OBE FRSE FRHistS is a leading Scottish historian. Best known for his controversial, ground-breaking and award-winning work on the Union of 1707 (*The Scots and the Union*, 2006, 2007, 2014), his most recent book is *Immortal Memory: Burns and the Scottish People* (2016). Currently Emeritus Professor at Dundee University, he was appointed in 2015 OBE for services to Scottish history education.

Index

Aberdeen, 34
Aberdein, Jenny, 13
Academy of Fine Art in Glasgow, 35
Act of the General Assembly 1711, 19
Act of Union 1707, 19
Adam, John, 21
Aldrich, Ruth, 100
Allan, David, 35
anti-subscriptionism, 23
Apter, Emily, 46
'Athenian Creed' (Witherspoon), 20
Auld Lichts, 18, 20, 21, 23, 24, 26–32
Austen, Jane, *Emma*, 16
Ayr, 88, 90
Ayrshire, 8–14
    as setting for Galt's fiction 15–33, 37, 60, 113
    'Ayrshire heresies,' 23

Bardsley, Alyson, 75, 76, 77, 79, 81
Benjamin, Walter, 'Work of Art in the Age of Mechanical Reproduction,' 123
Blackwood, William, 3, 50, 110, 129
'Blackwood Group,' 3, 4, 5, 125

Blackwood's Edinburgh Magazine ('The Maga'), xii, 2, 3, 65, 69, 95, 110, 113, 115, 116, 119, 125
Brooks, Peter, 112, 123
Brown, Callum, 91
Brown, George Douglas, *The House with the Green Shutters*, 1–2
Bryce, Thomas H., 40
Burlington, Canada, 59
Burns, Robert, 1, 7, 9
    'Address to the Unco' Guid, or the Rigidly Righteous,' 23
    'Holy Willie's Prayer,' 17, 18, 23, 24, 25
    'The Kirk of Scotland's Garland,' 23
    Muir on, 3
    Poems, Chiefly in the Scottish Dialect, 35
    satires, 18, 23
Butler, Samuel, *Hudibras*, 17

Calvinism, 17, 18, 19, 23, 134
Campbell, Archibald, 3rd duke of Argyll, 86
Campbell, Roy, 'Scotland's Neglected Enlightened' (essay), 35

Campbell, Thomas, 35
Canada Company, xii, 2, 44, 50, 52, 57, 58
Capote, Truman, *In Cold Blood*, 12
Carlyle, Thomas, 2
Chartism, 96
Checkland, S. G., 145n1
Chitnis, Anand, 36
chorus, use of, 9
Christensen, Jerome, 47
Church of Scotland, 17, 19
Circum-Atlantic commerce, 65
Coleridge, Samuel Taylor, 8, 11, 98, 104
colonialism, 40, 41–42, 48–52, 55, 57–69
commercialism, 89
common land, ownership of, 89, 90
Concise Scots Dictionary, 100
'conjectural histories,' 77, 117, 120, 122, 123
Convention of Royal Burghs, 86
Corn Laws, repeal of, 106, 107
corruption, 89
Costain, Keith, 36, 123
counter-Enlightenment, 4, 7, 18, 20, 22, 26, 33
Covenanting Wars, in fiction, 70–81
  The Brownie of Bodsbeck (Hogg), 70, 71
  Old Mortality (Scott), 70, 72–74
  Ringan Gilhaize, 70, 71, 75–81
Craig, David, 3, 4
Crawford, Robert, 39
Crockett, S. R., 4, 11
Croftangry, Chrystal, 126

Cullen, William, 40
Culloden Visitor Centre, 74

Daiches, David, 3
Darien expedition, 48–52
de Groot, Jerome, 75
dialect, 10, 11, 13, 15, 54
didacticism, 63, 65
Douglas, George, 163n1
Duncan, Ian, 36, 72, 73, 77, 79, 80, 116, 122
  Scott's Shadow: The Novel in Romantic Edinburgh, 5, 6

Edinburgh
  New Town, 86, 88
  Royal Visit, 38
  and Scottish Enlightenment, 34, 35, 85
  and use of vernacular, 35
Edinburgh and Glasgow Union Canal Company, xi
The Edinburgh Companion to James Hogg, 71
The Edinburgh Companion to Scottish Romanticism, 71
Edinburgh Monthly Magazine see *Blackwood's Edinburgh Magazine*
The Edinburgh Review, 2, 119
Edinburgh Theatre Royal, 6
Edinburgh University Press, 6, 7
Emerson, Ralph Waldo, 13
epistolary novels, 16, 27, 36
Erll, Astrid, 75, 78
Esterhammer, Angela, 6

feminism, 127–35
Ferguson, Adam, 117, 118
Fergusson, Alexander, 21, 22, 23

Fergusson, Robert, 35
Ferris, Ina, 71, 72, 73, 79
fictional autobiographies 60, 78
first-person narration, 16–17, 30, 31, 53, 54, 78, 138
Foulis, Robert and Andrew, 35
Foulis Academy, 35
Fraser's Magazine, 103, 104, 131
Frazer, Sir James, *Golden Bough*, 5
French Revolution, 38, 60, 83, 91

Galt, John
    accessibility of work, 15
    The Annals of the Parish, xii, 2, 10, 11, 12, 16, 21, 25, 26, 30–31, 37–38, 40, 41, 42, 60, 84, 86, 91, 92, 94, 110, 115, 116, 117, 123, 127
    The Appeal (play), xi, 6
    Autobiography, xii, 41, 99, 116
    The Ayrshire Legatees, xii, 11, 13, 16, 26, 27–30, 36, 38, 87, 88, 110, 113, 116, 117, 118, 120
    'The Battle of Largs' (epic poem), xi
    'Biographical Sketch of William Paterson,' 147n15
    biography, xi–xii
    death, xii
    drama, 6
    Bogle Corbet, or, The Emigrants xii, 38, 41, 42, 43, 57, 59, 64, 65–69
    'The Broken Heart,' 122
    The Entail, xii, 2, 4, 5, 11, 37, 45, 48–52, 54, 126
    'Essay on Commercial Policy,' 45
    The Gathering of the West, xii, 38, 87, 88, 95, 96–97, 108, 109
    'The Gudewife,' 131–32, 133
    'The Howdie,' 3, 129–30, 131
    'The Hurricane,' 114, 115
    The Last of the Lairds, xii, 4
    Lawrie Todd; or, the Settlers in the Woods, xii, 45, 52, 53–54, 57, 59–64, 68, 95
    Letters from the Levant, xi
    The Life and Studies of Benjamin West, xi
    life in Canada, 57–69
    The Life of Lord Byron, xii, 59
    The Literary Life and Miscellanies, xii, 12, 36, 43, 58, 70, 71, 84, 99, 119
    literary view of, 2–7
    The Lives of the Players, 6, 59
    marriage, xi
    'The Mem,' 9–11
    The Member, xii, 4, 98, 99, 102–08
    The New British Theatre (ed.), 6
    The Omen, xii, 3
    The Pastor (later *Annals of the Parish*), 110
    personality, 1–2
    poetry, 6
    political beliefs, 4, 58, 91, 98, 107, 119
    The Provost, xii, 4, 11, 12, 13, 41, 60, 84, 86, 87, 88, 89, 90, 91, 92, 93, 98, 99–102
    The Radical, xii, 104, 108
    'A Rich Man; Or, he has great Merit,' 135
    Ringan Gilhaize, xii, 32, 33, 70, 71, 75–81, 84, 126
    'The Russian,' 114, 121
    'The Seamstress,' 127–29
    Selected Short Stories, 4

Galt, John (*cont.*)
    short stories, 125–35
    Sir Andrew Wylie, of that Ilk, xii, 45, 46–47, 48, 110, 116
    Southennan, xii, 59
    The Spaewife, xii, 38
    'The Speculawtor,' 45, 54–56
    A Statistical Account of Upper Canada, xi, 83
    The Steam-Boat, xii, 42, 110, 111, 114–15, 117, 119–20, 122, 123
    Stories of the Study, 126–27
    'Tales of the West,' 13, 16, 110–24
    'theoretical histories,' 1, 5, 12, 13, 16, 65, 77, 84, 99, 104, 111, 116–17, 122, 123
    'Tribulations of the Rev. Cowal Kilmun,' 133–35
    Voyages and Travels, 123
    The Witness (The Appeal) (play), xi, 6
gender, 127–35
George III, King, 93–94
George IV, King, 38, 87, 107, 108
Glasgow, 22, 34–43, 85, 88
    industrialism, 39
    and Scottish literary history, 35
    post-Enlightenment, 37–43
    radicalism and rioting, 95
Glasgow Enlightenment, 34, 35–36, 37
Glasgow Literary Society, 35
Glasgow School, 34, 39, 40, 41
Glorious Revolution, 23
glossary, Scots and American, 63–64
Goderich, Canada, 58
Goldsmith, Oliver, *Vicar of Wakefield*, 16

Gordon, Ian A., 4, 5, 68, 108, 126
Gosta, Tara, 73
gothic short fiction, 125
grain, right of blocking, 92, 93
'Green Grow the Rashes' (song), 132
Greenock, 8, 85, 86, 88, 96
Greenock Library, 36
Gribben, Crawford, 70, 71
Guelph, Canada, 58

Hamilton, Thomas, 34
    The Youth and Manhood of Cyril Thornton, 38, 39, 40, 42
Hardy, Thomas, 9
Harris, Professor Bob, 85, 86
Hart, F. R., 5
    The Scottish Novel from Smollett to Spark, 4
Harvie, Christopher, 98, 102
Hawick, 90
heresy trials, 17, 21, 22–23
Herreshoff, J. K., 59
Hersey, John, *Hiroshima*, 12
Hewitt, Regina, 117, 150n11
    John Galt: Observations and Conjectures on Literature, History and Society, 7
Highlanders, Galt attitude to, 67
Hill, David Octavius, 94
'historical novels,' 71, 72
Hogg, James, 1, 3, 7
    The Brownie of Bodsbeck, 70, 71–72, 79
    The Private Memoirs and Confessions of a Justified Sinner, 25
    short stories, 125
Holmes, William, 103

INDEX

Holy Alliance, 106
Hook, Andrew and Sher, Richard (eds.), *The Glasgow Enlightenment*, 35
Hume, David, 32, 39
humour, 15–18, 27, 47 *see also* irony; satire
Hunterian Museum, Glasgow, 35, 39, 40
Hutcheson, Francis, 19, 32, 35, 40
hypocrisy, religious, 17–19, 22–25, 28, 30, 31, 33

imperialism, 38, 39, 42
industrial revolution, 8
irony, 16, 30, 31, 98, 104, 129, 130
Irvine, 8, 10, 11, 13–14, 85, 90
Ishiguro, Kazuo, 16

James, Henry, *The Portrait of a Lady*, 12
Jeffrey, Francis, 115
   'Secondary Scotch Novels,' 2
Jesuits, 21, 22
John Galt Primary School, Irvine, 8
John Galt Society, 6
Johnson, Paul, 145n1
Johnstone, Christian Isobel, 2, 3, 129–30
Jones, Catherine, 72, 73
Joyce, James, 'The Dead,' 12

Kailyard fiction, 2, 14
Kilmarnock, 88
Kilpatrick, James A., *Literary Landmarks of Glasgow*, 35, 40
Kilwinning, 14
King's Bench prison, 59
Klein, Kerwin, 74

Knausgaard, Karl Ove, 123
   My Struggle, 110

latitudinarianism, 20, 23
Law, John, 50
Lee, Harriet, *Canterbury Tales*, 119
Lee, Simon, 122
Les Lieux de Mémoire project, 74
literary ventriloquism, 15, 16, 18, 19, 79
'local memory,' 14
Lockhart, John Gibson, xi, 3, 5, 6
Lukács, György, 71, 72

Macconnel, James, 21
MacDiarmid, Hugh, 4
Macduff, 92
Mack, Douglas, 71
Mackenzie, Henry, 2
MacQueen, John, 79
   The Rise of the Scottish Novel, 5
Maitland, Sir Peregrine, 58, 59
Maxwell, James, 24, 25
May, Chad T., 152n42
Mayne, John, 'Glasgow' (poem), 145n44
McCracken-Flesher, Caroline, 120, 122
McCrie, Thomas, 70
McGill, William
   Christian Unity Illustrated, 23
   Practical Essay on the Death of Christ, 23
McIlvanney, Liam, 37
McKean, Professor Charles, 85
McNeil, Kenneth, 65
Meadowbank, Lord, 93
Meldrum, David Storrar, 2, 4
memorialisation, 40, 73–81
Millar, John, 35

miniaturism, 7
'Mississippi bubble,' 50, 51, 52
Mitchell, John, 39
Moderates, 18–20, 21, 26
Moir, David Macbeth
    'Farther Portions of the Autobiography of Mansie Wauch, Tailor,' 111, 112
    Life of Mansie Wauch, Tailor in Dalkeith, 112–13, 115
    'Wonderful Passage in the Life of Mansie Wauch, Tailor,' 111
Molière, *Tartuffe*, 17
Montrose, 94
Moore, Dugald, *The Bard of the North*, 38
moral benevolence, 19, 32
Morrison, Robert, 116
Muir, Edwin, 4
    'Scotland 1941' (poem), 3
Murie, Thomas, 88

nationalism, 3, 4, 5
nationality in fiction, 62, 63
The New British Theatre (journal), xi
New Lichts, 18–21, 23, 26, 27, 31, 33
New Monthly Magazine, 49
Nora, Pierre, 74, 75, 79
North America, 44, 52–54, 57–69
    Galt's career in, 58–59
    as fictional setting, 59–69

Paisley, radicalism and rioting, 96
parody, 19, 20, 77
Paterson, William, 49
Penny, George, 83
periodicals, popularity of, 39

Peterhead, 92
Philalethes *see* Walker, Thomas
Phillipson, Nicholas, 34
Philorthodoxus (pseudonym), 22
Philosophical Magazine, xi, 46
plot, 116–17
poetic monologue, 17
political novels, 98–109
    Galt as originator, 8, 11, 98
    The Member, 102–08
    The Provost, 99–102
    The Radical, 108–09
The Political Review, xi
Poovey, Mary, 122
Port Glasgow, radicalism and rioting, 96
'pre-Romantic' period, 1
Presbyterianism, 1, 5, 17, 19, 58, 63, 84
Presbytery of Ayr, 23
Presbytery of Irvine, 21, 22
presentist approach, 3
Princeton College, 19
Providence
    in *The Annals of the Parish*, 30
    and Glasgow improvements, 38
    importance in Galt's work, 36, 80
    in *Lawrie Todd*, 60
    in *Life of Mansie Wauch*, 112
    in *Ringan Gilhaize*, 33
    Presbyterian idea of, 1, 5
    in 'Tribulations of the Rev. Cowal Kilmun,' 133, 134
'provincialism,' 3
psychology of characters, 13
Puritan hypocrite, historical idea of, 17
Puritanism, 23

Radical War 1820, 95
radicalism
    in *Bogle Corbet*, 42, 65, 66
    Galt's reaction to, 95–97
    in *The Gathering of the West*, 109
    in *The Provost*, 91
    in Scott, 73
    Tait and, 129
Ramsay, Allan, 35
rationalism, 89
realism, 2, 16, 84, 135
Reform Act, 108
Reid, Robert, 86
Reid, Thomas, 35
Renfrewshire, 17–22, 24, 25, 26, 31, 33
Revolution of 1689–90, 19
revolutions, 83
Reynolds, Sir Joshua, 40
riots, 92, 93, 95, 107
Roman Catholic Emancipation, 106, 107
Romanticism, 2, 125
Roughhead, William, 4, 129
Royal Caledonian Asylum, xi

satire, 17, 18, 20, 23, 33, 38
Schoenfield, Mark, 51
'Scotland's Smaller Towns in the Era of the Enlightenment, 1745-1820' project, 85
Scots Magazine, 21, 22
Scott, Michael, 34
    Tom Cringle's Log, 41, 42
Scott, Paul, 68
Scott, Walter, 1, 4, 5, 7
    Chronicles of the Canongate, 126
    epilogue to *The Appeal*, xi
    epilogue to *The Witness*, 6
    Galt and, 3, 84
    humour, 15
    Muir on, 3
    political views, 3, 95
    Rob Roy, 40, 63, 118, 119
    short stories, 125, 126
    The Tale of Old Mortality, 70, 71–74, 77, 115
    'The Two Drovers,' 125, 126
    Waverley novels, 15, 36, 63
Scottish Enlightenment
    and commercial society, 37–38
    counter-Enlightenment, 4, 7, 18, 20, 22, 26, 33
    Glasgow Enlightenment, 34, 35–36, 37
    impact on Galt, 1, 16, 31, 32
    MacQueen on, 5
    waning of, 39, 40
    and urban improvement, 82
Scottish Romanticism, 1, 5, 6, 7
secularism, 3, 4
Shakespeare, William
    The Taming of the Shrew, 132
    Twelfth Night, 17
Sibbald, William, 86
Simpson, Kenneth, 60, 84
slavery, 40, 41–42, 66, 67
Smith, Adam, 32, 35, 36, 93
Smollett, Tobias, 36, 39, 40
    The Expedition of Humphry Clinker, 16, 30, 42, 113
Snodgrass, Charles, 105
speculation 44–56
    definition, 44
    The Entail, 45, 48–52, 54
    Lawrie Todd; or, the Settlers in the Woods, 45, 52, 53–54

speculation (*cont.*)
    Sir Andrew Wylie, of that Ilk, 45, 46–47, 48
Stelter, Gilbert, 42, 43
stereotypes, 47, 131, 132
Stevens, Wallace, 11
Stewart, Dugald, 65, 77, 117
subscription and circulating libraries, 91
Swann, Charles, 78
Swift, Jonathan
    Gulliver's Travels, 20
    A Modest Proposal, 17
Swing Riots, 107
Synod of Glasgow and Ayr, 21, 22, 23

Tait, William, 129
Tait's Edinburgh Magazine, 2, 3, 54, 129, 133
Tassie, James, 35
Thompson, Edward, 'moral economy,' 92
Thorburn, Grant, 52
Tilloch, Elizabeth, xi
Trumpener, Katie, 160n3
    Bardic Nationalism: The Romantic Novel and the British Empire, 5
Tulloch, Graham, 71
Twain, Mark, 'Celebrated Jumping Frog of Calaveras County,' 113

unionism, 2, 40, 63
University of Glasgow, 35, 36, 40
unreliable narrators, 16–17
urban improvement, 82–97
    competition and, 86, 87
    and cultural impact, 90, 91
Utilitarianism, 107, 108

vernacular Scots *see* dialect
Voltaire, 83

Walker, Thomas (pseudonym Philalethes), 22
Ward, John, 104
Waterston, Elizabeth, 43
Westminster Confession of Faith, 17, 18, 19, 20, 21, 22, 24
Wilie, David, 8
Witherspoon, John, 18, 21, 33
    Ecclesiastical Characteristics, 18, 19–20
    History of a Corporation of Servants, 20
Wordsworth, William and Coleridge, Samuel Taylor, *Lyrical Ballads*, 122

www.ingramcontent.com/pod-product-compliance
Lightning Source LLC
Chambersburg PA
CBHW071846230426
43671CB00012B/2078